Ariel A. Bloch

Studies in Arabic Syntax and Semantics

Ariel A. Bloch

Studies in Arabic Syntax and Semantics

Second revised printing

1991

Otto Harrassowitz · Wiesbaden

Die Deutsche Bibliothek – CIP-Einheitsaufnahme

Bloch, Ariel A.:

Studies in Arabic syntax and semantics / Ariel A. Bloch. –
2. revised printing. – Wiesbaden : Harrassowitz, 1991

ISBN 3-447-03147-6

Kreuzberger Ring 7c-d, 65205 Wiesbaden, produktsicherheit.verlag@harrassowitz.de

Publication of this book was supported by grants from the University of California and the National Science Foundation (Grant No. BNS 8418785)

Printed in Germany

ISBN 3-447-03147-6

For Chana

Contents

Abbreviations X

Preface XIV

I A Principle of Balancing 1

1. Pronoun Reduplication . . . .
2. Pronoun Reduplication for Focusing . . . .
3. Pronoun Reduplication in Coordination 2
4. Evidence from Medieval Grammarians and Modern Colloquials 4
5. Pronoun Reduplication in Apposition 5
6. Balancing 7
7. Stress as a Balancing Device 9
8. Pronoun Reduplication and Stress 10
9. The Two Uses of Pronoun Reduplication Contrasted 11
10. Coordinative vs. Comitative, Appositive vs. Vocative 12
11. Conclusion 13

II Direct and Indirect Relative Clauses 15

1. Method of Presentation 15
2. The Two Modes of Reference 16
3. Definitions 17
4. Specificity 18
5. The Notion of Category 22
6. Contextual Criteria 24
7. The Emphatic Indirect Relative Clause 25
8. Vocativic Utterances 27
9. Metaphors 34
10. Historical Reconstruction 36
11. The Medieval Grammarians' Approach 37
12. The Presentation in the Western Standard Grammars 38
13. The Broader Phenomenon 39

14. Conclusion 40

III "Be With" > "Encounter", "Come With" > "Bring" 41

1. From Comitativity to Objecthood 41
2. The Notion of the "Envisaged Scene" 44
3. The "Movement With" Notion 47
4. Hierarchical Comitativity 51
5. Bravmann's Theory 52
6. Conclusion 53

IV Presentative Structures and Their Syntactic and Semantic Development 54

1. Introduction 54
2. Nuclear, Amplified and Proclitic Structure 55
3. The Semantics of the Three Structures 61
4. Unmarked Sentences: The Role of the Semantics 63
5. From Amplified to Proclitic Structure by Syntactic Reanalysis . 69
6. The Special History of Pronominal Nuclear Structures 74
   6.1 The nuclear pattern *hā huwa ḏā* and its development 74
   6.2 The pattern in the Qur'ān 80
   6.3 The invariable pattern 82
   6.4 Incorporation of the post-nuclear substantival appositive . 84
   6.5 The affective base 86
   6.6 The development of the incorporating substantival nuclear structure 91
   6.7 Incorporation of the post-nuclear locative appositive . . . 95
   6.8 The special position of pronominal nuclear structures . . . 97
7. Conclusion 99

V The Historical Syntax and Semantics of *inna* 102

1. The Function of *inna* 102
   1.1 Description 102
   1.2 The larger picture: Devices functionally corresponding to *inna* 103
   1.3 Difference from other "emphasizing" devices, notably those for focusing and topicalization 105
   1.4 Use of *inna* as an independent morpheme 106
   1.5 The bi-directionality of *inna* 112

2. *Inna Zaydan*: Vestiges of a Historically Primary Nuclear Structure 113
2.1 The evidence 113
2.2 The semantic range in a general linguistic perspective . . . 115
2.3 The acc. of the head and other expressions of case notions . 118
2.4 The medieval grammarians' deletion hypothesis and its modern counterpart 122
2.5 The syntactic and semantic development 127
2.6 The Biblical Hebrew evidence 131
2.7 The modern colloquial evidence 133
3. Conclusion 136

Indices 137

Abbreviations

Arabiyya	*Al-ʿArabiyya, Journal of the American Association of Teachers of Arabic.*
Arberry	A. J. Arberry, *The Koran Interpreted.* New York 1955.
Baalbaki	R. Baalbaki, "Some Aspects of Harmony and Hierarchy in Sībawayhi's Grammatical Analysis", *ZAL* 2 (1979), 7–22.
Bakr	Y. Bakr, *Dirāsāt fī Fiqh al-Luġa al-ʿArabiyya.* Beirut, 1969.
Barth *Pron.*	J. Barth, *Die Pronominalbildung in den Semitischen Sprachen*, Hildesheim (G. Olms), 1967.
Barthélemy	A. Barthélemy, *Dictionnaire Arabe-Français (Dialectes de Syrie: Alep, Damas, Liban, Jérusalem).* Paris, 1935–1955.
Bayḍāwī	Al-Bayḍāwī, *Anwār al-Tanzīl* . . ., H. O. Fleischer ed. Leipzig, 1848.
Beeston	A. F. L. Beeston, *The Arabic Language Today.* London, 1970.
Blanc *CD*	H. Blanc, *Communal Dialects in Baghdad.* Harvard, 1964.
Blanc "Negev"	H. Blanc, "The Arabic Dialect of the Negev Bedouins", *The Israel Academy of Sciences and Humanities Proceedings* 4/7, Jerusalem (1970), 112–150.
Blau *An Adv.*	J. Blau, *An Adverbial Construction in Hebrew and Arabic*, in *The Israel Academy of Sciences and Humanities Proceedings* 6/1, Jerusalem (1977), 1–103.
Blau *BZ*	J. Blau, *Syntax des Palästinensischen Bauerndialekts von Bīr-Zēt.* Walldorf, 1960.
Blau *Chr. Ar.*	J. Blau, *A Grammar of Christian Arabic*, Louvain, 1966–67.
Blau *Emergence*	J. Blau, *The Emergence and Linguistic Background of Judeo-Arabic*, Oxford, 1965.
Blau "Jāḥ."	J. Blau, "Notes on Syntactic Phenomena in . . . Jāḥiẓ's *Kitāb al-Buxalāʾ*", *IOS* 5, Tel-Aviv (1975), 277–298.
Blau "Obs."	J. Blau, ". . . Observations on Syntactic Trends in Modern Standard Arabic", *IOS* 6, Tel-Aviv (1976), 158–190.
Blau *Jud. Ar.*	J. Blau, *A Grammar of Medieval Judeo-Arabic.* Jerusalem, 1980.
Blau *Orbis*	J. Blau, Review of W. Fischer *Dem.* (see below), *Orbis* 9/1, Louvain (1960).
Blau "Remarks"	J. Blau, "Remarks on Some Syntactic Trends in Modern Standard Arabic", *IOS* 3, Tel-Aviv (1973), 172–231.
Bloch *Chr.*	A. Bloch, *A Chrestomathy of Modern Literary Arabic.* Wiesbaden, 1974.
Bloch "*Damir*"	A. Bloch, "*Ḍamīr Al-Šaʾn*", *ZAL* 21 (1990), 30–9.
Bravmann *Studies*	M. Bravmann, *Studies in Arabic and General Syntax.* Cairo, 1953.
Bravmann "Linguistic Taboo"	M. Bravmann, "Semitic Instances of 'Linguistic Taboo'", in *Studies in Semitic Philology*, Leiden (1977), 465 ff.
Brock.	C. Brockelmann, *Grundriß der Vergleichenden Grammatik der Semitischen Sprachen*, Vol. 2. Hildesheim, 1961.
Buḫ. (ed. Krehl)	Al-Buḫārī, *Al-Jāmiʿ Al-Ṣaḥīḥ*, L. Krehl, ed. Leiden, 1862–1907.
Cant.	V. Cantarino, *Syntax of Modern Arabic Prose.* Indiana, 1974–1975.
Carter	M. Carter, "An Arab Grammarian of the Eighth Century A.D.", *JAOS* 93 (1973), 146–157.

Clark	E. Clark, "Locationals: A Study of the Relations between 'Existential', 'Locative' and 'Possessive' Constructions", *Working Papers in Language Universals* 3, Stanford (1970), 1–36.
Cohen	D. Cohen, *Dictionnaire des Racines Sémitiques*. Paris, 1970, 1976.
Comrie	B. Comrie, *Language Universals and Linguistic Typology*. Chicago, 1981.
Cowell	M. Cowell, *A Reference Grammar of Syrian Arabic*. Washington, D.C., 1964.
Feghali	M. Feghali, *Syntaxe des Parlers Arabes Actuels du Liban*. Paris, 1928.
Fischer-Bräunlich	A. Fischer and E. Bräunlich, *Schawāhid-Indices*. Leipzig and Vienna, 1934–1945.
A. Fischer "Schwur"	A. Fischer, "Grammatisch schwierige Schwur- und Beschwörungsformeln des Klassischen Arabisch", *Der Islam* 28 (1949), 1–105.
W. Fischer *Dem.*	W. Fischer, *Die Demonstrativen Bildungen der neuarabischen Dialekte*. The Hague, 1959.
W. Fischer *Gramm.*	W. Fischer, *Grammatik des Klassischen Arabisch*. Wiesbaden, 1972.
W. Fischer "Daß-Sätze"	W. Fischer, "Daß-Sätze mit *an* und *anna*", *ZAL* 1 (1978), 24–31.
W. Fischer (ed.) *Grundr.*	W. Fischer, ed., *Grundriß der Arabischen Philologie*. Wiesbaden, 1982.
Fitzmyer	J. Fitzmyer, *The Genesis Apocryphon of Qumran Cave I*. Rome, 1971.
Fleischer	H. L. Fleischer, *Kleinere Schriften*, Vol. 1. Leipzig, 1885.
Freytag	G. W. Freytag, *Kitāb Ašʿār al-Ḥamāsa maʿa Šarḥ ... al-Tibrīzī*, G. W. Freytag, ed. Bonn, 1828–1847.
Gen. Apocr.	*Genesis Apocryphon* (see Fitzmyer, above).
Goldenberg	G. Goldenberg, "Tautological Infinitive", *IOS* 1, Tel-Aviv (1971), 36–85.
Grotzfeld	H. Grotzfeld, *Syrisch-Arabische Grammatik*. Wiesbaden, 1965.
Guillaume	A. Guillaume, *The Life of Muhammad (A Translation of Ibn Ishaq's Sirat Rasul Allah)*. Oxford, 1955.
Ḥaqqī	Y. Ḥaqqī, *Qindīl Umm Hāšim*. Cairo (no date).
Havers	W. Havers, *Handbuch der Erklärenden Syntax*. Heidelberg, 1931.
Hetzron "Clitic Pronouns"	R. Hetzron, "Clitic Pronouns and Their Linear Representation", *Forum Linguisticum* 1/3, Lake Bluff, Illinois (1977), 189–215.
Hetzron "Presentative Movement"	R. Hetzron, "The Presentative Movement ...", in *Word Order and Word Order Change*, Charles N. Li, ed. Texas (1975), 347–388.
Ḫiz.	Al-Baġdādī, *Ḫizānat al-Adab*, Vol. 4. Cairo (Būlāq), 1882.
Howell	M. S. Howell, *A Grammar of the Classical Arabic Language*. Allahabad, 1880–1911.
Ibn Hišām	Ibn Hišām, *Sīrat Rasūl Allāh*, F. Wüstenfeld, ed. Göttingen, 1858–1860.
Ibn Saʿd	Ibn Saʿd, *Kitāb al-Ṭabaqāt al-Kabīr*, E. Sachau, ed. Leiden, 1904–1909.
Ibn Yaʿīš	Ibn Yaʿīš, *Šarḥ al-Mufaṣṣal*, G. Jahn, ed. Leipzig, 1882–1886.
IOS	*Israel Oriental Studies*
JAOS	*Journal of the American Oriental Society*
Joüon	P. Joüon, *Grammaire de l'Hébreu biblique*. Rome, 1947.
JSS	*Journal of Semitic Studies*
Kanafānī	Ġ. Kanafānī, *Al-Āṯār Al-Kāmila*, Vol. 1. Beirut, 1972.
(Al-)Kitāb al-Muqaddas	*Al-Kitāb al-Muqaddas ay Kutub al-ʿAhd al-Qadīm wa-l-ʿAhd al-Jadīd*. Beirut (no date).

Knobloch	J. Knobloch, *Sprachwissenschaftliches Wörterbuch*. Heidelberg, 1960–.
Kropfitsch	L. Kropfitsch, "Zu Fragen der Verbalkongruenz im Neuhocharabischen", *ZAL* 1 (1978), 32–45.
Lambdin	T. Lambdin, *Introduction to Biblical Hebrew*. New York, 1971.
Lambrecht	K. Lambrecht, *Topic, Antitopic and Verb Agreement in Non-Standard French*, in *Pragmatics and Beyond* 2/6, Amsterdam/John Benjamins B.V. (1981).
Landberg	C. de Landberg, *Études sur les dialectes de l'Arabie méridionale*, Vol. 2 (Daṯīnah). Leiden, 1905–1913.
Lane	E. W. Lane, *Arabic-English Lexicon*. New York, 1955–1956.
Lisān	Ibn Manẓūr, *Lisān al-ʿArab*. Beirut, 1955–1956.
Lyons *Introduction*	J. Lyons, *Introduction to Theoretical Linguistics*. Cambridge, 1968.
Lyons "Possessive, Existential ..."	J. Lyons, "A Note on Possessive, Existential and Locative Sentences", *Foundations of Language* 3 (1967), 390–396.
Maḥfūẓ *Ḫān*	N. Maḥfūẓ, *Ḫān al-Ḫalīlī*, Cairo, 1962.
Marçais *Gl. Takr.*	W. Marçais and A. Guiga, *Textes Arabes de Tarouna*, Vol. 2: *Glossaire*. Paris, 1958–1961.
Masʿūdī	Al-Masʿūdī, *Murūj al-Ḏahab*, Barbier de Meynard, ed., Vol. 6. Paris 1861.
Mitchell	T. F. Mitchell, *An Introduction to Egyptian Colloquial Arabic*. Oxford, 1956.
Mosel	U. Mosel, *Die Syntaktische Terminologie bei Sībawayh*. Munich, 1975.
Muraoka	T. Muraoka, "Emphasis in Biblical Hebrew", Diss. Hebrew University, Jerusalem, 1969.
Nöldeke *Mand.*	Th. Nöldeke, *Mandäische Grammatik*. Darmstadt, 1964.
Nöldeke *ZGr.*	Th. Nöldeke, *Zur Grammatik des Classischen Arabisch*. Darmstadt, 1963.
Palva	H. Palva, *Studies in the Arabic Dialect of the ... l-ʿAǧārma Tribe*, in *Orientalia Gothoburgensia* 2, Göteborg (1976).
Poebel	A. Poebel, *Das Appositionell Bestimmte Pronomen der 1. Pers. Sing. in den Westsemitischen Inschriften und im Alten Testament*, in *The Oriental Institute of the University of Chicago Assyriological Studies* 3, Chicago (1932).
Polotsky *Études*	H. J. Polotsky, *Études de Syntaxe Copte*. Cairo, 1944.
Polotsky "The Indirect Attribute"	H. J. Polotsky, "A Point of Arabic Syntax: The Indirect Attribute", *IOS* 8, Tel-Aviv (1978), 159–173.
Q	Qur'ān. References are to the standard Egyptian edition.
Rabin	Ch. Rabin, *Ancient West-Arabian*. London, 1951.
Reck. *AS*	H. Reckendorf, *Arabische Syntax*. Heidelberg, 1921.
Reck. *SV*	H. Reckendorf, *Die Syntaktischen Verhältnisse des Arabischen*. Leiden, 1895–1898.
Riwāyāt al-Aġānī	*Rannāt al-Maṯāliṯ wa-l-Maṯānī fī Riwāyāt al-Aġānī*, A. al-Ṣāliḥānī, ed., Vol. 1. Beirut, 1908.
Rosenhouse-Katz	J. Rosenhouse and Y. Katz. *Texts in the Dialects of Bedouins in Israel*, in *Occasional Papers on the Middle East* 3, University of Haifa, The Jewish-Arab Center, Institute of Middle East Studies, Haifa (1980).

Rubinstein *Ha-Mišpaṭ Ha-Šemani*	E. Rubinstein, *Ha-Mišpaṭ Ha-Šemani*. Israel, 1968.
Rubinstein *Ha-Ivrit Šelanu*	E. Rubinstein, *Ha-Ivrit Šelanu ve-Ha-Ivrit Ha-kduma*, in *Sifriyat "Universita* Mešuderet", Ministry of Defence, Israel (1980).
Saad "Comitative"	G. Saad, "The Comitative in Arabic: An Element of the Deep Structure", *An-Našra, Journal of the American Association of Teachers of Arabic* 7/2 (1974), 79–84.
Schmidt-Kahle	H. Schmidt and P. Kahle, eds., *Volkserzählungen aus Palästina*. Göttingen, 1918–1930.
Schub	M. Schub, "Direct and Indirect Relative Clauses", *Arabiyya* 11/1–2 (1978), 15–19.
Sībawayhi	Sībawayhi, *Kitāb*, H. Derenbourg, ed. Paris, 1881–1885. Unless a quotation specifies the Būlāq ed. (Cairo, 1316–1317), references are to the Derenbourg edition.
Spitaler	A. Spitaler, "*Mā Rāʿahū Illā Bi-* ...", in *Serta Monacensia, F. Babinger ... Dargebracht*, H. J. Kissling and A. Schmaus, eds. Leiden (1952), 171–183.
Spitta	W. Spitta, *Grammatik des Arabischen Vulgärdialectes von Aegypten*. Leipzig, 1880.
Ṭab.	Al-Ṭabarī, *Ta'rīḫ* ..., J. Barth, Th. Nöldeke, et al., eds. Lugd. Bat., 1879–1901.
WKAS	*Wörterbuch der Klassischen Arabischen Sprache*
WZKM	*Wiener Zeitschrift für die Kunde des Morgenlandes*
Wright	W. Wright, *A Grammar of the Arabic Language*. Cambridge, 1967.
ZAL	*Zeitschrift für Arabische Linguistik*
Zamaḫšarī	*Al-Zamaḫšarī, Al-Mufaṣṣal*, J. P. Broch, ed. Christiania, 1879.

Preface

In his *Arabische Syntax* (1921), H. Reckendorf singled out a broadly based historical analysis of Arabic syntax as a major desideratum; now, more than sixty years later, this demand has been reiterated in the *Grundriß der Arabischen Philologie* (1982) as a still-pressing need. In view of the general upsurge of interest in syntax in recent years, it is remarkable that there are surprisingly few studies of Arabic syntax, and that works of a diachronic orientation are virtually nonexistent in this field. The two initial chapters of this book are primarily descriptive in nature; the last three, constituting the major portion, are historical and comparative, dealing with basic mechanisms of syntactic and semantic change. It is in these three chapters that I hope to have made a contribution toward a historical syntax of Arabic.

The argumentation throughout this book rests on the crucial premise of the interconnectedness of syntax and semantics. This manifests itself, for example, in the attention I have paid to the meaningful distribution of related constructions, such as the direct and indirect relative clauses (ch. II) and the amplified and proclitic structures (ch. IV), or to the manifold ways in which abstract case roles are expressed in the surface structure (chs. III and IV).

I have taken my examples mostly from grammatical works and less often directly from texts. In those cases where the grammars name the sources, I have attempted as much as possible to examine the examples in context. This was especially important in chs. II and IV, where the semantic contrasts could not have been established without a close scrutiny of the contextual background.

In my discussion I draw upon hitherto scarcely noticed observations of the medieval Arab grammarians which shed new light on the historical development of basic syntactic structures. For example, certain vestigial (now long obsolete) uses of *inna* that are essential for the understanding of this particle's original syntax (ch. V) might have escaped our attention were it not for the fact that they were recorded by these grammarians. The ones I consulted are Sībawayhi, Zamaḫšarī, Ibn Yaʿīš and, to a lesser extent, Al-Baġdādī's *Ḫizāna*.

While my data are predominantly from Arabic, many of the linguistic phenomena discussed are of a much broader nature, having cross-language relevance. I therefore felt it legitimate to include examples not only from all periods and genres of Arabic (Ancient Poetic, Koranic, Classical, Middle, Modern Literary and Colloquial), but also from other Semitic (occasionally also non-Semitic) languages – provided, of course, that such examples manifested the same phenomenon. Thus it is above all the phenomena themselves that engaged my attention, and only secondarily their provenance. Because of the widespread occurrence of the phenomena, and their cross-language significance, the book addresses itself not only to the Arabist and Semitist but to the general linguist as well.

The following summary of the contents is offered primarily as a help to the general linguist who has little or no knowledge of Arabic.

In ch. I, "A Principle of Balancing", I discuss a feature that is widespread in Arabic as well as other Semitic languages. A bound pronoun will typically be reduplicated by the corresponding free form when followed by a coordinative or appositive, e.g.

⟨I-went I and-Zayd⟩ ⟨I-went I Zayd⟩
"I and Zayd went away" "I, Zayd, went away"

This feature – which, for brevity's sake, is exemplified here only by the subject position and the first person – is under no constraints, occurring in all syntactic positions and with all persons. In Arabic this reduplication is largely obligatory, as confirmed by a test which I conducted with speakers of diverse modern dialects. Statements by the medieval Arab grammarians confirm a similar situation for the earlier stages of the language.

I argue that any explanation of this feature must start from the one element that coordination and apposition have in common, namely that they involve entity terms that are syntactically on a par. I suggest, therefore, that the feature is to be explained as a device marking syntactic parity: through its reduplication by a free form, the pronoun in question is given a similar surface structure representation as its coordinative or appositive (hence my term "Balancing"). It is significant that this use of pronoun reduplication is confined to the condition of syntactic parity in the *strictest sense*, thus not extending to comitative ("with") constructions; this presents yet another argument in favor of a sharp separation between comitativity and coordination.[1]

Two other balancing devices, operative in Arabic and elsewhere, are briefly discussed for comparison, namely the repetition of the embedding matrix and the application of identical stress. Balancing devices are viewed as "perceptual simplifiers" serving above all to clarify grammatical relations, i.e. as having no *semantic* effect. For this reason, I make a sharp distinction – never fully recognized in the standard works on Semitics – between pronoun reduplication for balancing and pronoun reduplication for focusing, in which latter case the device is used for a specific semantic purpose (e.g. ⟨I-went I⟩ "*I* went away," ⟨We-want-you you⟩ "We want *you*").

1 Contra Lakoff et al., quoted Saad "Comitative".

Finally, because of the striking similarity in the functions of pronoun reduplication and stress – each of which is used for both balancing and focusing – I speculate about a possible genetic connection between these two devices. In a language such as Arabic where the position of stress within the word is regulated, stress cannot be used for a functional purpose such as to mark a bound pronoun for focusing or balancing. Pronoun reduplication may, therefore, have originated out of the need for such functional stressing, the free (reduplicating) pronoun providing a stressable "vehicle" outside the confines of the word.

Ch. II, "Direct and Indirect Relative Clauses", deals with a question of distribution. Arabic relative clauses (RCs) embedded in predicational constructions with first- or second-person subjects, i.e. type

I am/you are P who ... (P = predicate)

differ from all other RCs in that they display two distinct modes of reference: one in which the resumptive pronoun refers to the subject, and another in which it refers to the predicate. Depending on whether the first or second mode is manifested in a given case, I speak of a "direct" or an "indirect" relative clause. I show that the distribution, which has so far been treated as a case of purely random variation, is largely determined by syntactic and semantic criteria.

There are indications that the degree of specificity expressed in the head of the RC is a strong factor in the distribution under discussion. This is particularly noticeable at the two extreme ends of the specificity spectrum: "most specific" heads (typically, proper nouns and other one-of-a-kind entities) unmistakably favor direct RCs, while "most unspecific" heads (vague, indefinite pronouns meaning "someone [unmarked] who ...") just as clearly prefer indirect ones. Notions other than specific/unspecific that were found to govern the distribution of the two RC-types are: on the scene/off the scene; self-contained/categorized; plain/emphatic. All of these notions are shown to have clearly definable formal-grammatical, semantic and contextual correlates. The phenomenon is seen as a manifestation of a dichotomy which has very deep roots in language generally and which reveals itself in various other, seemingly unrelated ways. A few of these other manifestations are discussed for comparison.

Ch. III is the first of the diachronic chapters. Its title "'Be With'>'Encounter', 'Come With'>'Bring'" symbolizes two processes of semantic change, each involving a transition from an original, historically primary notion of proximity or comitativity to a notion of object, where "object" is understood as an umbrella term in the sense of abstract case grammar (i.e. for semantic roles such as patient, etc.) The most remarkable aspect of these two processes for linguistics is that the object notion develops in *verbless* sentences.

The first process occurs in sentences of this surface structure:

Iḏā anā bi-
⟨Suddenly I with⟩

resulting in a semantic change that can be presented informally: "Suddenly I (was) with/at/near/in the vicinity of a thing/person" > "suddenly I encountered a thing/person".

The second process takes place in a large number of sentences (I adduce here only two as examples) with original meanings surrounding a basic notion of *movement with* a thing or person. The formal exponents of this notion are the preposition *bi-* ("with," cf. the preceding sentence) and another preposition, *li-* or *ʿalā*, expressing movement in the direction of a target:

anā laka bi- ⟨I towards-you with⟩

kayfa lī bi- ⟨How towards-me with⟩

These semantic changes can be described by glosses such as:
"I towards you with the thing/person">"I bring you the thing/person"
"How towards me with the thing/person?">"How can I get the thing/person?"

There are various proofs that the change to objecthood has indeed taken place: 1. The terms governed by *bi-* in all these sentences are not constrained in terms of lexical-semantic categories. Thus, these terms may not only denote concrete entities, but also sense perceptions, abstract qualities, etc. – categories which preclude an interpretation according to the primary notion (e.g., there is no * Suddenly I was with a noise," but only "Suddenly I heard a noise"; no * How towards me with good health?", but "How can I achieve good health?"). 2. Variant constructions where the term in question, rather than being governed by *bi-*, is in the acc. case, etc.

I argue that these sentences are not only diachronically but also *underlyingly* verbless. The traditional postulates of implied (surface-deleted) verbs are shown to be untenable, except as explanatory ploys. The general interest of these sentences, then, is that they demonstrate a semantic role "object" that is not dependent upon the presence of a verb. We may speak here of "verb-free" objects (and, similarly, of verb-free agents, recipients or benefactives, cf. the roles of the other terms in these sentences). The usefulness of abstract case grammar for the description of these sentences can hardly be overstated.

The last two chapters form a unity of sorts because of the similarity of the syntactic processes described. Ch. IV, "Presentative Structures and their Syntactic and Semantic Development", sets the groundwork for the discussion. There are, on the one hand, structures that I call "nuclear" and "amplified," in which the presentative forms a sentential unit (nucleus) with a substantive or pronoun and, on the other, those I call "proclitic," in which the presentative does not form such a sentential unit. This dichotomy I found to be fundamental throughout the history of Arabic presentative syntax. To present the basic types schematically:

Nuclear	Amplified	Proclitic
hāḏā Zaydun	*hāḏā Zaydun munṭaliqan* (acc.)	*hāḏā Zaydun munṭaliqun* (nom.)
"There is Zayd"	"There is Zayd, departing"	"Look, Zayd is departing"

This syntactic dichotomy has a semantic correlate. The meaning of the nuclear and amplified structures is always determined by the deictic-concrete nature of the presentatives in their nuclei, while the proclitic structures are characterized by a great semantic diversity. They can, for example, be simply alerting (this is their basic meaning, and the only one reproduced above, "Look, ..."), but also argumentative, consequential, causal-explanatory – to mention but a few possibilities. In their capacity to express abstract clausal relations such as the last three, proclitic presentatives approach the semantic sphere that is commonly associated with conjunctions. Although this chapter deals only with a limited number of presentatives, I believe that the conclusions are valid to presentative syntax in general.

I argue that the proclitic structures are historically secondary, deriving from the amplified ones through a process of syntactic reanalysis in which the third component (a *Ḥāl*, or "subordinated" predicate) is raised to the status of a predicate and the presentative becomes dislodged from the nucleus. The semantic diversity of the proclitic structures is seen as a consequence of this development: once the presentative ceases to be an integral part of the nucleus, it loses its purely deictic-concrete meaning and becomes exposed, as it were, to contextual influences, thus acquiring new meanings. Various formal features as well as typological and comparative considerations suggest strongly the development from amplified to proclitic structure, rather than the other way around. Most important of these are the "left-over" features exhibited by the various proclitic structures, such as the inflectedness of the (proclitic) demonstrative presentative and the acc. case of the subject in the *inna*-structure (next chapter) – features which would be hard to account for if these structures were to be seen as other than historically derived as suggested, or if they were to be seen as having emerged in an independent genesis. From this also follows, of course, that no purely synchronic-descriptive approach could explain satisfactorily these features of the proclitic structures.

Pronominal structures exhibit the same properties as outlined above for the substantival structures (three-way distinction, syntactic and semantic contrast, reanalysis process). But some features on the level of the *nucleus* indicate what I would call a "primacy" of the pronominal over the substantival types. One of the more remarkable manifestations of this primacy is the fact that various modern Arabic dialects – independently of one another – developed a nuclear substantival structure by exactly the same procedure, namely by "grafting" a substantive onto a nuclear pronominal structure (the independence of the development is proved by the componential diversity of the various versions). I interpret these constructions as reflecting an original appositival (or "right dislocation", or "antitopic") syntax, i.e. type "there he is, the man". I demonstrate by examples from a number of languages that this syntax is particularly common in exclamatory or otherwise emotive-affective sentences (one misses this recognition in Lambrecht's monograph), and argue that the strong affinity of *presentative* sentences for this syntax – again, supported by comparative data – stems from their exclamatory-affective character.

The final chapter, "The Historical Syntax and Semantics of *Inna*", examines the function of that particle, corrects some misconceptions about it, and offers a reconstruction of its historical development in the light of new evidence. *Inna* emphasizes the speaker's certainty (or, in questions, his doubt) that what is said in the sentence is a fact, the truth, will surely take place, etc. – a function quite adequately rendered with *indeed*, *certainly*, *surely* and the like[2]. *Inna*, therefore, must be sharply distinguished from other "emphasizing" devices, notably those for focusing or topicalization, which pertain to a specific component of a sentence (i.e. subject, object, etc.). This distinction, though rather basic, has often been neglected by Western Arabists, including in the most recent literature, resulting in misleading statements about the function of the particle. One (largely unobserved) feature that is especially well-suited to highlight *inna*'s true function is its use as an independent morpheme to voice strong agreement with a preceding statement.

Among the traditional views of the particle that I examine critically is the one that describes it in terms of a presentative (either explicitly or by paraphrases with words like *look*, *behold*, *siehe*, *ecce*). This view is not based on textual attestation but on etymological-comparative considerations, above all the par-

2 Despite some overlap, the semantic category here under discussion is not identical with the one defined as "Fact" by P. and C. Kiparsky in their article of that title in *Progress in Linguistics*, ed. by M. Bierwisch and K. Heidolph, Mouton (1970).

ticle's cognates in other Semitic languages. Yet there is good evidence to support the notion of an *originally* presentative *inna* in Arabic. The evidence in question is an archaic sentence-type, *inna Zaydan* (acc.), whose vestiges were recorded by the indigenous medieval grammarians but were hardly noticed in Western grammatical works. The meanings of the examples range from deictic-concrete ("Voilà Zayd") to purely existential (with indefinite substantives), thus suggesting for this particle a direction of semantic development that is well-attested in many languages and for which I adduce further documentation (from Arabic, Hebrew, etc.). I explain the acc. within the original meaning as the exponent of an abstract case-role "object," and I show this case-role as characteristic of nuclear presentative structures, manifesting itself in a great variety of formal ways accross languages. My reference to a "purely" existential meaning is directed against the view held by the medieval grammarians, and also – interestingly for the history of linguistic thinking – by some contemporary scholars (e.g. John Lyons et al.), according to which all existential sentences are implicitly locative. I argue that this approach leads to an artificial analysis which in fact falsifies the meaning of these sentences.

Assuming that the type under consideration does indeed reflect an archaic nuclear presentative structure, I propose that it was the starting point for the formation of new presentative structures along the steps suggested in the chapter on presentative syntax. To present the two developments in synopsis:

Nuclear	Amplified	Proclitic
hāḏā Zaydun	*hāḏā Zaydun munṭaliqan* (acc.) →	*hāḏā Zaydun munṭaliqun* (nom.)
inna Zaydan	*inna Zaydan munṭaliqan* (acc.) →	*inna Zaydan munṭaliqun* (nom.)

The soundness of the hypothesis may be gauged by the fact that the structures upon which it is based are all actually attested, with the sole exception of the amplified one with *inna*, which has not survived (but for some possible reflexes of a noncanonic usage).

Here too, I see the semantic change involved – from the original notion of concrete deixis to one of emphasis – as linked to the syntactic reanalysis process by which the particle shifts from its nuclear to a proclitic status. I point to another case of precisely this syntactic/semantic contrast in Arabic, and yet another one that is typologically closer in Biblical Hebrew, where the presentative *hinnē* (the etymological cognate of *inna*) is deictic-concrete in nuclear status but as a proclitic serves (*inter alia*) for sentence-emphasis.

Finally, my reconstruction receives support from a rather unexpected source: a number of contemporary Bedouin dialects have preserved reflexes of *inna* with an unmistakable *presentative* meaning, in nuclear and proclitic positions. This at the same time highlights also a more general point, namely that the modern Arabic dialects may preserve ancient features more faithfully than the classical language.

***

A few technical remarks:

Unless preceded by §, references are to the page and, where necessary, to the page and the line. Lines counted from the end of the page are preceded by the minus sign.

Portions between ⟨ ⟩ are in morphemic transcription. I have used this device sparingly and only where essential for the sake of clarity.

* marks grammatically unacceptable sentences, as well as historical reconstructions (the reader should have no difficulty recognizing which of these two uses is intended in a given case).

As much as possible, I have kept the transcription faithful to that of the original texts.

For useful suggestions and comments I would like to thank H. Blanc, H. Bobzin, M. Carter, O. Gensler, G. Goldenberg, T. Givón, M. Goshen-Gottstein, R. Hetzron, D. Justice, G. Krotkoff, J. Matisoff, M. Schub, A. Spitaler, R. Steiner, K. Zimmer, M. Zwettler and, especially, J. Blau, who read the entire manuscript. I also would like to thank Florence Myer for typing the manuscript with her usual precision and care, and to record my special gratitude to my student and friend Benjamin Hary, who compiled the indices and offered penetrating criticism. This book is dedicated to my wife Chana who helped with her unfailing encouragement and her critical acumen.

Research on this book was supported by fellowships from the Social Science Research Council and the National Endowment for the Humanities, and its publication by grants from the University of California and the National Science Foundation (Grant No. BNS 8418785; any opinions, findings, and conclusions or recommendations expressed in this publication are those of the author and do not necessarily reflect the views of the National Science Foundation).

Berkeley (Calif.), July 1986 ARIEL A. BLOCH

In order to reduce production costs in this second printing, I was obliged to limit changes to corrections of misprints and other minor alterations. For the same reason, I was able to incorporate only a few of the suggestions made by reviewers. One of these suggestions deserves to be acknowledged here briefly; it concerns a point of general methodology. Because *coexistence* of source and resultant structure is the norm in the syntactic phenomena discussed in chapters IV and V, one reviewer felt that the relation between any such two structures should be conceived in terms of purely mentalistic notions like "primacy" and "derivation" rather than chronological sequence.

Berkeley (Calif.), November 1990 Ariel A. Bloch

Chapter I

A Principle of Balancing[1]

1. Pronoun Reduplication

In Arabic, as well as in other Semitic languages, a free personal pronoun may reduplicate a preceding bound pronoun, i.e., suffix or pronoun inherent in a finite verb. This device, which in all likelihood harks back to the earliest stages of this family of languages, will be referred to as "pronoun reduplication".

2. Pronoun Reduplication for Focusing

One use of pronoun reduplication is as a focusing device:

(1) *fa'ayna naṣībī anā min hāḏā nnafali*
⟨then-where share-of-me I of this the-booty⟩
"Where then is *my* share of this booty?" — Wright II 265 C

(2) *nubāyiʿuka anta*
⟨we-will-acknowledge-you you⟩
"We will acknowledge *you* as leader". — Reck. *AS* 281

(3) *mā ẓalamnāhum walākin kānū humu ẓẓālimīna* (var. *-ūna*)
⟨never we-wronged-them but they-were they the-wrongdoers⟩
"We never wronged them, but *they* did the wrong". — Q 43:76

Sentences such as (1)–(3) contrast semantically with non-focused ("plain") ones in which the bound pronoun is not reduplicated:

fa'ayna naṣībī min hāḏā nnafali
⟨then-where share-of-me of this the-booty⟩
"Where then is my share of this booty?" etc.

I call a "focusing device" any linguistic means of which languages avail themselves in order to put into relief the item of the sentence that contains the new or contrastive information, thus making this item stand out against the rest

1 This chapter is an enlarged version of an article that appeared in *Studia Orientalia Memoriae D. H. Baneth Dedicata*, Jerusalem 1979, 211–23.

of the sentence, which contains the presupposed or known information. An item so marked is the "focus" of the sentence. In the above sentences the focus is italicized. The term "focusing device" is conceived very broadly so as to encompass all the devices that have a similar semantic effect, such as clefting ("it is John who did it") and stress ("Jóhn did it"), to mention only two. For a brief summary of the major focusing devices of Arabic (other than pronoun reduplication), see § 1.3 of chapter V.

3. *Pronoun Reduplication in Coordination*

3.1 A second use of pronoun reduplication is the subject of this chapter. A bound pronoun in Arabic will typically be reduplicated when coordinated with a following substantive or pronoun:

(4) *baʿaṯanī anā wa-z-Zubayru/a*
⟨he-sent-me I and-Zubayr (nom./acc.)⟩
"He sent me and Zubayr". Reck. *AS* 342

(5) *baʿaṯanī anā wa'anta*
⟨he-sent-me I and-you⟩
"He sent me and you". Reck. *AS* 342

(6) *ḏikru ḫurūjihi huwa wa'aḫūhu*
⟨report-about departure-of-him he and-brother (nom.)-of-him⟩
"The report about his and his brother's departure" Brock. 224.9

(7) *taẓāfuruhu huwa wa-Abū Saʿdin*
⟨aid-of-him he and-Abū (nom.) Saʿd⟩
"His and Abu Saʿd's aid" Reck. *AS* 345

(8) *ittifāquhu huwa wa'aḫīhi*
⟨agreement-of-him he and-of-brother (gen.)-of-him⟩
"His and his brother's agreement" Wright II 326

On the fluctuations in the case marking in (4) and (6)–(8) see below, § 3.5.

(9) *ṣāma huwa wajamīʿu man maʿahu*
⟨he-fasted he and-all-of those-who with-him⟩
"He and all those with him fasted". Reck. *SV* 376

(10) *daḫaltu anā wahiya*
⟨I-entered I and-she⟩
"I and she entered". Reck. *AS* 332

And from the modern literary language:

(11) *annahu huwa walmaṭʿam ʿalā "ḥsābnā"*[2]
⟨... that-he he and-the-restaurant ...⟩
"(He assured us) that he and the restaurant were at our service"[3].
Bloch *Chr.* 9.–4

3.2 It may be mentioned in passing that Hebrew likewise reduplicates its bound pronouns in coordination:

... pen tiwwārēš attā ub̲ēt̲k̲ā ...
⟨lest you-come-to-poverty you and-the-household-of-you⟩
"Lest you and your household come to poverty". Gen 45:11

naʿaśē et̲ kol haddābār ... kaʾašer ʿaśīnū anaḥnū waʾab̲ōt̲ēnū
⟨we-shall-do obj. every the-thing as we-did we and-fathers-of-us⟩
"We will do everything as we and our fathers did". Jer 44:27[4]

The Hebrew usage of this device differs in detail from Arabic and will not be further considered.

3.3 We are not, however, dealing with a linguistic *rule*, since the reduplicating pronoun may be absent:

(12) *jaʿalnāhā wa-bnahā āyatan lilʿālamīna*
⟨we-appointed-her and-son-of-her a-sign ...⟩
"We appointed her and her son to be a sign unto all beings". Q 21:91

(13) *baʿḍu šaʾnī wawaladī*
⟨some-of concern-of-me and-(of) son-of-me⟩
"Some of my and my son's concern" Reck. *AS* 345.2

(14) *fīhi wa-ʿAbdi llāhi*
⟨with-him and-Abdallah⟩
"With him and Abdallah" Reck. *AS* 345.3

(15) *id̲ aqbalat wazuhrun*
⟨when she-came and-radiant-ones⟩
"When she and the radiant ones (fem.) drew near". Reck. *AS* 331.7

2 This word is marked as colloquial in the original text. Since the rest of the sentence, as well as most of the story, is in pure literary Arabic, a coll. reading: *inno huwwe* (with the uninflected -*o*) is unlikely.

3 Constructions of the type *kunnā anā wa-Fāṭimatu* (Reck. *AS* 332) do not involve pronoun reduplication (in contrast to *kuntu anā wa-Fāṭimatu*) and will not be dealt with here.

4 I thank M. Schub for the reference to these examples.

3.4 The patterns underlying (4)–(11) and (12)–(15), respectively, can be represented schematically as:

(16) A. bound pronoun + free (reduplicating) pronoun + wa- + coordinative
B. bound pronoun + wa- + coordinative

I am using the term "coordinative", and similarly "appositive" (see below), for the *second* of two items in coordination and apposition, respectively.

These two patterns of coordination do not have the same degree of acceptability, as will be shown (§ 4.).

3.5 A brief explanation is called for concerning the case endings of the coordinated substantives in the preceding Arabic examples. In pattern B these endings reflect the case of the bound pronoun (or, put differently: the syntactic relation expressed in this pronoun's embedding matrix, depending on whether it is suffixed to a verb, substantive, preposition, or is inherent in the verbal form), see the acc. in (12), the gen. in (14), the nom. in (15). In pattern A there are two possibilities: The coordinated substantives may likewise reflect the case of the bound pronoun, see the acc. in (4), the gen. in (8); or be in the nom., regardless of the case of the bound pronoun, see (4), (6), (7). Since the second possibility exists only in pattern A, never in B, the nom. (as in 4, 6, 7) ought to be seen as a surface structure adaptation to the inherent case of the free pronoun.

4. *Evidence from Medieval Grammarians and Modern Colloquials*

4.1 There are indications that the medieval Arab grammarians had a feeling of uneasiness towards pattern B. Sībawayhi (I 342–343), for example, accepts constructions according to this pattern as "correct" (*ḥasan*) only with a direct object, as in (12), but rejects them as "incorrect" (*qabīḥ*)[5] elsewhere, usually explaining such *qabīḥ* constructions in poetry as caused by the *ḍarūrat al-šiʿr* (the "Verszwang"). Since in reality, however, they occur also in prose (e.g., Reck *AS* 331, 344.–2), Sībawayhi's explanation is simply a measure of the low degree of acceptability he accords these constructions. Ibn Yaʿīš goes even one step further than Sībawayhi: while agreeing with him that pattern B is "correct" only with the direct object, he declares the option with reduplicating pronoun (pattern A) to be better yet (398.22)[6].

5 For this understanding of *ḥasan* and *qabīḥ* in Sībawayhi, see Carter 147.

6 Lit. "the best thing" (*aḥsan šay'*). The question of how the Arab grammarians viewed the relation between the two patterns (to be separated, of course, from their distribution in actual language usage) deserves a detailed investigation.

4.2 The evidence from the modern colloquials is even more decisive. I asked five native speakers representing four Eastern Arabic dialects[7] to translate the following into their colloquials:

(17) I saw him and Ḥasan.
(18) He and Ḥasan came.

All informants without exception rendered (17) and (18) according to pattern A:

⟨I-saw-him he and-Ḥasan⟩[8]
⟨he-came he and-Ḥasan⟩

Moreover, only a single informant (Allama) accepted as "also possible" a rendition according to pattern B for sentence (17):

⟨I-saw-him and Ḥasan⟩

While all without exception rejected such a rendition for sentence (18):

*⟨he-came and Ḥasan⟩[9]

5. *Pronoun Reduplication in Apposition*

Bound pronouns are also reduplicated before an appositive. Although in Arabic this is less well documented than reduplication with coordinatives, there is good evidence from other Semitic languages. Here again, the type with reduplication seems to be preferred over the one without it. The feature typically occurs with (though is probably not restricted to) pronouns of the first person. My examples are from modern literary Arabic (19), Aramaic (20) (Bibl. 20a, *Gen. Apocr.* 20b), and Phoenician (21):

(19) *bayna hāḏihi l'asrāri wanufūsinā naḥnu lbašar*
⟨between these the-secrets and-the-souls-of-us we the-humans⟩
"Between these secret forces (lit. secrets) and our souls, the souls of human beings" Bloch *Chr.* 40.1

7 Adnan Haydar and Salim Allama (Lebanon), Nagat al-Sanabary (Egypt), Kamal Abu Deeb (Syria) and Muhammad Kadhim (Iraq).

8 I am using only a schematic presentation since different dialects are involved.

9 All informants hesitated to come forth with a translation of my third sentence, "the house of him and Ḥasan". This may be due to the questionable grammaticality of this sentence, for which "his and Ḥasan's house", or "his house and Ḥasan's", etc., would probably have been less objectionable. But their reaction may also be due to the inherent ambiguity (is one house involved, or two?) – which of course would have existed also with any of the alternatives. It has been demonstrated by others that informants react with discomfort to ambiguity of "input" sentences.

(20) a. *uminnī anā Artaḥšastā malkā śīm ṭ'em*
⟨and-from-me I Artaxerxes the-king is-made a-decree⟩
"And I, King Artaxerxes, make a decree". Ezra 7:21

b. *wšbyqt 'nh 'brm bdylh' wl' qtylt wbkyt 'nh 'brm*
⟨and-I-was-spared I Abram because-of-her and-not I-was-killed and-I-wept I Abram⟩
"And I, Abram, was spared because of her and was not killed.
And I, Abram, wept". Fitzmyer 62.10-11

(21) *šm 'nk Yḥwmlk*
⟨the-name-of-me I Yḥwmlk⟩
"My name, the name of Yḥwmlk" Brock. 225.7

The feature is especially common in Daniel, occurring in this book's Aramaic as well as Hebrew passages, see Da 4:15; 7:15 and 8:1, 15; 12:5. For an attestation in Bibl. Hebrew see 1 Kings 1:26.

The mentioned preference manifests itself especially well when a translator uses pronoun reduplication where the source sentence does not have it. Thus, the *-ī* of (Bibl. Hebrew)

'aḏ šaqqamtī Dḇōrāh Jud 5:7

was understood by many as the common Hebrew ending of the first person sing. of the perf., including the Arabic translator (*Al-Kitāb Al-Muqaddas*), who rendered this verse:

ḥattā qumtu anā Dabūratu
⟨until I-arose I Deborah⟩
"Until I, Deborah, arose".

That this *-ī* is more likely an archaic second person fem. sing. perf. ending and the meaning of the sentence "Until you, O Deborah, arose" (the construction possibly to be interpreted according to § 10.2) is immaterial to the point under discussion. What alone matters here is the translator's understanding, which prompted him to use pronoun reduplication, thus deviating from the "Vorlage". The same is true of the Aramaic (Targum) rendition of this verse.

An appositional construction without the reduplicating pronoun is attested in Phoenician:

(22) ... *bšnt ʿsr wʾrbʿ lmlky mlk ʾšmnʿzr*
⟨in-the-year-of ten and-four to-reign-of-me king Išmnʿzr⟩
"In the year fourteen of my reign, the reign of King Išmnʿzr" Poebel 18.15[10]

The patterns underlying (19)–(21) and (22), respectively, are:

(23) A. bound pronoun + free (reduplicating) pronoun + appositive
B. bound pronoun + appositive[11]

6. *Balancing*

6.1. The statements of Sībawayhi and Ibn Yaʿīš (§ 4.1), as well as my test results (§ 4.2), show that pattern B in coordination has a low degree of acceptability in the linguistic systems of classical Arabic and the modern colloquials (in fact, it may be more correct to say that in the colloquials the use of pattern A is largely obligatory). Moreover, the evidence of Arabic and, to a greater extent, other Semitic languages points to a similar preference of pattern A over B with appositives (§ 5.) This remarkable behavior of pronouns across various languages can hardly be accidental and demands an explanation. Any explanation must take into consideration that the feature affects bound pronouns, not free ones, and that it occurs in coordination and apposition. Items in coordination and apposition are syntactically on a par – as is made explicit, for example, by their identical case in case-marking languages.[12] I consider pronoun reduplication, as in patterns A of (16) and (23), to be a means of making this syntactic parity explicit in the surface structure. This is achieved by adaptation of the morphological status of the pronoun to the morphological status of its coordinative and appositive, respectively: in patterns A both the pronoun and its coordinative/appositive are represented as *free* forms – in contrast to patterns B. In my interpretation, pronoun reduplication in coordination and apposition is to be classified together with the various other devices of the surface structure

10 For *mlk ʾšmnʿzr* in the sense of "king Išmnʿzr" (rather than "the reign of Išmnʿzr") see the next line in Poebel. I am grateful to M. Goshen-Gottstein for bringing Poebel's book to my attention. The discussion, esp. in the middle section of this par., has greatly benefitted from information provided me by Richard Steiner.

11 The constraints on pattern B in apposition reported Wright II 285 should be compared with actual usage. Cowell's formulation, 550, "A suffix pronoun itself cannot have modifiers, except as mediated by its corresponding independent form", rules out pattern B for Damascene. This parallels my informants' reaction to this pattern in coordination (§ 4.2.). Unfortunately, Cowell uses the term "modifier" rather vaguely; moreover, the two sentences he adduces are focus sentences, and thus do not illustrate his rule.

12 Where, of course, the marking indicates not just the syntactic parity but also a specific case *role*.

(such as case-marking), which languages use to signal syntactic parity.[13] I shall refer to all such devices as "balancing" devices.

6.2 Another balancing device which Arabic uses with bound pronouns is repetition of the governing word (verb, substantive, preposition) before the coordinative:

(24) *wadāhu wawadā Labīdan*
⟨he-paid-him and-he-paid Labīd⟩
"He paid blood money for him and Labīd". Reck. *SV* 497

(25) *wilāyatuhā wawilāyatu l-Kūfati*
⟨the-governorship-of-it and-the-governorship-of Kūfa⟩
"Its (i.e., Baṣra's) and Kūfa's governorship" Reck. *AS* 345

(26) *qad ʿaṭišnā waʿaṭišat dawābbunā*
⟨surely we-are-thirsty and-thirsty-are animals-of-us⟩
"We and our riding animals are thirsty". Reck. *AS* 332.2

6.3 In the balancing type of (24)–(26), the syntactic parity of the bound pronoun and its coordinative is overtly marked by the identity of their syntactic environments (their identical embedding matrix). The similarity between this device and pronoun reduplication is apparent. These are two different ways to the same end, viz., to avoid an "unbalanced" pattern B:

wadāhu huwa wa-Labīdan
⟨he-paid-him he and-Labīd⟩

wadāhu wa-Labīdan
⟨he-paid-him and Labīd⟩

wadāhu wawadā Labīdan
⟨he-paid-him and-he-paid Labīd⟩

and similarly for (25)–(26).[14]

In both cases there is a process of adaptation: pronoun reduplication adapts the items themselves to one another, while in (24)–(26) their syntactic environ-

13 In fact, the syntactic parity of the coordinatives in pattern A of classical Arabic may be viewed as doubly marked, i.e. morphologically, as just described, *as well as* by means of the two case marking systems mentioned § 3.5: The first system expresses this parity through the case identity with the bound pronoun, the second through the case identity with the free form. Of course, in the second system only the parity itself is marked (by the nom.), not the case role.

14 Reckendorf has recognized, at least implicitly, that pronoun reduplication and repetition of the governing word have the same underlying motivation, viz., to avoid the type of construction described here as pattern B. He sees in both devices "Störungen" of that pattern, see Reck. *AS* 331–2, esp. 331 n. 3, where he speaks of "tiefere syntaktische Gründe".

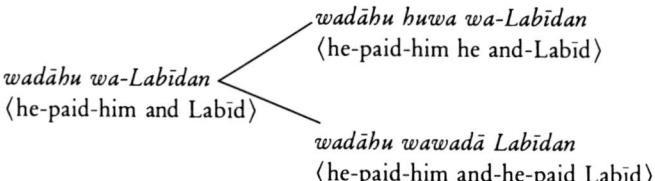

ments are adapted. Involved, then, are two types of surface similarity serving to mark syntactic parity.

6.4 It is possible to conceive of sentences (24)–(26), as well as pattern A sentences (4)–(11), as being derived from underlying patterns B by the application of different balancing devices. (Similarly, appositional pattern A constructions may be seen as derived from the corresponding patterns B.) In this approach it is immaterial whether patterns B actually exist in a speaker's linguistic system, or whether they are abstractions. Needless to say that such an approach is simply a way of presentation; it does not itself *explain* anything.

6.5 However, constructions such as (24)–(26) pose a problem of interpretation. Rather than representing a single sentence or phrase nucleus, as the above translations assume, they may represent two different nuclei, involving two separate notions: two events in (24) and (26) (e.g., "He paid blood money for him ... and he paid ..."), two different governorships in (25) (cf. note 9), etc. In this case the repetition has *semantic* reasons, i.e., we are not dealing with a parity-marking (balancing) device, cf. § 9. Of course, only the context can determine which of these two interpretations applies in a given case. [A similar question arises if, for example, in (modern) Hebrew the overt marker of the direct object (*et*) or the possessor (*šel*) were to be repeated before the coordinative. Are the sentences

pagašti et Dan ve-et Avivà
⟨I-met obj. Dan and-obj. Aviva⟩

habayit šel Dan ve-šel Aviva
⟨the-house of Dan and-of Aviva⟩

semantically different from (in the above sense), or identical with the sentences

pagašti et Dan ve-Aviva *habayit šel Dan ve-Aviva*?!]

7. *Stress as a Balancing Device*

There seems to be a tendendy to apply equal stress to coordinated items. I asked several native speakers of German to mark with (´) the stressed and with (˘) the unstressed words in sentences (27)–(29). In order to exclude stressing for the purpose of focusing, the persons were told that these sentences were intended simply to transmit information, without special emphasis on any word. Although the response was not uniform (as was to be expected, especially since linguistically untrained persons are not easily aware of stress), most of those questioned placed the markers as follows:[15]

(27) Er erzählte mĭr, daß ĕr drei Wochen lang krank war.

(28) Er erzählte mír und Fránz, daß ĕr drei Wochen lang krank war.

(29) Er erzählte mĭr, daß ér und Fránz drei Wochen lang krank waren.

What appears at first glance as odd stress behavior in these sentences becomes plausible in the light of the principle of balancing: pronouns were marked as unstressed, except when coordinated with a stressed item, as in (28)–(29).[16]

Pronouns, as is well known, typically tend to attach themselves to neighboring forms (verbs, substantives, particles) – a development which often results in loss of stress. On the other hand, pronouns also occur in independent positions as fully stressed forms.[17] Pronouns, therefore, are candidates par excellence for this kind of balancing-by-stress.

8. *Pronoun Reduplication and Stress*

It is tempting to speculate about a possible genetic relationship between pronoun reduplication and stress. Such a connection may seem less far-fetched if one considers that there is a remarkable similarity in the *functions* of these two devices. Stress is perhaps the most basic means of focusing (§ 2.) and, as was just demonstrated, it is also used for balancing. Both of these functions are expressed in Arabic by means of pronoun reduplication. Since the position of stress in an Arabic word is regulated[18], stress cannot be used within the body of the word for functional purposes, such as to mark a bound pronoun for focusing or balancing, e.g.

**ḍarabtuhú*	**baytí*
⟨I-hit-hím⟩	⟨house-of-mé⟩

15 I am omitting the stress markings that are not relevant to the present discussion, such as those on the verbs.

16 A similar test conducted with English speakers showed much less uniform results. I am unable to say whether this reflects an actual difference between the two languages involved, or some unevenness in my testing techniques.

17 Another phenomenon directly resulting from this double role of pronouns is discussed in A. Bloch, "Morphological Doublets in Arabic Dialects", *JSS* 16 (1971), 53–73.

18 Even what may occasionally appear as a free word stress in an Arabic dialect usually turns out to be determined by the underlying morphophonemic base, see Blanc "Negev" 120. Fluctuations in the word stress such as reported for the Yemen (see W. Diem, "Skizzen jemenitischer Dialekte", *Beiruter Texte und Studien* 13 (1973), 10–12), are certainly not typical for Arabic.

**minká*	**biʿtúm*
⟨from-yóu⟩	⟨yóu(pl.)-sold⟩

in contrast to a language such as German, where the pronouns are separate and, thus, may receive such functional stress. It is therefore conceivable that pronoun reduplication originated out of (or was at least enhanced by) the need to provide a vehicle for functional stressing:

ḍarabtuhu húwa	*baytī ánā*	*minka ánta*
⟨I-hit-him hé⟩	⟨house-of-me Í⟩	⟨from-you yóu⟩ etc.

The crux of this hypothesis is, of course, that the question of the origins of pronoun reduplication must necessarily be pushed back to the earliest stages of the Semitic languages, where very little is known about whether word stress was regulated or free.

9. *The Two Uses of Pronoun Reduplication Contrasted*

The use of pronoun reduplication for focusing (§ 2.) must be sharply separated from its use for balancing. In the first case, the device has a *semantic* effect, demonstrable in the contrast between sentences such as (1)–(3) and their plain counterparts. In the second case, pronoun reduplication is clearly not used for a semantic purpose (patterns A of (16) and (23) do not differ in meaning from the corresponding patterns B), but as a means to make explicit the syntactic parity of a bound pronoun and its coordinative or appositive.[19] The purpose behind this use of pronoun reduplication becomes evident if one compares it to other devices for expressing syntactic parity, such as the identical case marking of two items in coordination or apposition. These are primarily "perceptual simplifiers" (to use a fashionable term), which help to clarify grammatical relations. This, I believe, is the reason for the widely attested preference for patterns A – and constructions such as (24)–(26), in the first interpretation (§ 6.3) – over patterns B.

19 Failure to recognize this difference led Poebel 22 and Brock. 225.1–14 to put 1 Sam 25:24 (not 35:24, as in Poebel), 2 Sam 19:1, 2 Chron 35:21, which are unmistakable uses of pronoun reduplication for focusing, in the same category as Da 7:15, 8:1, where the device is employed for balancing. And in the same vein Nöldeke *ZGr.* lumps together the ex. in 48.1–2 *wayahjūnī* ... (balancing) with the preceding exx. (focusing).

10. Coordinative vs. Comitative, Appositive vs. Vocative

10.1 It must be emphasized that this use of pronoun reduplication is restricted to the condition of syntactic parity in the strictest sense. Thus, there is no pronoun reduplication if the coordinative is replaced by a comitative ("with" case), i.e.

(30) **baʿaṯanī anā maʿa z-Zubayr*
⟨he-sent-me I with Zubayr⟩
"He sent me with Zubayr".

(31) **daḫaltu anā maʿa z-Zubayr*
⟨I-entered I with Zubayr⟩
"I entered with Zubayr".

but only

(32) *baʿaṯanī maʿa z-Zubayr*

(33) *daḫaltu maʿa z-Zubayr*[20]

This is relevant to a problem that was being debated among some theoretically oriented linguists a few years ago. The evidence from Arabic presents yet another argument in favor of a *separation* between "and" and "with" constructions.[21]

10.2 We have seen (§ 5.) that bound pronouns will typically be reduplicated before an appositive in Biblical Aramaic. If, however, the substantive following a bound pronoun (of a second person) is a vocative, no reduplication will take place:

(34) *lāḵ elāh aḇāhāṯī mhōḏē umšabbaḥ anā*
⟨to-you god-of fathers-of-me thank and-praise I⟩
"To thee, O God of my fathers, I give thanks and praise". Da 2:23

"Whoever makes petition to any god or man
(35) *lāhēn minnāḵ malkā*
⟨except to-you king⟩
except to you, O king" Da 6:8

This, then, confirms once again that the use of pronoun reduplication discussed in this chapter is confined to the condition of syntactic parity in the strictest sense: This condition is fulfilled with the appositive (items in apposition being

20 Sentences such as (30) and (31) do occur, of course, as *focus* sentences (in the sense of "he sent *me* with Zubayr", "*I* entered with Zubayr"), but not as plain sentences ("he sent me with Zubayr", "I entered with Zubayr"), for which semantic value only (32) and (33) are correct.

21 See similarly Saad "Comitative" 79, against Lakoff and Peters.

syntactically on a par), but not with the vocative, whose syntactic role (or "case", in the abstract sense) is different from that of the bound pronoun. To be sure, it could be argued that the substantives in (34)–(35) might still be appositives, witness the attestation of pattern B in (22). However, pronoun reduplication in apposition is so common in Biblical Aramaic that it suggests a normed, obligatory feature, and it is therefore far more plausible that the substantives in question are vocatives. And this is, in fact, also the understanding of the New Oxford Annotated Bible and the King James Version, as well as *Al-Kitāb Al-Muqaddas*, which has here

> *iyyāka yā ilāha ābā'ī aḥmadu wa'usabbiḥu*
> ⟨to-you O god-of ...⟩

and

> ... *illā minka ayyuhā lmalik*
> ⟨except to-you O the-king⟩

Moreover, these two renditions may serve to illustrate the fact that the vocative is exempted from pronoun reduplication also in Arabic.[22]

11. Conclusion

11.1 Balancing, defined in the broadest possible way, is the creation of surface-structure similarity to mark syntactic parity. The discussion concentrated specifically on the creation of a "balance" between a bound pronoun and its coordinative or appositive: Through the reduplication of the pronoun by a free form the language makes explicit the syntactic parity between these items. In addition to pronoun reduplication, two other such devices, likewise involving pronouns, were dealt with marginally, namely balancing by means of the creation of an identical embedding matrix (§§ 6.2–6.3) and balancing through adaptation of stress (§ 7.).

Apart from a tentative suggestion (§ 8.), no attempt was made to speculate on the origins of pronoun reduplication in the Semitic languages. Our term "pronoun reduplication", therefore, implies nothing as to the genesis of the device[23],

22 Where, in contrast to Aramaic, it is usually overtly marked, i.e. by *yā*, *ayyuhā*, etc. That we are justified in speaking of a vocative also in Aramaic, despite its unmarkedness in this language, emerges from a sentence such as *malkā l'ālmīn ḥeyī*, Da 2:4. Here the imperative form of the verb allows only a vocative interpretation, "O king, live for ever!", and not *"May the king live for ever", *"Long live the king" or the like.

23 As far as I know, the only attempt to explain the genesis of pronoun reduplication within Arabic linguistics is Reckendorf's in *SV* 376.–1ff., rightly rejected Brock. 224.

but is of a purely descriptive nature. The descriptive usefulness of such a term becomes evident if one wants to distinguish between the device itself, on the one hand, and its uses (§ 9.) on the other.[24]

11.2 Finally, let us look at a phenomenon which at first glance seems similar to the one discussed in this chapter, but which ultimately must be sharply separated from it. There are, probably in all languages, some constraints against what one may call "imbalanced coordination". Thus, whereas a sentence such as (36) is acceptable, (37) is not:

(36) He drank slowly and with great enjoyment.
(37) *He drank slowly and a glass of port.

This is not refuted by the fact that an imbalanced coordination may occasionally be used deliberately, say, for a humorous effect, as in this line by Christian Morgenstern:

(38) Palmström, etwas schon an Jahren,
wird an einer Straßenbeuge
und von einem Kraftfahrzeuge
überfahren.

which is funny precisely *because* it violates this constraint (as would its equivalent in English "He was run over at a street corner and by a car"). The violation in (37) and (38) lies in the fact that the coordinated items belong to dissimilar categories, i.e. a manner adverbial and a direct object in the former example, a local adverbial and an agent of a passive verb in the latter one. Now, the phenomenon dealt with in this chapter is crucially different. The dissimilarity (or "imbalance") of the coordinates in sentences of type (37) and (38) is definable in terms of syntactic and semantic categories[25], whereas the imbalance underlying sentences of pattern B is morphological in nature, as argued above. Or, put differently: There is no constraint against coordinating a pronoun and a substantive – since they belong to the same large umbrella category of "entity terms" (or, if you will, NP's) – *unless* the pronoun is a bound form. Thus, although one may speak of an "imbalanced" coordination in both the case of pattern B and examples such as the last two, it is a categorially different kind of imbalance.

24 Under no circumstances can one accept the view that the free pronoun stands in an "appositional" or "attributive" relation to the bound pronoun, so Brock. 223.–12, Reck. *SV* 377.5, Poebel 22.5 (the designation 'Pronomina in Apposition' is likewise inadmissible for the syntactic structures dealt with Brock. 222). Appositives as well as attributes "narrow down", or identify more closely their referents, but no such function can be ascribed to the reduplicating pronouns.

25 See e.g. Paul Schachter, "Constraints on Coordination", *Language* 53/1 (1977), 86–103.

Chapter II

*Direct and Indirect Relative Clauses**

1. *Method of Presentation*

1.1 Grammars of Arabic occasionally include a paragraph on "relative clauses to a first- or second-person pronoun". The majority of these relative clauses are embedded in predicational constructions that can be symbolized as:

(1) I am/you are P who ... (P = predicate)

1.2 It is important that "relative clause" (henceforth RC) be understood as referring to a broad underlying category, encompassing not only the surface structures that are commonly meant when the term is used in its narrow sense, but also participial structures, such as (3)i, structures of the type *Naʿt Sababī*, as in (2)i, (13)–(14), etc.[1]

1.3 As with RCs in general, those under discussion can have substantival heads, e.g., (2)a–c, (3)a–c, or pronominal ones, e.g., (2)d–h, (3)d–h, (10)e–f. When the head is pronominal, the portion "P who" in (1) stands for "the one who", "someone who", etc. When it is substantival, that portion stands for "the man (woman, carpenter, etc.) who", "a man (woman, etc.) who".

Since the properties of the heads of RCs are of paramount importance to the phenomenon to be discussed in this chapter, I prefer to speak here of substantival and pronominal heads rather than of "attributive" and "nominalized" RCs, respectively. The pronominal heads to be dealt with are *man* and the set *allaḏī*.[2]

* I first introduced the term "direct and indirect relative clauses" in preliminary drafts for this study presented at the First North American Conference of Semitic Linguistics, Santa Barbara, California, March 1973, and at the 29th International Congress of Orientalists, Paris, July 1973. The term was subsequently adopted by M. Schub, who conducted further research on this subject (see Abbreviations). This chapter is an enlarged version of a paper that appeared in *ZAL* 5 (1980), 8–34.

1 It is of course only underlyingly that structures such as those just mentioned, whose surfaces share many properties with attributes, can be seen as RCs. On the *Naʿt Sababī* see now Polotsky "The Indirect Attribute".

2 The third pronominal head, *mā*, refers primarily to non-persons and it is therefore not surpris-

The set *alla*d̲*ī* is of concern here only when it occurs as head, not when it accompanies a (definite) head, as in (4) type B.

2. *The Two Modes of Reference*

The crucial grammatical feature by which the RCs under discussion differ from all others is that they exhibit two distinct modes of reference. Thus, the *ʿĀ'id* (i.e., resumptive pronoun, inherent in the verbal form, suffixed or free) in examples (2) refers to the personal pronoun, in examples (3) to its predicate.[3] I have attempted, as much as my material allowed it, to juxtapose similar constructions:[4]

(2) a. *innī mru'un ṣarʿī ʿalayka ḥarāmun* "I am a man whom you are not allowed to throw down". Reck. *AS* 423

b. *naḥnu unāsun baratnā lḥarbu* "We are people whom war emaciated". Nöldeke *ZGr.* 98.–7

c. *innā laqawmun lā narā lqatla subbatan* "We are people who do not consider it shameful to be killed". Nöldeke *ZGr.* 98.–12

d. *lasnā bilļad*̲*īna nuqātilu Muḥammadan* "We are not the ones who are going to fight against Muḥammad". Nöldeke *ZGr.* 99.14

(3) a. *innī mru'un fī Hud*̲*aylin nāṣiruhū* "I am a man whose helper is among the Hud̲aylis". Reck. *AS* 424

b. *kunnā unāsan yaʿlifūna l'ayāṣira* "We are people who feed with (desert) herbs". Nöldeke *ZGr.* 162 (100 n. 2)

c. *naḥnu qawmun tanazzalū* "We are people who have dismounted". Brock. 560.8

d. *lastu llad*̲*ī jafāhu* "I am not the one who treats him badly". Reck. *AS* 195.4

ing that it did not figure among the RCs under discussion. For the treatment of *man* and *alla*d̲*ī* (as well as *mā*) as heads of RCs see esp. Beeston 49.

3 The standard grammars of Arabic typically describe this dichotomy in terms of an alternation between a first- or second-person and a third-person resumptive pronoun, see e.g. the wording in Reck. *AS* 423, 443; Nöldeke *ZGr.* 98, 100; Blau *Chr. Ar.* 563–4; Blau "Remarks" 209–10; and similarly Nöldeke *Mand.* 456. Though factually correct, this description is linguistically inadequate. Such an alternation remains unmotivated and incomprehensible unless seen in terms of reference to two distinct antecedents, as above. Better in Cant. III 157.

4 Examples in this chapter are from classical Arabic and, much less frequently, from the modern literary language, the colloquials and Middle Arabic. Their provenance is always indicated.

e. *la'allī akūnu anā lladī anjū* "Perhaps I will be the one who saves himself". Nöldeke *ZGr.* 99.–13

f. *anta lladī laqītanī* "You are the one who met me". Reck. *SV* 622.3

g. *a'anti llatī stawda'tuki ssirra* "Are you the one to whom I entrusted the secret?" Reck. *AS* 443.–11

h. *naḥnu lladīna naḍmanu ššahra* "We are the ones who take upon themselves to safeguard the month". Nöldeke *ZGr.* 99.–17

i. *anā ššā'iru lma'rūfu wajhī* "I am the poet whose face is widely known". Reck. *AS* 443.–7

j. *anā rajulun lā māla lī* "I am a man who has no money". Cant. III, 157

e. *anā lladī ja'ala Ādama* "I am the one who created Adam". Brock. 589.–5

f. *anta lladī āṯāruhū* "You are the one whose remains ..." Nöldeke *ZGr.* 100.7

g. *anta lladī tarjū ṣṣa'āliku saybahū* "You are the one whose gifts the needy hope for". Reck. *AS* 443.–2

h. *naḥnu lladīna bakaw lahū* "We are the ones who wept for him". W. Fischer *Gramm.* 193.–15

i. *anā lmašhūru bi'abīhi* "I am the one known through his father". Reck. *SV* 536.–1

j. *kuntu mra'an laysa lahū min ahlin* "I was a man who had no family". Cant. III, 158

Examples (2)j and (3)j are modern literary; all the others in (2) and (3) are classical. The purpose behind this somewhat lengthy list of examples – apart from the demonstration of the two modes of reference – will become evident in § 4.4.

3. *Definitions*

3.1 There are several possible definitions for the Arabic RCs involving a first- or second-person pronoun. On the basis of the item referred to, i.e., a personal pronoun on the one hand and a substantive on the other, one may speak of "personal" and "objectified" RCs. In this study, however, we shall define these RCs from the viewpoint of the speaker: either the speaker refers directly to the "I" and "you", or he does so indirectly ("I am/you are *the man/woman/carpenter* who ..."). In one case he speaks about himself in the first person and addresses someone else in the second person – i.e., directly – and in the other he does both in the third person – i.e., indirectly. The indirectness in the latter case is due to the fact that what is said about the "I" or "you" is said *via* the predicate.

On the basis of this distinction, I propose the terms "direct" and "indirect" RCs.[5]

3.2 These terms apply not only to predicational constructions (1) but also to vocative utterances, which likewise exhibit two modes of reference in their embedded RCs. Since vocativic utterances differ in several respects from the predicational constructions, they will be treated separately, See § 8.

3.3 At this point a clarification of the terminology is called for. It will be shown that the notions "direct" and "indirect" have correlates on the semantic and contextual levels. But this is not how the terms themselves are to be understood. They are based strictly and exclusively on the inner, context-free criterion of the two modes of reference. In other words, a given RC will be called "direct" or "indirect" irrespective of whether it does or does not correlate with these semantic notions in a given context. In this (context-free) sense, the terms may be used, for example, as convenient labels for typological purposes. Thus, one may speak of a "direct-RC language" or an "indirect-RC language", depending on which of the two modes a given language uses, predominantly or exclusively.

4. *Specificity*

4.1. The head of a RC – any RC, not just of those that are here under discussion – may denote a specific, narrowly definable, particular entity, or it may denote one of a more unspecific, general, vague nature. One may speak, abstractly, of a scale or hierarchy, the two extremes of which would be a "most specific" and a "most unspecific" head, respectively.[6] But this is not only an abstract concept. The following is a ranking of the major RC-types of classical Arabic according to such a specificity scale:

(4) A.	*Laylā llatī qālat*	Layla who said
B.	*almar'atu llatī qālat*	the woman who said
C.	*imra'atun qālat*	a woman who said
D.	*allatī qālat*	the one (fem.) who said
E.	*man qālat*	someone (fem.)/the one (fem.) who said
F.	*man qāla*	someone (unmarked) who said

5 In order to avoid a confusion in the terminology, I must point out that "direct" and "indirect" are occasionally used in a different sense, so e.g. in Polotsky's article, see note 1.

6 "Particular" might be better suited than "specific", especially because the latter is sometimes used in the sense of "pertaining to a certain species", which is not what is intended here. But I settled for "specific" because "particular" has no equivalent (*"imparticular") at the other end of the scale.

The heads of these RC-types can be described in formal-grammatical terms such as "definite", "indefinite"[7], "pronominal", "substantival". In this respect, then, the notion of specificity can be said to have surface structure correlates.

Let us emphasize in order to avoid a misunderstanding that our model (4) represents the invariable third person *ʿĀʾid* that characterizes all RCs other than those involving a first- or second-person pronoun, while only the latter exhibit the variability (dir. and indir. mode) that is the subject of this chapter. This ought to be kept in mind when in the following we assign a given dir. or indir. RC to one of the six types of that model.

4.2 There are clear indications that the degree of specificity of the head is a strong determining factor in the distribution of the dir. and indir. RCs. Our observations on this particular point are based on data from classical and, to a lesser degree, middle and modern literary Arabic. The conclusions on the prevailing distributional trends do not apply, however, to one well-circumscribed category, namely the vocative formulas of the classical language, where the indir. RC has become largely standard usage, see § 8.2.

4.3 Consider the following sentences:

(5) a. *anta Ādamu llaḏī ḫalaqaka llāh*
"You are Adam whom God created". Nöldeke *ZGr.* 99

b. *anta Mūsā llaḏī ṣṭafāka llāh*
"You are Moses whom God chose". Brock. 589

c. *anta Ilyās allaḏī atġayta Banū Isrāʾīl*
"You are Elias who has seduced the sons of Israel". Blau *Chr. Ar.* 564

d. *anā, Ṭarṭyūs, allaḏī katabt*[8]
"I, Tertius, who wrote" Blau *Chr. Ar.* 563

e. *anā lmāḥī llaḏī yamḥū biya llāhu lkufra*
"I am the Eradicator with whose help God erases godlessness".
Buḫ. (ed. Krehl) II 389.-5

7 The categories of definiteness and specificity have been related to one another already by the medieval grammarians, who distinguish between *taʿrīf* and *taḫṣīṣ*, respectively, albeit on the basis of different criteria, see e.g. Wright II 198D, 260D. For an understanding and critical evaluation of the use of these terms see H. Gätje, "Zum Begriff der Determination und Indetermination im Arabischen", *Arabica* 17 (1970), 225–51.

8 That the relation in this particular case is appositional, not predicational, is irrelevant to the argument.

f. *innā šīʿatuka llaḏīna narjū fī ṭāʿatika*
"We are your adherents who desire to obey you".
Nöldeke *ZGr.* 162 (100 n. 1)

Examples c–d are Middle Arabic, the others in (5) are classical. The heads are proper nouns, or definite substantives of such a high degree of specificity as to come close to that of proper nouns, as is the case in e–f. In e, the Prophet is speaking of his "Names", one of which is *almāḥī*. In f, ʿAli's adherents are addressing him. Although probably not yet used here as the *name* it later came to be, the high specificity of the word *šīʿa* in this sentence is evident. That such heads are to be placed at the very top of the specificity scale (4) hardly needs an explanation, since they denote entities that are unmistakably identifiable in the particular situations of the utterances in question and are, at least in the case of the proper nouns, "one of a kind".

4.4 Now, within this category of specificity all the recorded examples had dir. RCs.[9] This becomes even more significant in view of the fact that the proclivity for dir. RCs gradually decreases as the heads become less specific. Thus, while dir. RCs are still unmistakably in the majority in the next rank on the specificity scale, i.e., among examples of (4) type B[10], no pattern of preference for either dir. or indir. RCs could be detected in types C and D, see examples (2)a–h and (3)a–h.[11] This points to a correspondence between the notion "specific" and the

9 For the one exception see § 9, end. Of course, if a language standardizes or at least manifestly favors indir. RCs in all categories, indir. RCs are very likely to be used also for proper nouns. This seems to be the case, for example, in Assyrian, where an indir. RC with a proper noun head is quoted Brock. 591.–3. Whenever standardization is at work, the speaker is not free to choose between the two modes, but is bound by the standard which the language imposes. In such cases, obviously, there can be no meaningful distribution.

10 A few examples: *anā ṣṣabiyyu llaḏī tarabbaytu fī dārika* Brock. 589.16; *anā ṣāḥibu ddanānīri llaḏī jiʾta ʿindī* Nöldeke *Mand.* 459.–15; *antumu nnafaru llaḏīna qāla fīkum* ... Nöldeke *ZGr.* 162 (100 n. 1); *alasta lʿabda lʾaswada llaḏī kunta* ... Wright II 324 C. I have not checked colloquial data against the specificity scale in any systematic way, but it may not be entirely coincidental that my only type B example with an indir. RC comes from a colloquial: *ana ssakka illi aʿṭēte jarrit ilmāl* Blau *BZ* 262.–8.

11 This is further corroborated by examples where both modes alternate within a single RC, such as: *innī mruʾun yaḏubbu ʿan ḥarīmī* Brock. 560.10; *anta llaḏī tarjūka Qaysun lifaḍlihī* Reck. *AS* 444.3; *an takūna llaḏī taḏhabu maʾṯuratu qawmika ʿalā yadayhi* Nöldeke *Mand.* 459.–4, of which the first is type C, the second and third type D. Brockelmann's claim that "*allaḏī* ruft doch häufiger schon die 3. Person hervor", for which he quotes: *naḥnu llaḏīna bāyaʿū Muḥammadan* Brock. 589.–10, *antumū llaḏīna iḏā zujirū staqdamū* Brock. 589.–7 is refuted by the variants or near-correspondences with dir. RCs: *naḥnu llaḏīna bāyaʿnā Muḥammadan* Nöldeke *ZGr.* 100.10, *naḥnu llaḏīna iḏā zujirnā staqdamnā* W. Fischer *Gramm.* 192.9. Again, it is type D within which the alternations occur in both examples. (Nöldeke's observation, *ZGr*

dir. RCs – a correspondence that has its most radical expression with heads possessing the highest specificity value.

4.5 At the other end of our specificity scale we find *man*. I have ranked it lower than *allaḏī* on that scale for the following reasons. *Allaḏī* is inflected (obligatorily in classical and modern literary Arabic) and thus denotes number and gender, concepts which the uninflected *man* is unable to express. These *can* be expressed by the *ʿĀʾid* of the *man*-clause, i.e., in (4) type E, but the language often chooses not to avail itself of this possibility[12], thus achieving an utterance of the greatest degree of unspecificity and vagueness, type F.[13] Furthermore, though *man* can be definite, it is more regularly indefinite[14], a fact which associates it more closely with absence of specificity than *allaḏī*, which is commonly definite.[15] Finally, the *man*-clause is quite often followed by a specifying *min*-phrase, while the *allaḏī*-clause is less frequently (in the modern literary language never) so followed[16], a difference which reflects *man*'s inherent lower specificity. All of this, then, marks a distinct line of separation between these two heads on the specificity scale. And, again, the difference is mirrored by the distribution of the RCs under discussion. While the head with the higher specificity, *allaḏī* (type D), still belongs to that "grey" intermediate area where no marked preference for either the dir. or indir. RC could be detected, see § 4.4, the head with the lower specificity, *man*, exhibited a clear preference for indir. RCs: of a total of ten recorded *man*-RCs in the classical and the modern literary language, i.e., (10)a–f, (17), (18)a, and notes 25, 31, a single one had the direct mode, viz. example (17).

100.10, that *bāyaʿnā* does not fit the meter of that verse, only *enhances* the linguistic value of this example.) I do not think it is coincidental that these alternations occurred precisely in types C and D, not in other types: it is an indication of the absence of any preference for either of the two modes in these two types.

12 W. Fischer *Gramm.* 192; Reck. *AS* 432–3. Also cf. Beeston 49.

13 It is more a matter of terminological bias than of substance whether one prefers to speak of this type as "most unspecific" or "least specific". I, for one, like to see "unspecific" as a category in its own right, definable not just by "absence of specificity".

14 Reck. *AS* 432, and esp. W. Fischer *Gramm.* 192.–5. For the modern literary language see Cant. III 173. Even if it should turn out that the type *marartu biman muḥsinin*, in which *man* functions as head of an attributive phrase, is no more than a grammarian's invention to prove *man*'s indefiniteness (cf. Reck *AS* 290.1–2, and n. 1), it does have a point at least insofar as there is certainly no corresponding definite **marartu bimani lmuḥsini*. But the whole question of this aspect of *man* deserves close scrutiny. It may turn out that what *man* really *marks* is only "unspecific", and that the contrast definite/indefinite is here annulled.

15 For another correlation: definite = more specific, indefinite = less specific, see (4) types B, C.

16 Reck. *AS* 438–9 vs. 440; W. Fischer *Gramm.* 193; Cant. III 179.

4.6 In sum, the preceding has shown a distinct correlation between the degree of specificity of the head and the distribution of the RCs under discussion. Proper nouns, which rank highest on the specificity scale, together with the adjacently located definite substantives, showed a clear preference for dir. RCs, while the manifestly unspecific *man* exhibited the same proclivity for indirect ones. Thus, it is at the two opposite ends of the scale – as one would expect – that the correlation is most clearly expressed, while the "grey" middle area (types C–D) showed no marked preference either way.[17]

5. *The Notion of Category*

5.1 As is known, CA has a RC-type (usually constructed asyndetically) whose head denotes a category or "genus".[18] This type, too, exhibits both the direct and the indirect mode:

(6) a. *anta lmarʾu taʿfū ʿani lḫanāti lkibāri* "You are a man who forgives the greatest sins". Brock. 559

b. *anta lmarʾu tafʿalu mā taqūlu* "You are a man who does what he says". Reck. *AS* 424.1

(7) a. *anā lmarʾu lā taʿyā ʿalayhi maḏāhibuhū* "I am a man to whom his ways are not inaccessible". Reck. *AS* 424

b. *anta lwazīru lā yuʿṣā* "You are a vizier whom one does not defy". W. Fischer *Gramm.* 194.7.

c. *mā anta bilmarʾi abtaġī riḍāhu* "You are not a man whom I desire to please". Reck. *AS* 339

17 I have included only the more common types of RCs in the specificity scale, excluding from consideration those for which attestation is less copious, such as the RCs that fall under the term in its wider sense (§ 1.2). However, some of these may also exhibit similar distributional tendencies. Thus, compare example (2)i, whose definite substantival head puts it on a par with type B on the specificity scale and which exhibits the direct mode, with (3)i, which has a lower specificity (it could be paraphrased by type D: *anā llaḏī šuhira biʾabīhi*), and which shows the indirect mode. On the other hand, there are examples among those less common types that do not fit into the picture. E.g., in *innanī samḥun muḫālaqatī* "I am someone who is easy to get along with" Nöldeke *ZGr.* 98.–3, one would have expected the indirect mode, since its head is manifestly unspecific and indefinite (one would here paraphrase with *man*, not *allaḏī*). It is conceivable that constructions whose surfaces differ from those of the common RC-types also differ from them, at least in part, with respect to notions such as specificity and definiteness and, therefore, may exhibit somewhat different distributions of the two modes.

18 The head's definite article, accordingly, is said to be *litaʿrīfi ljins*, Wright II 318 B* (cf. I 269 B); Reck. *AS* 413–4; Reck. *SV* 524.

d. *innaka lalkarīmu lā yuṭʿanu fī ḥasabihī* "You are a nobleman whose good reputation cannot be contested". Brock. 560

e. *innaka lmarʾu narjūhu wanantaẓiru* "You are a man such as we are hoping and waiting for". Nöldeke *ZGr.* 162 (101 n. 1)[19]

The semantics of these sentences would be more faithfully rendered by paraphrases such as "You are the kind of man who ...", "You belong to the category of viziers who ...", etc.

5.2 The indirect examples are obviously in the majority. Though the sampling is small, I do not think that this ratio is coincidental. It becomes especially meaningful if one compares it with the reverse ratio exhibited by the (commonly syndetic) RCs whose heads denote specific and definite entities, i.e., (4) type B, see § 4.4 and the exx. in note 10. The difference ought to be understood in terms of the semantic notions involved. Whereas the heads in (4) type B are individual and self-contained entities, sentences (6)–(7) have the individual in mind only insofar as he belongs to a larger category of individuals with comparable properties. Thus, the vizier in (7)b is assigned membership in the category of viziers who have the characteristic of not allowing disobedience; the man in (6)a is classified among easily forgiving people, etc. There are clear indications that heads of RCs involving notions such as "class" or "category" prefer the indirect mode. Cf. also § 8.10–11. The same appears to apply when the head is a superlative phrase. Superlatives are by their very nature class-oriented: an individual entity is compared with other entities of the same category and is found to hold a higher rank than all the others with regard to some property. I have only a single example of this sort, but its indirect mode seems distinctly determined by this notion. While an individual entity, i.e., the *umma* in question, is implicitly compared within the category of *umma*'s in (9), no such comparison is involved in (8), where that entity is seen as self-contained:

19 Nöldeke *ZGr.* understood this particular example to be an asyndetic RC with a specific head, see ibid. 101. But the context of this verse in the *ʿIqd*, as well as the word *almarʾu* – as in five of the above examples – seems to me to favor the generic interpretation. This is also Brockelmann's understanding of a variant of this verse, ibid. 553.–10 ("Du bist ein Mann wie wir ihn ...").

(8) *annā ummatun akramanā llāhu* "that we are a nation whom God has honored". Reck. *SV* 538

(9) *kuntum ḫayra*[20] *ummatin uḫrijat linnāsi*[21] "You are the best nation ever brought forth to men". Q 3:110

RCs with generic heads differ of course from RCs whose heads are superlatives in many regards. But the two types have one important aspect in common, namely, the implied reference to the *category*. In this sense I believe there is a similar motivation behind the (prevalent) indirect mode in the generic type and the indirect mode of (9).

5.3 Thus, there seems to be a single, relatively simple rationale behind the inverted ratios mentioned § 5.2: heads representing self-contained entities prefer dir. RCs, while generic and other classifying, categorizing heads prefer indirect ones.[22] From the standpoint of the distributional tendencies involved, therefore, unspecific and generic heads stand together in opposition to specific, self-contained heads.[23]

6. *Contextual Criteria*

The approach in the preceding paragraphs was primarily structural. It was shown that particular RC-types – more accurately, particular types of head – prefer the direct mode, others the indirect one. The abstract notions discussed were seen as properties of these RC-types. But this approach presents only one part of the picture. In the following we shall examine to what extent other than structural criteria play a role in the distribution of these modes – criteria such as the actual situation in which a given utterance is made and, rather significantly, the *point of view of the speaker*. Abstract

20 Not *ḫayru*, as in Reck. *VS* 538.

21 I am not dealing here with the difference in the number agreement of *umma*, i.e., pl. in (8), fem. sing. in (9). Alternations of this sort are quite widespread with human collectives, cf. e.g. Q 3:113 *ummatun qā'imatun yatlūna āyāti llāhi*.

22 It could be argued that indefinite heads of (4) type C, such as the frequent *imru'un*, often have a general meaning undistinguishable from that of generic heads, and it is true that in such cases there is some overlap between these two types. But it is a decisive difference whether the notion "category" is only implied or whether it is overtly marked, as in the case of the *Lām al-Jins*. Furthermore, type C is of course associated not only with heads like *imru'un*, but also with highly specific, individualized ones such as in (24), to mention but one instance.

23 This itself would be a sufficiently strong argument to propose a closer look at the relationship between the notions "unspecific" and "categorial".

notions like "specificity", "category", etc., will still be dealt with, only now no longer as structure-based but as related to nonstructural criteria like those just mentioned. These criteria will be summarily referred to as "contextual".

7. The Emphatic Indirect Relative Clause

7.1 Reckendorf uses "portentous or emphatic indefiniteness" ("prägnante oder emphatische Indetermination") for a well-known and powerful stylistic device of classical Arabic. A person in love, for example, might speak of "a heart" when he has his own in mind: *uʿazzī qalban mustahāman* "I am consoling a lovesick heart"; or it may be said that someone *ajāba rabban daʿāhu* "followed a master who summoned him", meaning God, etc. For a discussion and examples see Reck. *AS* 199–200, and cf. ibid. 194; *SV* 163. My understanding of the phenomenon, as presented in the following paragraphs, differs from Reckendorf's in one basic respect, see note 32 end.

7.2 What creates the portentous, ceremonious, occasionally mysterious effect of utterances such as these (simply "emphaticity" in the following) is the discrepancy between what a speaker is really talking about, which is a familiar and known entity, and the oblique and unspecific way he chooses to talk about that entity. Typical candidates for this way of presentation are the love-stricken heart, as in the above example, the slain hero addressed in a eulogy, etc. But whether or not an entity will be so presented in any given situation depends on the speaker's attitude, his point of view. Of interest to our particular subject is a case like this:

> *in baqītu laʾarḥalanna biġazwatin taḥwī lġanāʾima aw yamūta karīmun*
> "If I remain alive, I shall participate in a warring expedition that yields booty – unless a nobleman should die". Reck. *AS* 200

where the speaker shifts from a direct to an indirect reference to himself: "I survive" → "a nobleman dies".[24] This demonstrates rather well the connection between emphaticity and indirect reference.

7.3 It was demonstrated earlier that the indirect mode is an outstanding characteristic of the *man*-RC (§ 4.5). We have seen, furthermore, that *man* is the unspecific head par excellence. In view of these two factors, one would expect *man*-RCs to be a suitable device for the expression of emphaticity, a notion so

24 Comm.: *aw yamūta karīmun yaʿnī nafsahu.*

intimately linked to oblique reference and vagueness. The following sentences are amenable to such an interpretation:

(10) a. *yā man lā yamūtu (i)rḥam man yamūtu*[25]
"O the one who does not die, have mercy upon him who dies". Reck. *SV* 606

b. *yā man hāḏā šaʾnuhu naḫuṣṣuka bilʿibādati walistiʿānati*
"O the one whose characteristics are thus, we worship you alone and to you alone we turn for help". Bayḍāwī 7.12[26]

c. *yā man aḥassa bunayyayya llaḏayni humā samʿī waṭarfī faṭarfī lyawma muḫtaṭafu*
"O the one who saw my two little sons, who were my hearing and my eyesight – my eyesight has today been snatched away". Wright II 320D

d. *miṯlu qatlika hadda qawmaka kullahum man kāna yaḥmilu ʿanhumū lʾaṯqāla*[27]
"Something like your being killed weighs heavily down on your people, O the one who used to carry their burdens". Reck. *AS* 435.–5

e. *antum yā maʿšara lʾanṣāri man lā yunkaru faḍluhum*
"You, O Ansar, are people whose excellence does not go unrecognized". Reck. *SV* 622

f. *qultu man anti faqālat anā man šaffahū lwajdu waʾablāhu lkamad*
"I said: Who are you? So she said: I am someone who has been afflicted by an all-consuming passion and deep grief". ʿUmar *Dīwān* 115.12[28]

The addressee in a–b is God; in c the emphaticity is not connected with the addressee(s)[29] but with the bereavement of the speaker; d is from a eulogy in which a friend addresses a slain hero; in e a venerated group of allies is addressed; f has, in addition to its obvious emphaticity, an air of mystery that is produced by the obliqueness of the reply.[30] All of these are very typically emphatic contexts.[31]

25 For a variant without *yā* see Wright II 87B.

26 From Bayḍāwī's commentary on *iyyāka naʿbudu*.

27 For the absence of a vocative marker (cf. note 25) see § 8.3.

28 Quoted from the ed. by P. Schwarz, Leipzig 1901–9. I am indebted to G. Goldenberg for having brought this verse to my attention.

29 This could be an address to a specific person, as Wright understood it ("O thou who sawest ..."), or it could be meant in an encompassing sense, for which cf. (16) a–b.

30 In this context where it refers to a woman, *man šaffahū* is (4) type F. For an emphatic use of *man*, but outside of the RCs under discussion, see Reck. *AS* 199 n. 1.

31 One further example whose context I was not able to check, but which might belong here, is *yā man yuḥākī lbadra* ..., Brock 590.1.

7.4 It was argued that the way of presentation in cases such as (10) is not dictated by the objective reality but by the speaker's attitude towards that reality. In other situations the speakers might have chosen to present exactly the same entities in a nonemphatic way. I suggest that, e.g., an utterance with *anā llatī* ... would be a nonemphatic counterpart of f, etc.[32] Because of their mentioned properties, *man*-RCs are ideal devices for the expression of emphaticity.

8. Vocativic Utterances

8.1 Vocativic utterances with embedded RCs (type: O you people who ...) constitute a category in their own right.[33] In this category there is a sharp

32 One may describe the discrepancy between such two presentations in terms of a specificity scale corresponding to the one according to which the heads of RCs were ranked (4). Thus, an underlying "I am the one who ..." would become "I am someone who ..." in f, corresponding to a shift from D to F. Similar shifts downward on the specificity scale could be postulated for the other cases in (10), with *yā ayyuhā llaḏī/llaḏīna* etc. postulated as underlying in cases such as a–c. Downward movement on that scale means increase of emphaticity. The same would apply to "my love-stricken heart", which would become "a love-stricken heart" in the surface structure, corresponding to a transition from B to C; and to an underlying "*Allāh* who called him", or "The Lord who ...", which would become "a lord who ...", reflecting a shift from A to C, etc. My approach differs from Reckendorf's (see § 7.1) in that I consider the relevant criterion to be "unspecific", not "indefinite". The reason is the *man*-RCs that were discussed above. We have seen that *man* can be both definite and indefinite, § 4.5, but it is *always* unspecific. Since *man*-RCs are strongly involved in expressing the sort of emphaticity that Reckendorf is talking about, I think something like "emphatische Unbestimmtheit" would be a better term for the phenomenon, taking German "unbestimmt" to be the equivalent of "unspecific" as used here. (In fact, Reckendorf himself uses "unbestimmt", *AS* 199.6.) Or, to put it another way: I believe that the basic ingredient in the emphatic value of utterances such as those under discussion is unspecificity rather than indefiniteness, and that it is the emphatic *man*-RCs that prove it.

33 The dichotomy of reference could here be described in a formalized way if one postulated that underlying any vocativic utterance of this kind is a second-person pronoun, which does not appear in the surface structure, followed by an appositive representing the adressee:

O you A who ... (A = appositive)

The postulate of such a second-person pronoun would be supported not only by the corresponding predicational utterances of address, where that pronoun actually appears in the surface structure – you are P who ..., see (1) – but also by the fact that some languages regularly have an overt second-person pronoun in their vocativic utterances, e.g., American "Hey, you guys", German "O Ihr ...". As in the predicational construction, here too the head can be pronominal or substantival (see passim in § 8), yielding two realizations of the portion "A who", cf. § 1.3. When the RC embedded in this vocativic utterance is direct, its *ʿĀʾid* refers to the personal pronoun, i.e., the underlying "you"; when it is indirect, the *ʿĀʾid* refers to its appositive.

difference between classical Arabic on the one hand and the modern literary language and the colloquials on the other.

Vocativic Utterances in Classical Arabic

8.2 In the classical language the indirect mode has been conventionalized to such an extent as to practically deserve the label "standard".[34] This applies above all to the numerous formulas whose common feature is the presence of an overt vocative marker, i.e., *yā*, *yā ayyuhā*, *alā ayyuhā*, *yā ḏā*, *a-*, etc.[35]

Excursus

The predominance of the indirect mode with the vocative has been noticed in Arabic as well as Syriac.[36] Since there is no intrinsic reason why this should be so – one does find the direct mode, at least sporadically, in Arabic and elsewhere[37] – an explanation is called for. I propose that the Qur'ānic language may offer an explanation for Arabic. As is known, an overwhelming number of the vocativic utterances in the Qur'ān are addressed to the believers, most often in the form of *yā ayyuhā llaḏīna āmanū*. It is conceivable that the indirect mode was here originally motivated by a notion such as "encompassing generality" of believers. This becomes plausible if one considers that the phrase *allaḏīna āmanū* by itself, at least at the very early period of the Prophet's mission, probably meant no specific group of people or nation, e.g., in its use in: *inna l'insāna lafī ḫusrin illā llaḏīna āmanū waʿamilū ṣṣāliḥāti watawāṣaw bilḥaqqi* (Q 103:2–3). In this interpretation, then, *allaḏīna āmanū* would have come close to marking the "category" of believer, in which case the indirect mode of *yā ayyuhā llaḏīna*

Needless to say, such a presentation has no explanatory value. It simply serves to make explicit the element which vocativic utterances and corresponding predicational constructions have in common.

34 I am talking here and in the following only about the mode within the vocativic utterance proper. The frequent shift to a direct address (imperative) outside of its confines is here of no concern.

35 I shall mention here only a random sampling of these formulas: Apart from its extremely frequent *yā ayyuhā llaḏīna āmanū*, the Qur'ān has *yā ʿibādi llaḏīna āmanū* (39:10), *yā ʿibādiya llaḏīna asrafū ʿalā anfusihim* (39:53), *yā ayyuhā llaḏī nuzzila ʿalayhi ḏḏikru* (15:6). For further examples the standard grammars may be consulted, e.g., Reck. *AS* 425.2, 425 n. 1, for which cf. Nöldeke *ZGr.* 162 (100 n. 2, last expl.); Reck. *AS* 444.9–10; Wright II 85.–1; 90.1; 93.3–4; Brock. 560.–6; 589.–1. Standardization of the indirect mode may even have extended beyond the realm of the relative to other subordinated clauses, such as the *Ḥāl*, see Wright II 85.–2.

36 Nöldeke *ZGr.* 100; Brock. 591.

37 E.g., Brock. 591.–4. For Arabic see below.

āmanū could be explained along the lines of §§ 5.2, 8.10–11. Once so established in what was undoubtedly a basic (perhaps *the* basic) type of formula of address, the indirect mode could then have been standardized.

8.3 On the other hand, vocativic utterances that deviate from these standard formulas present a different picture. Consider:

(11) a. *aʿūḏu biʿizzatika llaḏī lā ilāha illā anta*
"I take refuge in your might, O you beside whom there is no god".
Nöldeke *ZGr.* 100

b. *baʿda nadīmayya llaḏayni bakaytukumā*
"After (you), my two drinking companions for whom I wept".
Reck. *AS* 443

Cases such as these suggest that the standardization of the indirect mode did not extend to vocativic utterances which in some way or another do not conform to the canonic patterns. The exact nature of the deviation may vary, see § 8.5. In the case of (11)a–b, the outward manifestation of the deviation is the absence of an overt vocative marker.[38] In the light of the preceding, the following hypothesis may be proposed: whereas the indirect mode was all but standardized within the canonic formulas[39], outside of these formulas both modes were available to the speaker. Indeed, a minimally contrastive pair such as (11)a:(10)d strongly supports this contention.

8.4 The status of the vocativic utterances with *yā man* vis-à-vis the standard formulas is uncertain. It cannot be ruled out that here, too, the indirect mode is due to the same process of standardization. However, since *man* exhibits that mode also elsewhere – i.e., not only in nonstandard vocativic formulas, see (10)d and note 25, but also in predicational constructions, (10)e–f – it seems far more likely that it is this pronoun's unspecific nature that imposes the indirect mode, as was suggested earlier.

38 Exx. (11)a–b differ from the canonic patterns also in other respects, but these cannot be discussed at this time.

39 I have encountered only a single example: *yā mūqidan nāran liġayrika ḍawʾuhā* "O the one who has enkindled a fire whose glow someone else enjoys", Reck. *AS* 111.6, which seemingly contains an exception. But in this case the utterance involves a RC of the second degree, i.e., the one whose head is *nār*, and this may account for the speaker's falling back into the direct mode. Cf. also note 34.

8.5 Another vocativic utterance that remained exempt from the standardization of the indirect mode, albeit for a different reason than in type (11), is:

(12) *minajliki*[40] *yā llatī tayyamti qalbī wa'anti baḫīlatun bilbadli ʿannī*
"Because of you, O you who enslaved my heart, yet are giving yourself only sparingly to me".[41]

Zamaḫšarī and Ibn Yaʿīš declare this *yā llatī* as deviant (*šāḏḏ*) because it presents the "inadmissible sequence of the vocative marker and the definite article"[42] – a sequence which is indeed found nowhere in the canonic types. This verse may illuminate the history of modern colloquial *yalli*. It is possible that some old Arabic dialect(s) possessed a vocative formula of the type **yā llaḏī*, **yā llatī* of which a single specimen was preserved in this verse, and that this formula is the historical forerunner of *yalli*.[43] We cannot know to what extent this formula actually penetrated into the classical language. But we can see why it would have been rejected by the grammarians: it allowed the direct mode in its RC, thus contravening the standard pattern in this point, § 8.2, and may have in addition been associated with colloquial usage.

8.6 Thus, (10)d, (11)a–b and (12) indicate that, outside the confines of the standard vocativic formulas, the speaker was free to choose between the direct and the indirect mode. In this realm, and only here, could his choice have been motivated by contextual criteria such as those discussed. We shall now examine the contexts of each of these examples. In (11)b the speaker addresses his two drinking companions. That these are two *specific* persons is recognizable from the very form of the RC, (4) type B. It is immaterial that these two may have never existed outside of the speaker's mind and that they probably represent the standard "two companions". What matters is, here again, not only real, objective truth, but the situational, subjective truth of the moment of utterance, and from this point of view these are two very real, concrete persons, so presented by the direct mode of address. In the two remaining examples with a dir. RC, the high degree of specificity, the "one of a kind" nature of the addressee, is plainly evident: in (11)a, God's oneness is the very message of the RC, and in (12) it is that particular lover, none else, that the poet is addressing. Here, as well as in (11)b, the addressees might have been "on the scene" at the time the address was made, in which case this would be an additional motivation for the use of the

40 For *min ajliki*.

41 For this anonymous verse see Sībawayhi I 269.10.

42 Ibn Yaʿīš 170.–1 ff. Such a sequence is found in Middle Arabic, see Blau *Chr. Ar.* 361 B.

43 Here *allaḏī* lost its inflection, just as it did outside of the formula. On the early loss of *allaḏī*'s inflection see Blau *BZ* 263.–12 ff.

direct mode (see § 8.7). It is, however, more likely that the direct mode has been chosen simply to "concretize" absent persons. On the indirect mode of (10)d, § 7.3.

Some Colloquial Vocativic Utterances

8.7 It comes as no surprise that in a language where both modes are available, dir. RCs would be preferred in situations where an addressee is visibly "on the scence" or otherwise immediately identifiable to the speaker. This distribution is evident in the following use of a vocativic curse-formula with a *Naʿt Sababi*-type RC in Bīr Zēt:

(13) *ya manʿūl abu šēbič* (14) *ya manʿūl abu šēbha*
"O the one whose white hair be cursed!"

where the old woman so addressed is in the presence of the speaker in (13), while he uses (14) in her absence.[44]

8.8 A meaningful distribution of the two modes was found also in other colloquial RC-types. Thus, *yalli* is used with the direct mode, *ya mīn* (*mən*) with the indirect one in the following:

(15) a. *qālu: mīn ačalha? mīn ačalha? wqālu: yalli ačaltha ʿalēk il amān* "They said: Who ate it? Who at it? And they said: O you who ate it, we guarantee that no harm will come to you [for having eaten it]".

b. *fēnak yalli bəddak ṭṭalleq marṭak*? "Where are you, O you who wants to divorce his wife?"

(16) a. *qāl: ya mīn yḥibbni yjīb šaqfit nār wḥamlit ḥaṭab* "He said: O whosoever loves me bring me some fire and a load of wood".

b. *ya mən šafəlna* ..." "O whosoever can find for us [such and such a lost object]".

The pair (15)a–(16)a is from Bīr Zēt; (15)b–(16)b could qualify as general Syr. Pal. (its exact provenance could not be determined).[45] The contrast manifested in these sentences is highly significant to the subject at hand. While *yalli*

44 As observed by Blau *BZ* 262. Similarly "on the scene" are the addressees in two further dir. RCs of the type *ya manʿūl* ... referred to Blau *BZ* 258.5–6.

45 For (15)a–(16)a see Schmidt-Kahle I 244.–16 and 104.–4, respectively, both referred to Blau *BZ* 262. For (15)b–(16)b see Barthélemy 917; 801.12.

with the direct mode is normally used for identified addressees that are directly spoken to, e.g.

> *ahla wsahla yalli čunt ḏ̣āyifna*
> "Welcome, O you who has become our guest",
> where the addressee is the bridegroom at the wedding ceremony;
>
> *yalli btiṭbaẖu ʿaššams*
> "O you who (have to) do their cooking in the sun",
> spoken in contempt to a group of poor women,

and cf. *ya* + addressee + *elli* in

> *ya s(i)yādi elli tiwaḥḥadu llāh*
> "O you gentlemen who profess belief in the unity of God",
> spoken by beggars in the street,[46]

I have singled out (15) a and b because they cannot be so interpreted. In (15)a the speakers are forty robbers in a cave who, having just sat down to feast on some meat which they had prepared, discover that one of the forty pieces is missing. They do not know who the thief is – it could be anyone among them, or someone else (the reader alone knows that it is the poor fellow who is hiding in the same cave, the story's protagonist). The choice of the dir. RC may be motivated here by an "on the scene" notion, if the robbers assume that the culprit is one of them – a likely assumption given the nature of their profession. The same could be true of (15)b, if it were, say, uttered by a judge who assumes the addressee to be among the people assembled before him in the courtroom and who chooses this form of expression to cause him to come forth. But even if the speakers in (15) a and b assume the addressees to be present, they certainly do not speak *to* them. The direct address is made "into the air", figuratively speaking. In this regard (15) a and b differ, contextually, from the three structurally similar exx. just quoted and from exx. such as (13) and (17), where the addressees are visibly identifiable by the speakers at the moment of utterance and are directly spoken to. Obviously, the choice of a dir. RC in (15) a and b cannot have the same motivation. All that can be said here with certainty is that the speakers in both cases assume the addressee to be a single male person. It is in this respect that (15) a and b contrast with (16) a and b, where the addresses are made to "any person who ...", or "all persons who ...". Again, we are dealing with a formal dichotomy, in this case:

> *yalli* with direct RC vs. *ya mīn* (*mən*) with indirect RC

that expresses notional contrasts such as "specific", "limited" vs. "unspecific",

46 Exx. from Pal., Leb. and Eg., see Brock. 590.6–9 (where the Leb. ex. is misquoted; its original reads as presented above).

"encompassing". Furthermore, these data have a significance to the general discussion, insofar as they demonstrate the dir. RC to be a meeting ground of the seemingly unrelated notions of "on the scene", on the one hand, and "specific" on the other. A possible associative link between these two notions might be "concrete". See also § 8.6 *in fine*.

Vocative Utterances in Modern Literary Arabic

8.9 Of the following, (17) is by Maḥfūẓ, (18) a and b by Jibrān:[47]

(17) *yā man tuḥibbūna l'almāna*
"O you who love the Germans"

(18) a. *yā man tubīnuhā nnafsu*
"O you whom the soul announces"

b. *yā ayyuhā llaḏīna unzilat ʿalayhim āyātu ljamāli*
"O you upon whom the tokens of beauty have descended"

Normally, modern authors feel free to use both dir. and indir. RCs in vocativic utterances, and one may therefore expect to find some motivated distributions. The speaker in (17) talks to a group of friends at a social gathering. This is a clear case of the use of a dir. RC for an "on the scene" situation, with the addressees identifiable by the speaker and directly spoken to.[48] I was unable to check (18)a in its context, but it seems unlikely that the address is made to any concrete entity physically presenting itself to the speaker, whatever its identity may be. Rather, the context of (18)b confirms, and the wording of (18)a suggests, that we are dealing in both cases with a particularly elevated and sublime subject matter – which fact would in itself all but prescribe the use of a canonic formula with its standard indirect mode.

8.10 Contrastive pairs by a single author in a single context are especially well suited for an examination of the distribution of the two modes:

47 (17) Maḥfūẓ *Ḫān*, 276.7. (18)a–b Jibrān, quoted Cant. II 219 (where the misprint *aljimāl* is to be corrected), and III 175. For the context of (18)b see Jibrān *Al-Majmūʿa al-Kāmila li-Mu'allafāt Jibrān Ḫalīl Jibrān al-ʿArabiyya* Beirut: Dār aṣ-Ṣādir (no year), 263.3. I am grateful to H. Bobzin for this reference.

48 A *man* with dir. RC appears in a *qaṣīda* in which a leader of the Druses addresses God: *yā man kalāmak bayn kāfin wnūn ..., yā man qawlak liššay' kun fayakūn*, referred to in Brock. 590.9–10. As the wording indicates, this is semi-literary usage; it is therefore excluded here from consideration.

(19) *ayyuhā ttuʿasāʾu ayyuhā l'amwātu llaḏīna taẓunnūna anfusakum aḥyāʾan* "O you unhappy people, you (living) dead who deem yourselves alive"

(20) *ayyuhā lwāqiʿiyyūna ssaṭḥiyyūna llaḏīna lā yarawna mina lwāqiʿi siwā wajhihi ẓẓāhiriyyi* "O you superficial realists who see nothing but the outward face of the material world"

Exx. (19) and (20) are from the concluding pages of ʿAbd al-Malik Nūrī's story *Našīd al-Arḍ*.[49] Contrary to what one may presume at a first glance, they do not contrast along the lines of "on the scene" vs. "off the scene". The addressees, who are the same in both instances, are intended to symbolize a certain type of human beings whom the author criticizes for deplorable qualities of character and mind. We shall consider whether the distribution of the two modes is here meaningful in any sense.

8.11 In (19) these people are described as what they *are*: unhappy humans who have a wrong notion about themselves. On the other hand, (20) speaks of their attitude to life and the world, their Weltanschauung. They are described – or better, perhaps, classified – as realists. The notion *category* comes to mind: they are assigned class membership in the category of "realists". The impression of a categorizing, labeling attitude on the part of the author is heightened by his use of semi-philosophical terminology (*al-wāqiʿ* "the real, material world", *wāqiʿiyy* "realist, positivist"). There is no single way to conceptualize the difference. In terms of the attitudes displayed by these people, one may speak of a contrast: towards self, inwardly vs. towards the world, outwardly. Or one could speak of the way the entities are seen in each case: as self-contained in (19), and as assigned to a larger class, categorized, labeled, in (20).[50] The relation of the latter dichotomy to notions discussed earlier is self-evident.

9. *Metaphors*

9.1 In commenting on (21)a, Nöldeke says: "Natürlich ist in einem Falle wie *wakuntu sinānan* ... nur die 3. Person im Relativsatz möglich; das Bild muß hier ja durchgeführt werden". This somewhat too apodictic statement neverthe-

49 Quoted V. Monteil, *Anthologie bilingue de la littérature arabe contemporaine*. Beirut (no year) 81.3 and 79.10, respectively. (19) is quoted in Blau "Remarks" 210.

50 Inclusion in a larger category is, of course, a well-known powerful device of insult: compare the relatively mild "you silly guys" with, say, "you silly Americans".

less contains a basic truth, namely that in this category – one may call it "metaphoric" predication – indir. RCs are the common and predominating usage:

(21) a. *wakuntu sinānan yaḫriqu ljilda ḥadduhū*
"I am a spearhead whose sharp edge tears the skin open". Nöldeke *ZGr.* 98 n. 1

b. *anta sayfun ... sallahū llāhu*
"You are a sword ... that God unsheathed". Reck. *AS* 424

c. *antum samā'un yu'jibu nnāsa rizzuhā*
"You are a sky whose thunderous roar amazes man". Reck. *AS* 424

9.2 In view of the logic of the metaphorical image (in Nöldeke's sense), metaphors with dir. RCs are certainly unexpected. And yet they do occur:

(22) a. *wa'innī la'arjū 'ājilan an taruddanī mawāhibuhū baḥran turajjā mawāhibī*
"And I do hope that soon his gifts will turn me into a sea whose gifts are hoped for". Brock. 559[51]

b. *iḏā anta ḥummilta l'amānata far'ahā wakūnanna quflan lā yarūmuka fātiḥun fa'inna lisāna lmar'i ... bimā yaḫfā 'alā nnāsi bā'iḥun*
"If you are charged with a trust (or: trusteeship), keep watching over it. Be a lock that no one would attempt to open. For a man's tongue ... reveals that which is hidden from people". Reck. *AS* 424[52]

The significance of cases such as (22) is, in the simplest sense, the plain fact that they occur at all. In this respect, the category of metaphors, more sharply perhaps than any other category of examples dealt with in this chapter, demonstrates how deeply rooted the phenomenon of the two modes really is. The importance of these examples lies precisely in the fact that they violate the logic of the metaphor. The speaker in (22) abandons the metaphorical image – the sea in a, the lock in b – for the "real" entity behind it, i.e. the "I" and "you" which the metaphor was supposed to replace. One might be tempted to suggest that in cases like these the message was more in the foreground, more important to the speaker, than the image. But while it still remains doubtful whether the deviations in (22) have a meaning of their own, different from that of the corresponding indir. RCs, there can be no doubt about the meaningfulness of the dir. RC in a case such as:

51 For this version of the verse see Abū Tammām *Dīwān*, ed. Muḥ. 'Abduh 'Azzām, Cairo 1964[2] (= Ḏaḫā'ir al-'Arab, 5), I, 215, where other variants are also listed.

52 For the whole quotation of (22)b see *WZKM* (reference in Reck. ibid.).

(23) *anā lḫubzu lḥayyu llaḏī nazaltu mina ssama*
man akala minhu lā yamūt
"I am the living bread that came down from Heaven.
Anyone who eats of it shall not die". Blau *Chr. Ar.* 564

Here the message is central – Christ in person descending from Heaven – while the image, i.e., Christ as manna, is relegated to the following sentence.[53]

Although the next example has nothing to do with metaphoricity, I am including it here because it resembles (23), in that it involves an entity that "manifests" itself in more than one way and the speaker chooses to focus on one of these manifestations:

anta Riḍwānuni llaḏī adḫalanī hāḏā lfirdawsa biḥūrihi lʿīni
"You are Riḍwān who brought me into this Paradise with its wide-eyed houris".
Bloch *Chr.* 80.–2

The Person here addressed as Riḍwān (this is the name of the guardian of Paradise) is the friend who previously introduced the speaker to the nightlife pleasures of Cairo. The speaker, who at this time has reached a fairly advanced stage of intoxication, actually believes (or at least pretends to believe) that he is in Paradise. The use of the indir. RC evokes the Heavenly guardian letting him enter Paradise, while the use of a dir. RC (*adḫaltanī*) would have instead focused on the "real thing" on earth, i.e. the friend who just brought him to a shady bar.

10. Historical Reconstruction

One occasionally encounters statements such as the one by Reckendorf, *SV* 536, alleging that the RCs which I call direct demonstrate that "the relative clause still enjoys a fair degree of independence". Such statements typically result from the confusion of synchronic facts and diachronic interpretations. RCs may indeed have *originated* from independent clauses[54], and the dir. RC in fact offers strong support to this view.[55] E.g., a sentence such as:

(24) *innī Ġālibiyyun ḫarajtu min ġayri fāqatin*
"I am a Ġālibite who has set out (though) not because of need".
Reck. *SV* 536

53 So observed by Blau *Chr. Ar.* 564 n. 76.

54 E.g. Beeston 49.

55 Cf. Blau *Chr. Ar.* 564 n. 75.

may be plausibly traced back to *"I am a Ġālibite. I have set out . . .". But in the synchronic system of the language, direct (like all other) RCs are definitely subordinated.

This reconstruction, however, raises a problem. RCs other than those involving a first- or second-person pronoun are reconstructable in the same way as dir. RCs, e.g.

(25) *inna s-Sīda kānat qabīlatan tuqātilu yawma rraw'i dūna nisā'ihā*
"The Sīda were a tribe who used to fight for their women on the day of horror". Brock. 553.7

may originally have been: *"The Sīda were a tribe. They used to . . .", but indir. RCs are not reconstructable in that way. For example, (24) could not be analyzed diachronically in this fashion if its RC were indirect. This suggests a different genesis of indir. RCs. The most likely conjecture seems to be that the dir. RCs and the regular ones reflect the original independence, while indir. RCs are historically secondary, having been formed by analogy to the (unmarked) norm of the regular RCs once subordination had been established.

11. The Medieval Grammarians' Approach

The medieval grammarians that I have consulted display a normative-prescriptive attitude towards the phenomenon. According to Tibrīzī, quoted Freytag 51, 147, the indir. RC is considered *wajh* "structurally correct", the direct one *qabīḥ* "structurally incorrect, ill-formed".[56] The criterion is the *'Ā'id* (Tibrīzī uses Ḍamīr): it must be a third-, not a first- or second-person pronoun. No explanation is given for this decree, but the reason appears self-evident. Since the dir. RC is, after all, nothing but a particular kind of RC, it "ought" to behave like the (unmarked) norm. With its third-person *'Ā'id*, the indir. RC was felt to be in conformity with that norm, while the direct one was considered a deviation.[57] But the medieval grammarians were forced to admit that the dir. RC does occur quite frequently. In the words of Māzinī, quoted Freytag 51: *lawlā ṣiḥḥatu mawridihi watakarruruhu laradadtuhu* "were it not for the fact that it [i.e., the dir. RC] occurs repeatedly and in good literary sources, I would have rejected it". In other words, since it occurs in sources which otherwise reflect

56 For *qabīḥ* in this sense see Carter 147.

57 A prescriptive attitude is also displayed by Wright, who is probably echoing the Arab grammarians when he says, II 324, that "the *'Ā'id* originally was, and strictly speaking, ought to be a pronoun of the third person". The attempt to justify the prescriptive verdict by a diachronic argument has nothing to support itself, see above § 10.

"best" Arabic (such as ancient poetry), the dir. RC had to be accepted, though only as an anomalous item that is not to be used as a model.

The explanation of these "incorrect" RCs is rather interesting. In discussing:

(26) *wamā anā binniksi ddaniyyi walā llaḏī iḏā ṣadda ʿannī ḏū lmawaddati aḥrabu*
"I am not a contemptible weakling, nor someone who becomes furiously enraged when the lover turns away from him".

Tibrīzī says, ibid. 147: *kāna yajibu an yaqūla walā llaḏī iḏā ṣadda ʿanhu ḏū lmawaddati yaḥrabu … lākinnahu lammā kāna lqaṣdu fī lʾiḫbāri ilā nafsihi … ḥamala lkalāma ʿalā lmaʿnā* "He should have said … *ʿanhu*, … *yaḥrabu*, but since he was talking about himself, he constructed the utterance according to the meaning". The terminology is here distincly semantic, i.e. *alqaṣdu fī lʾiḫbār*, lit. "the intention of the report"[58] and *ʿalā lmaʿnā*. One may be tempted to represent the phenomenon, as seen here by Tibrīzī, in terms of an "underlying" semantic component, reflected in the direct RCs – a component that "ought not" to surface at all – and a surface-structure component, reflected in the indir. RCs, where a structural adjustment (a "correction", in the spirit of the prescriptive approach) takes place, in that the *ʿĀʾid* is made to be in the third person. This interpretation is also supported by the terminology used in Ibn Yaʿīš, where the first-person *ʿĀʾid* of a direct RC is said to be *ḥamalan ʿalā lmaʿnā*, while the third-person *ʿĀʾid*, which "should" have been used, is referred to in terms of surface structure (*lafẓ*), namely as *lafẓ(u) lġayba*.[59] Modern reformulations of this kind, to be sure, are always somewhat risky.

12. The Presentation in the Western Standard Grammars

While most grammars correctly observed that the mode which I call indirect predominates in the vocativic utterances of the classical language, their statements on the distribution elsewhere are of very little use. Here one is left with the impression of an utterly unprincipled alternation between the two modes.[60] The reason for this presentation in the grammars may be the circumstance that a large number of the recorded examples are of types C–D on our scale (4), where there is indeed no observable preference for either mode, as we have seen § 4.4. But we have also seen that a clear distributional principle emerges when one leaves this "grey" area, moving either upward or downward on that scale. This,

58 In the discussion of another dir. RC the word *murād* "intention" is used, ibid. 51.

59 See Ibn Yaʿīš 494.2–6. See also similarly Zamaḫšarī, as described in Schub 16.

60 See Wright II 324; Reck. *AS* 423–4; 443–4; Nöldeke *ZGr.* 98–100; Brock. 559–60. On Brokkelmann's attempt to find a rationale in a specific case see note 11 above.

however, could not have been recognized in the standard grammars, which failed to look for and isolate types of RCs around which the modes tend to cluster, such as those with proper-noun heads, generic heads, etc.

13. The Broader Phenomenon

The phenomenon discussed in this chapter reflects a dichotomy which has very deep roots in language generally, and which reveals itself in various other ways. Let us mention here in random fashion a few other manifestations of that dichotomy. In Semitic languages, for example, the imperative and the jussive (the latter preceded by *li-* in Arabic) are a second- and third-person command, respectively:

iftaḥū lbāb	*liyaftaḥū lbāb*

Similarly, second- and third-person suffixes of *kull-* contrast in utterances of address in Syriac and Biblical Hebrew (Brock. 590 n. 1):

šmaʿ(ū) kullḵōn ʿammē	*šimʿū ʿammīm kullām*
"Listen all ye nations!"	"Listen all ye nations!"
	daʿ(ū) kullhōn bnay ṭohmeh
	"Know all ye kinsmen of his!"

Finally, consider the contrast between quoted and reported speech after verbs of saying found in numerous and unrelated languages, as in:

He said to him: "I don't want to go".	He said to him that he didn't want to go.
He said to him: "You are a fool".	He said to him that he was a fool.[61]

Obviously, these are different phenomena. I mention them here only for the one element which they have in common with each other and with the RCs discussed in this paper. They exhibit the contrast:

first- or second- vs. third-person pronoun,

a contrast which in all of these cases is associated in some way with the notions "direct" and "indirect". In this sense, then, these are manifestations of a single, deeply underlying notional dichotomy in language.

61 Changes such as those involving tense and mood, which in some languages accompany the shift from quoted to reported speech, are of no relevance in the context of the phenomenon under discussion.

14. Conclusion

In some sense we were dealing here with a feature of linguistic variation. But this so often misused term needs a strong qualification. To be sure, there are no "conditions" or "constraints" in the narrow linguistic sense, and certainly no "rules of grammar" that govern the distribution of the dir. and the indir. RCs. There was hardly any category in which one mode was found to be prevailing that did not also exhibit the other, at least sporadically. And even if it should turn out that there is a category which consistently exhibits only one mode, it could not be stated apodictically that the other *could* not also be generated.[62] However, the absence of easily statable conditions by no means implies that we are dealing with a random variation. I hope to have shown that the distribution of the Arabic dir. and indir. RCs corresponds to notions such as specific/unspecific; on the scene/off the scene; self-contained/categorized; plain/emphatic – notions which have clearly definable formal-grammatical as well as contextual and semantic correlates.

62 Again, I am talking here strictly about Arabic. On this point see esp. note 9.

Chapter III

"Be With" > "Encounter", "Come With" > "Bring"

1. *From Comitativity to Objecthood*

1.1 This chapter's title is an oversimplified symbolization of two processes of semantic change, each involving a transition from an original, historically primary relational notion of proximity or comitativity[1] to a notion of object, where "object" is to be understood as a term for an abstract case-category in the sense of the definition in § 2.3.2 of chapter V. The following is an attempt to trace these processes in a number of sentence-types of classical Arabic.

Consider the following examples:

(1) a. *falammā tawassaṭtu ddarba iḏā anā biṣawtin*
"When I had gotten midway along the road, I suddenly heard a noise".
Wright II 157D

b. *marra nāsun min Jurhumin bibaṭni lwādī fa'iḏā hum biṭayrin*
"People from (the tribe of) Jurhum were walking in the bottom of the wadi when they suddenly encountered/saw birds". Reck. *SV* 476

c. ... *fa'iḏā anā biẓulmatin šadīdatin*
"... when I suddenly became aware of a great darkness". Reck. *SV* 477

(2) a. *baynā huwa yasīru iḏā birahjin*
"As he was walking along, there was suddenly a cloud of dust".
Wright II 157D

b. *ṯumma maḍaytu fa'iḏā bifusṭāṭin*
"Then I continued to walk, and there was suddenly a big tent".
Reck. *SV* 478

c. *wanaḥnu fī lḥadīṯi wa'iḏā biḍajjatin ʿaẓīmatin ʿalā lbābi*
"As we were talking, there was suddenly a great noise at the door".
Wright II 157D

1 The term "comitative" has been used for some time in the general linguistic literature, see e.g. Lyons *Introduction* 295, and cf. terms such as "ablativus comitativus" and "dativus comitativus" in Knobloch. In Arabic linguistics the term has been used by Saad, "Comitative" (though he investigates comitative relations other than those to be dealt with here).

As is known, the traditional interpretation postulates that these two sentence types, i.e. (1) *iḏā anā/huwa bi-Zaydin* and (2) *iḏā bi-Zaydin*[2], "imply" some form of *aḥassa, šaʿara, baṣu(i)ra*, etc. – all of which are verbs of perception governing their object by means of *bi-*.[3] Viewed from a strictly methodological point of view, there is nothing objectionable in this way of presentation, *as long as* is it understood as simply a convenient way of ascribing a notion of object (in the sense of the above-mentioned definition) to the term governed by *bi*, rather than as implying that an actual verbal form has been deleted from the surface-structure, for which assumption there would be no support (cf. § 2.3.2.2 of ch. V). Let us examine to what extent an object notion can in fact be ascribed to the term governed by *bi-* in these two sentence-types.

1.2 An object notion is directly observable in the very meanings of sentences of type (1). This can be made explicit in a convenient way by means of a schematic paraphrase such as "suddenly I/he perceived (saw, heard, became aware of, etc.)/encountered (met, came upon, etc.)[4] a thing/person".[5] On the other hand, an object notion is not similarly observable in sentences of type (2), where an argument for such a notion can ultimately be made only on an inferential basis, i.e. by comparison with the (directly observable) object notion of type (1)[6], or on the basis of theoretical considerations such as Bravmann's, see § 5. below. I shall limit myself in the following to a discussion of types such as (1), (4), (5)–(11), where an object notion is observable (or "transparent") in the very meaning of the sentence, since it is these sentence-types that are most suited to demonstrate the semantic change that is the subject of this chapter.[7]

2 A word on a few marginal features of these two sentence-types. The term governed by *bi-* in both types can of course be pronominal, i.e. *iḏā anā/huwa bihi, iḏā bihi*. I have encountered no examples of type (1) where the free pronoun is of the second person, i.e. no **iḏā anta bi-Zaydin*. Presumably this is simply due to the fact that one does not normally tell an addressee about the latter's own experience, rather than being indicative of an inherent linguistic constraint. For the alternation *fa'iḏā* ~ *wa'iḏā* ~ *iḏā* in these sentence types see Reck. *SV* 478.

3 Reck. *SV* 476 n. 1, Wright II 158A, Fleischer 374.–4.

4 On the relation between the notions "encounter" and "perceive" see below.

5 Such paraphrases are in fact occasionally found in the texts themselves, as e.g. when the event related in (1)b is described by means of a verb in a parallel account: *nazalū fī asfali Makkata fara'aw ṭā'iran* "they had camped in the lowest part of Mecca when they saw a bird", Reck. *SV* 476. For another such alternation between the (verbless) type (1) and a verbal account compare *fa'iḏā hiya biṣawtin* "... she suddenly heard a voice", Buḫ. (ed. Krehl) II 345.9 with *samiʿat ṣawtan* "she heard a voice", ibid. 342.–1.

6 Fleischers's wording in 374.–3 appears to indicate that he was aware of this difference in the "transparency" of the object notion between types (1) and (2).

7 I shall also refrain from discussing the difficult problem of the historical relation between types (1) and (2). Suffice it to say that of the scholars that have made suggestions on this issue,

1.3 The most plausible historical reconstruction of type (1) known to me is the one offered by Brockelmann, who suggests that originally *bi-* was used here in its basic, i.e. strictly "prepositional" meaning. Accordingly, he paraphrases his model-sentence of this type, *iḏā huwa bihudhudin lahā*, as follows:

> "da traf er einen Wiedehopf von ihr", eigentlich
> "da war er bei einem Wiedehopf". Brock. 36.18[8]

While Brockelmann's reconstruction is convincing, his paraphrase is too simplistic, since it glosses over what in fact is a difference between two distinct semantic categories (or, more precisely: abstract case categories).

As I see it, there are on the one hand the original meanings of the preposition *bi-*, i.e. those of spatial proximity, physical togetherness, comitativity (*at*, *with*, *in the vicinity of*, *together with*, and the like).[9] We may plausibly suggest that these are the indigenous, *historically primary* meanings of *bi-* in this sentence-type. On the other hand, there are the synchronically observable meanings which, as we have just seen, fall under a category of "object". Therefore, the historical reconstruction proposed by Brockelmann requires the assumption of a change from the former to the latter category of meanings. A likely semantic change of this kind, occurring at a point where these two categories of meaning come closest to each other, could be symbolized in a gloss such as:

> (3) "suddenly he was with/at/near/in the vicinity of a thing/ person" > "suddenly he encountered a thing/ person".[10]

It stands to reason that such a change from the former to the latter category of

Brockelmann and Spitaler agree in viewing type (2) as historically secondary, differing only in detail insofar as Brock., 36, sees it as derived from (1) by a process of pronoun deletion in cases where this pronoun was easily "retrievable" from the preceding context, while Spitaler, 176 n. 1, considers (2) as resulting from a blend between (1) and the type *iḏā Zaydun*. For Bravmann's view see § 5 below.

8 For the sake of clarity, I have replaced Brockelmann's abbreviations "eig." and "bei einem W." with their unabbreviated equivalents.

9 For the use of *bi-* with specifically *these* meanings see examples such as *qaryatun bibābi l-Qāhirati* "a village close by the gate of Cairo", *ištarā lḥimāra bilijāmihi* "he bought the donkey together with its bridle", *nazala biqaylin* "he stayed with (dismounted at, etc.) a Ḥimyarite king", Wright II 156Cff., Brock. 362 (= § 236)ff. On the close connection between the notions of spatial proximity and comitativity see Brock. 364.–8. See also the terms *ilṣāq*, *ẓarfiyya*, *muṣāḥaba*, *mulābasa* in Wright II 163.–1ff.

10 It is not clear from Brockelmann's rendition of his model-sentence (see above) whether he really recognized such a semantic *change*, or whether he merely intended a paraphrase. This vagueness is evident also in Spitaler's rendition: *iḏā anā bihi* ... "da (war) ich bei ihm" = "da traf ich ihn" (176 n. 1). Only on a simple truth level can these two meanings be "the same". Linguistically, the presentation is flawed insofar as it equates what in fact are two distinct semantic categories, as outlined.

meanings was strongly aided by the semantics of the embedding frame of type (1), i.e. the presentative *iḏā* (the "*Iḏā* of Suddenness", also discussed § 2.3.4 of ch. V). This will be understood if we realize that the notion "be with/at, etc.", taken by itself, is a static notion, whereas "suddenly be with/at, etc." is dynamic, implying a *transition* from one state to another. In other words, it is likely that the semantic shift symbolized in the model (3) was to a large extent enhanced by the very notion of transition implied in the presentative *iḏā*. One may, thus, say that type (1) bears within itself the seed for this development.

1.4 It must be emphasized, however, that our model (3) can account for the actual meanings observed in type (1) only if we understand "to encounter" in its broader sense, i.e. as encompassing not merely that notion's concrete meaning (of "coming to be close to") but also its expanded sense of "to experience, become aware of, perceive". This type of expansion of the rudimentary, concrete meaning is of course a familiar phenomenon in verbs such as Engl. *to encounter, meet, find, come upon*, Arabic *laqiya*[11], etc. That we are indeed justified in postulating a similar expansion of the semantic range of "to encounter" for the right-hand portion of our model (3) is suggested by the fact that *bi-* occurs not only with substantives denoting physically palpable, concrete entities, but – significantly for our argument – also with those denoting entities perceived by the senses, such as a voice, eg. (1)a[12], or a darkness, as in (1)c. In the case of a substantive of the latter kind, obviously, "encounter" can be understood only in an expanded sense as outlined. Thus, examples with substantives denoting sense perceptions are of a special significance, insofar as they exhibit a further step in the semantic development of type (1), indicating how well established indeed the shift from a notion of comitativity, proximity, physical connectedness to one of objecthood (3) is in this sentence-type.

2. *The Notion of the "Envisaged Scene"*

2.1 Another sentence-type that must be discussed in this context is:

(4) a. *ka'annaka biġurābi lbayni*
"It is as if you can already hear the raven of separation". *WKAS* I 5.26 left

11 Which means not only "to meet, find, encounter" in the concrete sense but also "to perceive by the sense and by the sight"; see e.g. Lane, Suppl. s.v. *liqā'*.

12 Or as in *innī ḏāta laylatin fī manzilī iḏā anā biṣawtihi yasta'ḏinu 'alayya* "I was one night in my home, when I suddenly heard his voice asking me to let him come in", Reck. *SV* 478.12, or in Buḫ. II 345.9, quoted note 5 above.

b. *ka'annī bika tanḥaṭṭu ilā llaḥdi*
"It is as if I see you being lowered into the grave". Wright II 158B

c. *faka'annakum bi-l-ʿArabi qad waradū bilādakum*
"It is as if you (pl.) can already see the Arabs, having just invaded your land". *WKAS* I 5.31 left

d. *ka'annī bikitābi l-Ḥajjāji qad atāka*
"It is as if I see Al-Ḥajjāj's letter having just reached you". Reck. *SV* 589.1[13]

Examples (4)b–d show this sentence-type as it most often occurs, namely with a circumstantial amplification[14], while (4)a exhibits it in its unamplified form. The relevance of (4) to the preceding discussion is obvious. We are dealing here, again, with the expression of an unmistakable object notion in a sentence-type whose embedded nucleus consists of a personal pronoun and a term governed by *bi-*, the same two components that constitute the nucleus of type (1).[15] But while these characteristics strongly suggest that (4) has likewise undergone the change from an original notion of proximity or comitativity[16] to an object notion, the process itself seems here to be different from the one proposed for type (1). This will be explained in the following.

2.2 In the light of our proposed reconstruction, we may represent the presumed original meaning of sentences of type (4) in paraphrases such as (using the more commonly occurring examples, with an amplification, as our model): "It is as if

13 For the use of *ka'anna* in the sense of "it is as if" (rather than simply "as if") see Reck. *AS* 539. –8ff. For more exx. of type (4) see Nöldeke *ZGr.* 51.3–6, *WKAS* I 4.33 right ff.

14 The circumstantial (*Ḥāl*) status of the amplification is evident in corresponding *syndetic* examples with *wa-* (the *Wāw al-Ḥāl*) such as *ka'annī bikum waqad ḥaṣaltum fī ḏālika lyawmi* "it is as if I see you having already gotten to that day (i.e. the Day of Judgment)", Fleischer 375.6; *ka'annī bikum ġadan waqad laqītum ahla š-Ša'mi* "it is as if I see you tomorrow having encountered the Syrians", Nöldeke *ZGr.* 51.3; *ka'annī bihim wa-l-laytu afḍalu qawlihim* "it is as if I see them, 'if only . . .!' being their most prominent word", *WKAS* I 5.6 left. In view of the existence of these syndetic parallels, one will reject Reckendorf's suggestion that constructions such as (4)b–d (as well as similar ones of type (1)) have been formed "in analogy" to constructions with verbs of perception, see Reck. *SV* 520. – 10, 588. – 5, *AS* 387.4.

15 A few distributional features may be mentioned here in passing. I have encountred type (4) only with the first and second, not third person pronouns (i.e. no **ka'annahu bi-Zaydin*), to which cf. Cant. II 301, who found this type only with the first person in the modern literary language. For a similar selectional peculiarity in type (1) see note 2 above. Furthermore, only pronominal subjects were recorded in types (1) and (4), i.e. no **iḏā ʿAmrun bi-Zaydin*, nor **ka'anna ʿAmran bi-Zaydin*. The latter peculiarity seems to me of a special linguistic significance. We may be dealing here with constructions that are inherently restricted to *pronominal* subjects.

16 Although Brock. 36.18 speaks only of type (1), it is clear from Brock. 364.8 that he applies the same reconstruction also to type (4).

I am with you as you are being lowered into the grave", "It is as if you (pl.) are already with the Arabs, they having invaded your land", etc. Such paraphrases serve to bring to the fore a crucial point, namely that sentences of type (4) evoke a mental image of an action or event, something one may call an *envisaged scene*.[17] Thus the envisaged scenes in the just-quoted examples are, in an informal description: "you being lowered into the grave"; "the Arabs having invaded the land".[18]

I suggest that the preposition *bi-*, with its rudimentary meaning, was used here from the outset to conretize how vividly real that envisaged scene is to the speaker (*ka'annī* ...) or the addressee (*ka'annaka* ...) – so real, that is, as if the speaker or the addressee were physically present. If one takes this explanation as a guideline, it is not difficult to see how these sentences might have gone through a process of reinterpretation by which the notion of the envisaged scene prevailed over the primary, conrete notion of physical presence *at* that scene, so that the term governed by *bi-* came to assume the relational status of "thing/person, etc. envisaged, imagined, mentally perceived". According to this explanation, then, we are dealing with a process by which an implied notion ("envisaged scene") prevails over a surface-marked notion (comitativity, proximity), effecting a reinterpretation of the relational status of the entity term in question.

2.3 One may ask how we can be certain that the *bi-* in types (1) and (4) has not in fact retained the original meaning. There are two arguments against such an assumption. The first is based on the kinds of substantives that occur in these two sentence-types. To those denoting sense perceptions, already mentioned earlier, one may add substantives denoting abstract concepts, as in the following example of type (4):

(4) e. *faka'annaka biddunyā lam takun wabil'āḫirati lam tazal*
"You should conceive of your earthly life as if it had never existed at all, and the afterlife as if it will exist forever". *WKAS* I 5.21 left

Substantives belonging to those two categories not only impose the interpretational limitations mentioned § 1.4, but – significantly to the present argument – also rule out that the intended relational notion in exx. such as (1)a, c or (4)e is

17 In this regard sentences of type (4) have a similarity with the reports of visions or dreams. The notion of something mentally perceived or imagined is even more prominent in a similar type that exhibits a verb of seeing: *ka'annī anẓuru ilā ddimā'i bayna l'amā'imi* "it seems as if I see blood between the turbans", Reck. *SV* 588, and further examples *WKAS* I 4.19,45 right.

18 Formally, the envisaged scene comprises the term governed by *bi-* plus the amplification. However, even in a case such as (4)a, where there is no amplification, one may speak of a "scene" because of what this image implies, i.e. "the raven of separation croaking".

one of proximity or comitativity. Or, formulated differently: one may be physically *with*, *at*, *in the vicinity of*, etc., a concrete entity, such as a thing or person, but one may not be in the same concrete sense *with*, *at*, *in the vicinity of*, say, an abstract concept or a visual or acoustic perception, such as "the earthly life", "the hereafter", "a voice", "a darkness". One could almost go so far as to say that entity terms of this kind "force" an object interpretation. Ultimately, however, this is merely a partial argument, because it excludes comitativity and proximity only for the substantives in these particular exx. The really decisive criterion remains the actually observable meanings of these sentence-types in the synchronic system of the language – meanings which confirm an object notion, rather than a notion of proximity or comitativity, for the entity term governed by *bi-*.[19]

3. *The "Movement With" Notion*

3.1 Finally, consider a group of sentence-types in which the term governed by *bi-* covers a range of object notions of, approximately, "thing/person, etc. brought, taken, seized, gotten hold of, obtained":

(5)	a.	*mā jā'a bika* "What brought you (here)?"	Brock. 364 n. 1
	b.	*utiya l-Ḥajjaju bimra'atin* "A woman was brought to Ḥajjāj".	Reck. *SV* 244.5
(6)	a.	*ʿalayya bi-l-ʿAbbāsiyyi* "Get me the ʿAbbāsi!"	Nöldeke *ZGr.* 142.–5 left
	b.	*ʿalaykumā binnāqati* "Get yourselves the she-camel!"	Reck. *AS* 354.–1
(7)	a.	*anā lakunna bihi* "I shall bring him to you".	Nöldeke *ZGr.* 51.1
	b.	*anā laka biḏālika* "I am going to fetch this thing for you".	Reck *AS* 240.2
(8)	a.	*fakayfa lī bihāḏā lmāli* "How can I get hold of this money?"	*WKAS* I 499.17 right

19 Of the two glosses provided for type (4) in W. Fischer *Gramm.* § 365 n. 1: *ka'annī bika* "es ist, als ob ich es mit dir zu tun hätte", "es ist, als ob ich dich vor mir sähe", the first one is inspired by the reconstructed meaning of *bi-* (cf. ibid. § 294: *bi-* "in Verbindung mit", and § 280b: "der Gegenstand, mit dem man es unversehens zu tun hat ..."), while the second reflects the actual meaning of this type in the synchronic system.

b. *kayfa lī biyadin tanāluki*
"How could I get a hand that would reach you?" — *WKAS* I 499.34 right

c. *kayfa laka bihi*
"How can you get hold of him?" — Nöldeke *ZGr.* 50.–6

(9) *hal lakum bisayyidi ahli š-Ša'mi*
"Can you get the commander of the Syrians?" — Nöldeke *ZGr.* 50.–1

(10) *min ayna lī birāḥilatin*
"From where can I get hold of a she-camel?" — Reck. *SV* 311.–9

(11) *man lī binnisā'i llatī tulā'imunī*[20]
"Who can get for me the women that will suit me?" — Reck. *SV* 243.–7

Types (5)–(11) exhibit a different kind of object notions than those observed in (1) and (4). Nevertheless, these two groups of sentences must be viewed together, since they have undergone the same *type* of semantic development (i.e. from comitativity, proximity, etc. to objecthood) that is the subject of this chapter.

3.2 I suggest that sentence-types (5)–(11) underwent semantic changes that may be symbolized informally by glosses such as:

jā'a bihi "he came with him" > "he brought him" (5), and similarly with other verbs of motion;

'alayya bihi "towards me with him!" > "bring him to me!", *'alayka bihi* "towards you with him!" > "seize, take, get hold of, grab him (in essence: bring him onto yourself)!" (6);

anā laka bihi "I towards you with him" > "I bring him to you" (7), etc.[21]

What these paraphrases attempt to reproduce is the one significant element that is shared by all of these sentence-types in their original meanings, namely the notion of *movement with* a thing or person. The formal exponents of this notion are the comitative *bi-* in combination with either a verb of motion, as in (5), or a verbless utterance of type (6)–(11) in which a preposition *'alā* or *li-* expresses movement in the direction of a target, the target being the person represented in the pronominal suffix of *'alā* and *li-*.[22] It is this notion of

20 So, rather than *tulā'imī*, Reck. ibid.

21 For these semantic shifts see Reck. *SV* 243, 311, *AS* 237.–3ff. Our interpretation in the following is essentially identical with Reckendorf's, but differs in that it emphasizes the directionality expressed by the prepositions *li-* and *'alā*.

22 Although in classical Arabic *li-* more typically marks the possessor or the benefitting person, its original notion of directionality is still sufficiently transparent in exx. such as Brock. 377, *WKAS* II 11.9 right ff., and cf. usage such as *huwa laka* "it is yours" (as it were "it goes to you"), Reck.

"movement with" that constitutes the essential common trait of all of types (5)–(11) in their original meanings[23], and which is the single most important element underlying the process of change to objecthood.

3.3 Here too, various semantic expansions can be observed. Thus, from the concrete object notion of "thing/person to be physically taken, seized, gotten hold of" developed the corresponding expanded notion of "something abstract (a quality, characteristic, a goal, etc.) to be achieved, acquired, guaranteed", as in:

(12) a. *ʿalaykum bilʾadabi/biṣṣabri*, etc. (cf. (6))
"Take upon yourselves (or "get" yourselves) cultural refinement/patience". Reck. *SV* 311.–7

b. *kayfa laka binnajāʾi* (for b and c cf. (8))
"How can you escape?" Reck. *SV* 311.14

c. *fakayfa lī biʾan arāki*
"So how can I see you?" *WKAS* I 499.38 right

d. *man laka bilʿīšati rrāḍiyati* (cf. (11))
"Who can provide for you (or guarantee you) a pleasant life?"
WKAS II 15.10 left

Examples such as (12) speak unmistakably – and better than others – for objecthood rather than comitativity in the synchronic system of the language, see the arguments § 2.3. Insofar as the terms governed by *bi-* are *abstracta* – "cultural refinement", "patience" (a), "escaping" (b), "seeing you" (c), "a pleasant life" (d) – these examples reflect a further step in the semantic development as compared with examples (6)–(11), viz. a step in the direction of an "expanded" object notion in the sense of § 1.4.[24]

SV 218.–8. In the case of *ʿalā*, directionality may not be the historically primary notion (that is, if the interpretation Brock. 391 is correct), but the preposition has certainly acquired a directional meaning in cases such as *ḫaraja/hajama/daḫala/ḥamala/saqaṭa/qadima*, etc. + *ʿalā*, where the term governed by *ʿalā* marks the target or goal, see also Wright II 167D, 168C, W. Fischer *Gramm.* § 302b, Reck. *SV* 209.–6,–5. In their original meaning, command formulas of type (6) may be compared with Engl. *away with him!*, Germ. *weg mit ihm!*, *her mit dem Hut!* (in the sense of "give me the hat!"), etc.

23 One will not agree with Bravmann "Linguistic Taboo" 479, who postulates an "implied" verb of motion in type (11), nor with Wright II 172B, where the same explanation is proposed for type (6). Recognition of the directionality of *ʿalā* and *li-* makes such postulates superfluous.

24 A few exx. of other kinds of semantic expansion affecting these sentence-types: "To seize, take" of type (6) yields the expanded meaning of "to attack, conquer", as in *ʿalaykum birrijāli* "attack these men!", *ʿalaykum bi-l-Yamāmati* "take (i.e. conquer) Yamāma!" Wright II 172D, Nöldeke *ZGr.* 142.–2 left. Or, *atā bi-*, *jāʾa bi-* "to bring", type (5), develop the secondary meaning of "to

3.4 A different argument for objecthood rather than comitativity is provided by the occasional use of *maʿa* in conjunction with the *bi-* in sentences of type (5), as in *ḏahabat bihā maʿahā* "she took her away with her", *mālun ḫarajtu bihi maʿī* "money which I took out with me", etc. The meaning confirms object status for the term governed by *bi-*, while the comitative notion is expressed by *maʿa*, as was observed already by Reckendorf, *SV* 244, *AS* 239.

3.5 The object status of the term governed by *bi-* is also supported by the occasional occurrence of variant types exhibiting the acc. case. Thus, the type *ʿalayka bi-Zaydin* (6) has an acc. variant:

(13) a. *ʿalayka ḏawī Faḍālata*
"Get the murderers (lit. those) of Faḍāla!" — Reck. *SV* 339.3

b. *ʿalaykahā*
"Get her!" — Reck. *AS* 113.12

Another such verbless command formula, *ruwaydaka bi-Zaydin*

(14) a. *ruwaydaka bil'amri*
"Handle the matter slowly, with care!" — Reck. *AS* 113.–3

b. *ruwaydaka sawqan bilʿawāzimi*
"Drive the old camels gently!" — Wright II 78C

likewise exhibits an acc. variant:

(15) a. *ruwayda ʿAliyyan*
"Treat ʿAli gently!" — Reck. *SV* 338.10

b. *ruwaydakanī*
"Treat me gently!" — Wright II 78C[25]

Despite the marginality of these variants in the acc. case, their mere existence is linguistically revealing. I suggest that these are adjustments of the surface structure to the semantics: In the types with the acc., the object status of the term governed by *bi-* gets its "appropriate" surface representation. Such an adjustment presupposes that the original notion (comitativity) is no longer transparent in the synchronic system of the language.

A remark in passing on the likely reconstruction of the type *ruwaydaka bi-* (14): Meanings such as that of *arwada* (IV) "to move or act gently, slowly", *rūd^{un}* "gentle manner of moving or acting" (e.g. Lane s. r. *rwd*) suggest a

produce", as in ... *fa'tū bisūratin* Q 10:38, and "to give birth" as in *atā bi'awlādin*, Reck. *SV* 244.1. Here again, the expanded meanings are the most indicative of the shift to objecthood.

25 In this command formula, *ruwayda* usually (though not obligatorily, see (15)a) has a second person pronoun suffix representing the addressee, see Reck. *AS* 289.

semantic development along the lines of "move slowly, gently with (thing/person)!" > "treat, handle (thing/person) gently!", which is of course in line with the interpretation proposed § 3.2.

4. *Hierarchical Comitativity*

The semantics of constructions with *verbs of motion* + *bi-* deserve a special attention. A sentence such as *ḏahaba bihi ilā ssūqi* means, in its comitative reading, "he took him along to the market place". Now, a close look at this meaning reveals an important detail: Although both persons participate together in the act of going to the market (the exponent of this comitative notion being the preposition *bi-*)[26], they do so in different roles, namely the person represented by the subject of the verb as the initiator, promoter, the controlling or otherwise dominant agent, the other as the more passively participating agent (one may apply here the notion of "control", see e.g. Comrie 52ff.). We may speak of a "hierarchical" comitativity, i.e. where there is a "primary" and a "secondary" participant. It is easy to see that this hierarchical comitativity is inherently conducive to a reduction of the secondary participant to the status of an object, i.e. "he (primary) took him (secondary) along" > "he brought (took, carried, etc.) him".[27] It is instructive, from a contrastive point of view, to compare these constructions with those of the sequence *verb of motion* + *maʿa*. Throughout the history of Arabic, the latter constructions remained strictly comitative in meaning, e.g. *ḏahaba maʿahu ilā ssūqi* "he went with him to the market place" never developed an object notion. Their different historical fate is to be attributed to the fact that the specific hierarchy observed in constructions *verb of motion* + *bi-* does not obtain in those with *maʿa*.[28]

26 The element of comitativity is also what separates *ḏahaba bi-* from *aḏhaba*, for which see W. Fischer (ed.) *Grundr.* I 75 (although the difference is formulated there from the viewpoint of agenthood of the subject of the verb, not comitativity).

27 The degree of establishment of objecthood may to some extent depend on the verbal lexemes involved. An extreme case is *jāʾa bi-*, where objecthood appears to have completely ousted comitativity, at least in the modern literary language (perhaps also under the influence of colloquial *jāb* "to bring"). In many instances, however, the decision as to whether a given combination *verb of motion* + *bi-* is to be understood as expressing comitativity or objecthood will depend on contextual criteria.

28 In fact, if constructions with *maʿa* express any hierarchy at all, it is the reversal of the one just observed for *bi-*. Thus, according to Saad "Comitative" 82, it is the entity that is governed by *maʿa* that has the primary rank. It is obvious that this state of affairs prevents the reduction of that entity to an object status.

5. *Bravmann's Theory*

At this point an explanatory theory that addresses itself inter alia to some of the sentence-types discussed in this chapter should be examined briefly. Bravmann, quite correctly, links the *bi-* in types such as *jā'a bi-Zaydin* (5) and *man lī bi-Zaydin* (11) with the semantic values of "to come with" and "to bring", but then proceeds to attribute the very same values also to the *bi-* of the two types with the "*iḏā* of surprise or suddenness" discussed earlier, *iḏā anā / huwa bi-Zaydin* (1) and *iḏā bi-Zaydin* (2). He does this by conjecturing that the suddenly or unexpectedly appearing entity in (1) and (2) is described by the language as being brought "into the scene (quasi by some outside [unknown] power)". In accordance with this interpretation, he paraphrases his model sentence for type (1), *iḏā huwa bihudhudin*: "suddenly he [noticed]: [there was (or came) 'it'] with a hoopoe".[29] While I do not deny that there are phenomena of language calling for such explanations[30], I can see nothing to support the postulate of an "unknown power" that comes with the entity in question onto the scene in the two sentence-types under discussion.[31] By extending the notion ("object notion" in our terminology) of "thing/person, etc. brought" that is expressed in types such as (5) and (11) to type (1), Bravmann is in effect disregarding the actual meanings of this sentence-type, which fall under a notion of "thing/person, etc. encountered/perceived", see § 1.2. Nor is there any justification for ascribing the notion of "thing etc. brought" to type (2). As stated earlier, no object notion is observable in the meanings of sentences of type (2) – in contrast to those of type (1). If an argument can be made at all for such a notion in type (2), then only on an indirect, inferential basis. But in such a case one would rather be inclined to infer an object notion as in (1) – the type with which (2) is most closely related – not as in types such as (5) or (11), as Bravmann's theory suggests.[32]

29 Bravmann "Linguistic Taboo" 477–82, and esp. 481 for the discussion of type (1). Here and in the following, the parentheses and brackets in the quotations from Bravmann are in the original.

30 E.g., Latin *si hominem fulminibus occisit*, or its German equivalent *wenn es einen Menschen mit dem Blitz erschlagen haben sollte*, both adduced by Bravmann ibid. 480. In a case such as this, the very syntax – made explicit in a literal rendition "if it should have killed a man by lightning" – as well as the numinous nature of the message itself fully support the view that this is an instance of linguistic "Taboo", implying the notion of an unknown power at work (or, better perhaps, of an unspecified supreme force, see Havers § 86 and cf. § 83).

31 I also do not understand Bravmann's reasoning that by describing the suddenly appearing entity as being placed into the scene by that unknown power, instead of describing it as coming on its own initiative, the language is somehow lessening the frightening effect of its sudden appearance, ibid. 480, 482.–8ff. In my opinion, such a presentation would increase, not diminish, the frightening effect, precisely by evoking such an ominous "unknown factor".

32 I find Bravmann's *syntactic* analysis as hard to accept as his semantic interpretation. Thus, he

6. *Conclusion*

It was argued that in a number of sentence-types of Cl. Arabic the term governed by *bi-* underwent a change from what was originally a relational (or "case") notion of comitativity, proximity, etc., to a notion of object. Two different changes of this kind were recognized, one establishing an object notion paraphrasable as "thing/person encountered / perceived, envisaged", in types (1) *iḏā anā/huwa bi-Zaydin* and (4) *ka'annī/ka'annaka bi-Zaydin*; and another establishing an object notion of "thing/person brought, taken, seized, gotten hold of, obtained", in types (5) *jā'a bi-Zaydin*, (6) *ʿalayya/ʿalayka bi-Zaydin*, etc., through type (11). The arguments for an object status of the term in question are based above all on the meanings of the sentences, including the meaning (class membership) of some of the substantives involved, see esp. §§ 1.4, 2.3, 3.3. Moreover, the object status manifests itself in occasional variants, including acc.-variants of some of these *bi-* types, see § 3.4–5.

A more general aim, of both this chapter and chapter V, esp. § 2.3.2, was to demonstrate an approach that takes the relational ("case") roles of entity terms as its point of departure. Specifically, I hope to have shown that a relationally understood concept of *object* can be meaningfully used in the description of a large variety of sentence-types. Insofar as most of these sentence-types are verbless, we are dealing here with object notions that may be termed "autonomous", i.e. not depending on the presence of a verbal form. In order to do full descriptive justice, one would of course have to mention also the other semantic roles that manifest themselves in these sentence types – such as *agent*, i.e. the subject pronoun in (1), (4), (7), (11);[33] or *recipient*, *benefactive*, etc., represented by the terms governed by *ʿalā* and *li-* in (6)–(11) – but a discussion of these points would go beyond the limits of our specific topic.[34]

suggests with respect to type (1) that "this pronoun (as in *iḏā huwa bihudhudin*) is to be considered as not standing in a direct syntactic relation to the prepositional phrase with *bi-* following it. Rather, this pronoun should be regarded as a(n originally) separate (independent) form of expression (an independent idea)", ibid. 481.–7. I fail to understand this suggestion: How could such an originally separate pronoun have been secondarily incorporated into a preexisting *iḏā bi-Zaydin* (2)? And how did it come to be placed *between* the two components of this sentence-type?! Whatever the relation between types (1) and (2) may be – it has been explained far more plausibly by Brockelmann and Spitaler, see above note 7.

33 In the terminology of semantic roles, the subject pronoun of a sentence such as "suddenly I/he saw a ..." (1), or "it is as if you see ..." (4) represents an *experiencer*. However, since Arabic (like English) treats experiencers just like initiators of actions, I see no reason to speak of these pronouns other than in terms of agents. On this point in general see Comrie 55.

34 It should be obvious that many of the traditional standard terms would be totally inadequate descriptively for these sentence-types. A case in point is "Prädikat" used in Reck. *AS* 308.–8 in reference to the portion *bi-Zaydin* in type (1).

Chapter IV

Presentative Structures and Their Syntactic and Semantic Development

1. Introduction

1.1 By "presentative" I mean a linguistic form, typically a particle, which serves (at least in the most basic use) to alert the hearer or draw his attention, a function paraphrasable by words such as *look*, *behold*, Germ. *siehe*, Lat. *ecce*, Fr. *voilà*, etc. The aim of this chapter is to describe some of the major *types* of Arabic presentative sentences and discuss their syntactic and semantic development. In keeping with this outlook, the data will be arranged by syntactic and semantic criteria, not by the usual classification into classical, middle, modern literary and colloquial Arabic. The provenence of the examples, however, will of course be noted in each case. Although this chapter deals only with a limited number of presentatives, I believe that the conclusions are valid to presentative syntax in general.

1.2 Presentative constructions have been discussed, at least sporadically, in works on Arabic and Semitic linguistics under headings such as "demonstrative Interjektionen", Brock. 635.–15; "demonstrative Satzeinleitungspartikel", W. Fischer *Dem.* 157–201 (a chapter that is especially rich in material), and the term "presentative" has been used in the more recent literature, e.g. Blau *An Adv.* 1, 4 and passim; Blau *Chr. Ar.* 461 ff.; Blau *BZ* 202; Blanc "Negev" 144.–2; Cowell 564 ("presentational particle", and see esp. n. 1, containing an insightful remark on the uniqueness of presentative constructions). Occasionally the term is ill chosen, as when Palva 29.10 applies it for what in truth is the "concretizing" use of the demonstrative (described e.g. in W. Fischer *Dem.* 85 ff. and Blau *BZ* 19.–2 ff.).

It ought to be pointed out that "presentative" is at times used in a different sense, esp. in works of a more theoretical outlook, e.g. "Presentative Movement" in the title of Hetzron's article, where it is applied to a postulated transformational process, and again differently in L. E. Breivik "On the Interpretation of Existential *There*", *Language* 57/1 (March 1981) (where *there* in a sentence such as "there are polar bears in Norway" is viewed as a "subject NP and a presentative signal", 23.19).

2. *Nuclear, Amplified, and Proclitic Structure*

2.1 Any self-contained sentential unit of presentative meaning will be referred to as a "nuclear presentative sentence". These are some of the common types in schematic presentation:

(1) Arabic	a.	*hāḏā Zaydun*	
	b.	*iḏā bi-Zaydin*	"Here is Zayd"
	c.	*iḏā Zaydun*	
	d.	*hā anā ḏā*	
		hā anta ḏā	"Here I am/you are/he is", etc.
		hā huwa ḏā etc.	
Hebrew	e.	*hinnē hāʾīš*	"Here is the man"
	f.	*hinnēnī* etc.	"Here I am", etc.[1]

2.2 A nuclear presentative sentence may contain no more than a presentative particle[2] and a substantive or pronoun, as in (1)a, c, e, f; or it may contain additional components, e.g. a preposition, as in b; or a demonstrative component, as in d. Moreover, a nuclear presentative sentence may have different semantic values, such as "Here/There is (comes, appears, etc.) the man/a man"; "Suddenly there was (appeared, came) the man/a man", etc. (the above renditions, necessarily schematized and simplified, do not reflect this heterogeneity). But what unites these and, for that matter, all nuclear presentative sentences – irrespective of formal and semantic differences in detail – is a basic *type* of meaning that underlies them, i.e. (schematically) "Here/There is X", with X standing for the substantive or pronoun. Such a substantive or pronoun will be referred to as the "head" of the nuclear presentative sentence. Thus, the salient criterion in this approach is semantic, allowing us to consider widely different types such as in (1) as belonging to a single basic category.[3] This category will be referred to as the "nuclear presentative structure".

1 For the types with *iḏā* and *hinnē* see (2) of ch. III and (14), (17) of ch. V.

2 "Presentative particle" (or briefly "presentative") will be applied in this chapter to primary presentatives, as well as to word-classes secondarily used as presentatives, such as the demonstrative pronouns in Arabic, see next paragraph.

3 W. Fischer *Dem.* 164 recognizes the sentential nature of what is termed here nuclear presentative sentences, but one cannot accept his terminology for these sentences, such as "scheinbares Prädikat" for the pronoun in *ha hūwa* "There he is", or "Kopula" for the one in *ha hiyya ddār*

2.3 Already in the earliest available texts, Cl. Arabic uses its *demonstrative pronouns* as presentatives. In the following exx. the demonstrative pronoun is a constituent of a nuclear presentative sentence:

(2) a. *hā'ulā'i banātī in kuntum fā'ilīna*
"Here[4] are my daughters, if you must do it".
(Lot to the people of Sodom) Q 15:71

b. *qāla yā bušrā hāḏā ġulāmun*
"He said: Good news! Here is a young man".
(the water-drawer, seeing Joseph in the well) Q 12:19

c. *qāla ayna Mālikun qīla hāḏā Mālikun*
"He asked: Where is Mālik? They said (lit. it was said): Here is Mālik".
Nöldeke *ZGr.* 48.–1

d. *faqāla Abū Bakrin hāḏā 'Umaru*
wahāḏā Abū 'Ubaydata fa'ayyahumā
ši'tum fabāyi'ū
"Whereupon Abu Bakr said: Here is
'Umar and here is Abu 'Ubayda,
so swear allegiance to whomever you want of the two". Reck. *SV* 414.2[5]

2.4 It is worth mentioning that medieval Arabic grammar has well recognized the presentative function of the demonstrative pronouns. Thus, Sībawayhi (I 218.13) speaks of it in terms of *tanbīh* ("to alert, call attention to"), distinguishing it sharply from their more common, i.e. identifying function.[6] He says about the model sentence

hāḏā 'Abdu llāhi munṭaliqan
"Here is Abdallah, departing":

"Here is the house". Nuclear presentative sentences differ in more than one respect from regular nominal sentences ("Nominalsätze"), and the mechanical transference of the nomenclature used to describe the latter to the former is not recommended.

4 An English translator of sentences of types (2) and (3) vacillates between renditions with "here is ..." and "there is ...". My decision in this matter was based entirely on my judgment as to which of these two possibilities is the more fitting in a given context (see e.g. the situation in which (3)a is spoken) and is therefore of no linguistic significance. Although Cl. Arabic has demonstrative pronouns for the near as well as the distant deixis, it is typically the former that are used as presentatives, the latter being far less common in this capacity (see e.g. Nöldeke *ZGr.* 49.9,10). Much more data would be needed to determine whether the use of these two sets as presentatives is semantically contrastive.

5 For the full quotation of (2)d see Ṭab. I 1842.8.

6 Here and in the following, I am using "identifying" in a loose sense so as to encompass not only strictly identifying predication ("this is John/my brother", etc.) but also classificatory, or qualifying predication ("this is an Englishman/a horse", etc.). On types of predication see e.g. Beeston 66.

walmaʿnā annaka turīdu an tunabbihahu lahu munṭaliqan lā turīdu an tuʿarrifahu ʿAbda llāhi li'annaka ẓananta annahu yajhaluhu faka'annaka qulta (u)nẓur ilayhi munṭaliqan
"The meaning is that you intend to draw his (i.e. the hearer's) attention to him (i.e. Abdallah) as he is departing. You do *not* want to identify Abdallah to him, thinking that he did not know him. Rather, it is as though you had said: Look at him, as he is departing".[7]

2.5 Although there can be little doubt that this demonstrative-pronoun with-presentative-meaning is related to the identifying demonstrative[8], and although both exhibit the same type of gender and number agreement – namely with the substantive[9], the functional-semantic contrast is reason enough to make a sharp distinction between them. Moreover, there is at least one *distributional* factor that goes along with the functional difference. As is well known, a pronominal copula (the *Ḍamīr al-Faṣl*)[10] is often used between the demonstrative and a definite substantival predicate, thus *hāḏā (huwa) rrajulu* "this is the man".[11] But it is not used when the definite substantive is the head of a nuclear presentative sentence. Put differently, for the meaning "here/there is the man" there is only *hāḏā rrajulu*, not **hāḏā huwa rrajulu*: As the typical exponent of identifying predication the copula is excluded from nuclear presentative sentences.[12] The functional contrast under discussion may also manifest itself in other ways.[13] Coll. Damascene possesses a fem. demonstrative pronoun *hayy* and a homonymous presentative particle. A sentence such as *hayy wāḥde tānye* can therefore mean both "this is another one (fem.)" or "here is another one (fem.)". But the demonstrative *hayy* is a member of an inflectional set and the form selected must agree with the predicate (i.e. *hāda wāḥed*, *hayy wāḥde*, etc.), as is the case in classical Arabic, whereas the presentative *hayy* remains uninflected, see Cowell 552, 564.[14]

7 Cf. also Ibn Yaʿīš 235.12–14.

8 For a plausible contextual situation in which an identifying demonstrative pronoun might assume a presentative meaning, see W. Fischer *Dem.* 185.9ff.

9 On this type of agreement in general see Beeston 67. Also now Bloch "*Damir*" 35–6.

10 As emphasized already by Fleischer 725 n. 1, this term is to be rendered as "pronoun of distinction" (i.e. between clause status and phrase status), not "pronoun of separation", as e.g. in Wright II 259 B, et al.

11 Contrary to what is frequently taught, this pronoun may be missing even in cases of potential ambiguity (at least in the classical language), witness the alternation *ḏālika lfawzu lʿaẓīmu* ~ *ḏālika huwa lfawzu lʿaẓīmu* in the Q, passim; and see esp. Reck. *AS* § 141.1 vs. § 141.2.

12 The pronoun in a presentative sentence such as *ha hiyya ddār* is not a copula (see note 3 above), but must rather be understood according to § 6.4.2–3 below.

13 Consider esp. the difference in the pronominalization, § 6.8.2 below.

14 Cowell's strictly synchronic statement in 564 is in need of some clarification, because the fem.

2.6 A nuclear presentative sentence may occur unamplified, as in (2). Or it may occur with some amplification, e.g. a relative clause:

hāḏihi sabʿu miʾati dīnārin uwajjihu bihā ilayka
"Here are seven hundred dinars that I am sending to you".[15] Masʿūdī 110.–1

But more typically the amplification is circumstantial (*Ḥāl*). Like other *Ḥāls* it exhibits the acc. when the morphology permits case marking:

(3) a. *hāḏā ʿUmaru bnu l-Ḫaṭṭābi mutawaššiḥan bissayfi*
"(Out) there is ʿUmar b. al-Ḫaṭṭāb, girded with a sword".
(person announcing that ʿUmar is standing at the door)

b. *hāḏā Ḥuṣaybun ṣaḥīḥa ljildi*
"Here is Ḥuṣayb, uninjured (lit. sound of skin)".

c. *hāḏā l-Farazdaqu sājidan*
"There is Farazdaq, prostrating himself".
a–c: Nöldeke *ZGr.* 49.8, 141 (49/2).

Notice that items functionally corresponding to the Arabic *Ḥāl* quite commonly amplify nuclear presentative sentences also elsewhere, as in the following French and English sentences:

Here I am, *surrounded* by water.
There he was, *sitting* in his chair.
There was Pooh, *sitting* on his branch.
Me voilà *vieux*.
Voilà mon homme *au désespoir*.
Voilà notre homme *pincé*.
Mes funestes pressentiments, les voilà *accomplis*.[16]

(I have italicized the item that corresponds to the *Ḥāl*.)

2.7 But there are also sentences with the item in question in the nom. case:

(4) "The Messenger of God had fallen asleep with his head on his chest while he was in the hut; then he woke up and said: Rejoice, Abu Bakr, God's help has come to you;

demonstrative *hayy* (fuller form *hayye*, Grotzfeld 21) appears to have a different source than the presentative, see W. Fischer *Dem.* 52ff., 179ff.

15 An ex. such as this is especially well suited to demonstrate how the transition from an identifying ("these are ...") to a presentative meaning might have occurred in the demonstrative pronouns. See note 8 above.

16 The Engl. sentences are from A. A. Milne's *Winnie-the-Pooh*. For the French ones see F. Brunot, *La Pensée et la langue* (Paris 1922) 8–9.

a. *hāḏā Jibrīlu āḫiḏun biʿināni farasin yaqūduhu ʿalā ṯanāyāhu nnaqʿu*
look, Gabriel is holding the rein of a horse,
leading it, with dust on his front teeth". Reck. *AS* 107.–5[17]

"I have suffered a rupture and Bišr saw it and forgave me,
b. *wahāḏā ʿaṭāʾī mardūdun fī bayti lmāli*
and look, my pay can be returned to the treasury". Reck. *SV* 406.–2[18]

It will be argued in the following that this case contrast reflects a contrast in the underlying syntactic structures. Whereas the substantive in (3) is the head of the embedded nuclear sentence and thus is linked with the demonstrative, the substantive in (4) is the subject and the participial form (in the nom.) the predicate, while the demonstrative has the syntactic status of a proclitic. Accordingly, I shall recognize these three structures (terms are my own),

(5)	Nuclear:	*hāḏā Zaydun*	as in (2),
	Amplified:	*hāḏā Zaydun munṭaliqan*	as in (3),
	Proclitic:	*hāḏā Zaydun munṭaliqun*	as in (4).

An approximate English correspondence of the contrast between the amplified and the proclitic structure would be:

There is Pooh, sitting on a branch.
Look (behold, etc.), Pooh is sitting on a branch.

2.8 There is another purely formal criterion which, though different from case marking, likewise reflects the underlying structure. In the *absence* of an entity term (i.e. substantive or pronoun) constituting a sentential nucleus with the demonstrative the structure is obviously proclitic. This type of proclitic structure is exemplified in the following sentences (of which the first is classical, the others middle Arabic):

17 For the full quotation see Ibn Hišām I/1 444.–6. One of the mss. has *āḫiḏan* in the margin (see ibid. II 118.–3), i.e. suggesting "Here is Gabriel, holding ..." as in type (3) above, and Guillaume has the same translation. This reading too fits this context, but the version in the nom. cannot of course be so interpreted. I have no explanation for the nom. *muḥīṭun* in the ex. Reck. *AS* 107.–3, where only the var. with the *Ḥāl*, *qad aḥāṭa bihi* (ibid. n. 3) appears to make sense.

18 For the full quotation see Ṭab. II/2 873.–2. Reck ibid. mistook *hāḏā ʿaṭāʾī* for an attributive phrase with an irregular word order ("this my pay ..."). For the correct reading see Blau *Orbis* 206. On this point in general see Fleischer 749–50 and esp. Nöldeke *ZGr.* 50.14–18.

(6) "ʿUmar b. ʿAbd al-ʿAzīz sent for me and Muzāḥim (early one morning) ..., so we came to him
walam yaddahin walam yatahayyaʾ faqāla
a. *hāḏā ʿajiltum ʿani ddahni*
before he had anointed and prepared himself, so he said:
Look, you have come so fast that
I did not yet anoint myself". W. Fischer *Dem.* 161.–13[19]

b. *hāḏā qad atawka ṯalāṯat(u) nafar*
"Behold, three men have come to you".

c. *hāḏā naktub*
"Behold, we are writing".

d. *wahāḏā biṣalāwāt alqiddīs Mār Afrem*
ḫallaṣ Allāh almadīna
"And behold, because of the prayers of St. Ephram
God saved the city". b–d: Blau *Chr. Ar.* § 363.3

In these sentences the demonstrative pronoun is uninflected, i.e. in the invariable third masc. sing.[20] (on the significance of this point see § 5.2.2 below). Thus, not only sentences of type (4) but also those of type (6) reflect the proclitic structure, together contrasting with sentences of types (2) and (3) in which the demonstrative constitutes a sentential nucleus with a substantival head.

2.9 The three-way distinction between nuclear, amplified and proclitic structures is the cornerstone of Arabic presentative syntax in general. This distinction can also be formulated, alternatively, with regard to the syntactic status of the presentative particle: One may speak of nuclear presentatives, i.e. that are components of a nucleus (whether the structure is unamplified or amplified), and proclitic ones. Although many of the examples adduced in this chapter involve demonstrative pronouns used as presentatives (referred to as "demonstrative presentatives"), sentences with other presentatives will also be considered, see especially the colloquial constructions in § 6.4.1 ff. below.

19 For the full quotation of (6)a see Ibn Saʿd V 296.–1. W. Fischer (ibid.) renders *hāḏā ʿajiltum* ... "da habt ihr euch aber mit dem Salben beeilt", but the context in Ibn Saʿd suggests rather that the caliph is talking about his own anointment, not that of his two visitors.

20 This is true also of the other exx. in Blau *Chr. Ar.* § 363.3, with the sole exception of *wahāḏihi lmarra ṯṯāniya qad baʿaṯanī ilayka*. But this is not a presentative sentence (as Blau's own rendition "it is the second time that he has sent me to you" clearly shows), and the same seems to me to apply to the sentence adduced ibid. p. 466.12.

3. The Semantics of the Three Structures

3.1 Let us emphasize here right away in order to avoid a misunderstanding that the argument for the distinction between an amplified and a proclitic structure would not be sufficiently strong if it were based only on purely formal criteria. This applies specifically to the acc./nom. contrast – a contrast which is neutralizable, as we have seen note 17 above. Rather, it is our contention that this and some of the other surface-structure criteria to be discussed (see § 5.2.2 below) are manifestations of underlying, essentially *semantic* distinctions, and that these distinctions may or may not find an expression in formal criteria. In the following we shall examine the basic semantic correlates of the syntactic (formal) distinctions.

3.2 The meaning of a presentative sentence of the amplified (and for that matter also the nuclear) structure is determined by (1) the concrete, deictic meaning of its presentative, and (2) by the fact that the time is the *present* from the viewpoint of the speaker-observer. These two factors impart to a presentative sentence of the amplified structure a distinct sense of immediacy and concreteness, of a "scene" unfolding before the eyes at the time of utterance: Here is (stands, comes) X, . . .ing!

In contrast, a presentative sentence of the proclitic structure is not bound to any specific time: It may be the speaker's present, as in (4)a, or any other time, e.g. referring to an event occurring prior to the time of utterance, (6)d, or subsequent to it, (4)b.[21] This difference becomes especially evident when the presentative sentence pertains to a subsequent event, as in (4)b, or in:

> *huwaḏā*[22] *tābūtu ʿahdi sayyidi kulli l'arḍi*
> *ʿābirun amāmakum fī l-'Urdunni*
> "Behold, the ark of the covenant of the Lord of all
> the earth is to pass over before you into the Jordan".
> Jos 3:11 (*Al-Kitāb Al-Muqaddas*)

The same wording but with an amplified structure (participle in the acc.) would yield:

> *"There's my pay, being returned . . ."
> *"There is the ark . . ., passing before you",

thus clearly falsifying the intended meaning.

21 Needless to say, the "time" notions are used here very loosely, simply to contrast the amplified and the proclitic structure, without any commitment to the question of tense/aspect.

22 For *huwaḏā* as a presentative see below § 6.3.1.

3.3 Moreover, while the meaning of the nuclear and amplified structures is homogeneous, being determined by the deictic-concrete nature of the presentatives in their nuclei, the proclitic structure exhibits a wide range of meanings. The semantic heterogeneity of the proclitic structures will occupy us at various points in this chapter, but the feature itself can be demonstrated to some extent already on the basis of the scanty material adduced so far. In its most basic use, a presentative sentence of the proclitic structure simply alerts to an event that is happening at the time of utterance (much the same as this is true of the two other structures), i.e. "Look, Gabriel is holding ...", (4)a, "Look, three men have come ...", (6)b. But this certainly could not be said of a sentence such as "Look, my pay will be returned ...", (4)b, which alerts to an intended action or promise. It is addressed to Al-Ḥajjāj by a soldier who had been disobedient and is now pleading for clemency. In sentences of this kind the speaker attempts to convince the hearer by means of arguments, and one may therefore speak in such cases of an argumentative use of the proclitic presentative structure, for which cf. also exx. (9)b, (27)d.

3.4 One may compare here the argumentative use of the Bibl. Hebrew presentative *hinnē* in an instance such as the following. Samson's wife complains bitterly to him for refusing to reveal to her the riddle that he had put to her countrymen. He replies:

> *hinnē lə'āḇī ūlə'immī lō(') higgattī*
> *wəlāḵ aggīḏ*
> "Look, I have not told my father or mother,
> so shall I tell you (lit. and to you I shall tell)?" Jud 14:16[23]

3.5 It is essential for the understanding of the proclitic structure that much of its semantic heterogeneity is the result of *extensions* of the rudimentary alerting meaning. Such extensions occur because a presentative sentence of the proclitic structure may be used not only to draw attention to a concrete event ("Look, three men ..."), but also to express some abstract semantic relation. For example, a sentence of this structure may acquire a causal-explanatory sense: "Don't be angry at him. Look, he didn't mean to offend you" = "after all, he didn't ..."; or be used argumentatively (as we have seen); or to mark the consequence of an action, etc. In fact, in their capacity to express abstract semantic relations such as these, proclitic presentatives may come close to the functional range that is commonly associated with conjunctions. For exx. see below (18)[24], (27)e–f.

23 For another argumentative sense of *hinnē* see Jud 6:15.

24 On the inclusion of (18) among the proclitic structures see § 6.1.4.2 below.

4. *Unmarked Sentences: The Role of the Semantics*

4.1 We have seen earlier that there are certain formal criteria which unambiguously mark a presentative sentence as amplified or proclitic, §§ 2.6–2.8. But there are many presentative sentences that exhibit no surface criteria by which their underlying structure can be determined (here referred to as "unmarked"). These are sentences of the sequence: demonstrative presentative + substantive + finite verb, and a less common group of the sequence: demonstrative presentative + substantive + prepositional phrase. In this section we shall examine to what extent a semantic analysis of these sentences in their contexts may suggest a "reading" of their underlying syntactic structure.

4.2 In many instances involving the sequence with a finite verb the context allows for either interpretation:

(7) a. *hāḏā l-Aʿšā qad nazala bimā'inā*
Amplified: "Here is Al-Aʿšā, having settled down at our watering place".
or
Proclitic: "Look, Al-Aʿšā has..." Nöldeke *ZGr.* 49.15

"They said: Father, what more can we desire?
b. *hāḏihi biḍāʿatunā ruddat ilaynā*
Amplified: Here is our merchandise, returned to us".
or
Proclitic: Look here, our merchandise has been..." Q 12:65

And from the modern literary language:
"And she pointed to her daughter and went on to say:
c. *hāḏihi Nawāl jā'at litarāka*
Amplified: Here is Nawāl, having come to see you".
or
Proclitic: Look, Nawāl has come..."[25] Maḥfūẓ *Ḫān* 265.–1

25 In addition to the structural ambiguity, there exists of course also the ambiguity between a presentative and an identifying reading. Thus, while the person in (7)c is well known to the addressee (she is the girl he used to be deeply in love with), which rules out an identifying reading, *"this is Nawāl, having come ...", contexts such as the following, in which a person unknown to the addressee is introduced:
hāḏā ġulāmunā abaqa minnā Bayḍāwī, to Q 12:19
hāḏā ʿabduka ... qāla lī kaḏā wakaḏā *Riwāyāt al-Aġānī* 2.4.
also allow an identifying interpretation ("this is our servant, having escaped ...", etc.).

These sentences fulfill the semantic conditions of the amplified structure, see § 3.2 above.[26] On the other hand, they may also be interpreted as proclitic sentences with an alerting demonstrative presentative, i.e. as in (4)a or (6)b (in which case the inflection of the demonstrative has to be understood in the light of § 5.2.1 below). One occasionally finds this interpretational ambiguity reflected in translation variants, as when the verb in (7)b is rendered as a *Ḥāl* by Nöldeke *ZGr*. 49.14, "Da ist unser Geld, uns wiedergegeben", but as a predicate in Arberry, "See, our merchandise here is restored to us".[27]

4.3 On the other hand, there are contexts that favor one interpretation over the other:

(8) "Al-Ḥulays ... had passed by Abu Sufyān b. Ḥarb as the latter was striking the side of Ḥamza's mouth with the point of the spear ... whereupon Al-Ḥulays said: O Banū Kināna,

a. *hāḏā sayyidu Qurayšin yaṣnaʿu bibni ʿammihi kamā tarawna laḥman*
here is the leader of the Qurayš, treating his cousin like meat, as you can see (i.e. mutilating his corpse)". Nöldeke *ZGr*. 49.16[28]

"When the Prophet saw them (i.e. the Qurayš) descending from the (hill) ʿAqanqal ... into the valley, he said: O God,
b. *hāḏihi Qurayšun qad aqbalat biḫuyalāʾihā wafaḫrihā ... allāhumma aḥinhumu lġadāta*
here are the Qurayš with (lit. having come with) their vanity and boastfulness ... O God, wipe them out this morning". Ibn Hišām I/1 440.6–8

"Suddenly there was a knock at the door, so he said: Look who it is. They went out and there stood Al-Muḥallaq's messenger, delivering his message. So they went back to him and said:

26 In the amplified reading, the perfect of the verb marks a resultative and static state of affairs (as opposed to the dynamic meaning of an imperfect, e.g. *hāḏā l-Aʿšā yanzilu* "Here is Al-Aʿšā, settling down ..."), see Reck. *SV* 552–3, Cant. III 250.

27 Needless to say, evidence drawn from translations has at best a secondary significance as compared with the independent examination of a sentence's meaning in its context.

28 For the entire context quoted here see Ṭab. I/3 1418.12ff.

c. *hāḏā rasūlu l-Muḥallaqi l-Kilābiyyi atāka bikayta wakayta* (Out) there is the messenger of Muḥallaq the Kilābite with (lit. having come to you with) such and such a message".
Nöldeke *ZGr.* 49.–15[29]

When seen in their contexts, each of these three sentences evokes the sense of a concrete *scene* being described – Abu Sufyān mutilating the corpse; the Qurayš having descended from the hill; the messenger having come to the door – which points in the direction of the amplified (*Ḥāl*) structure.[30] In ex. (8)a this understanding is furthermore supported by the words *kamā tarawna* ("as you see"), which suggest an event that is happening before the eyes of Al-Ḥulays and his fellow warriors. Consider also that the portion *yaṣnaʿu ... laḥman* is paralleled by an unambiguous circumstantial clause in the preceding sentence (*wahuwa yaḍribu* "as he was striking ..."). Finally, notice that the situation of (8)c – announcing the presence of someone at the door – is the same as in (3)a, where the *Ḥāl* is overtly marked.

4.4 In contrast to (8), the contexts of the following sentences seem to favor an interpretation according to the proclitic structure:

(9) "Then (i.e. upon being informed of the makeup of the army facing him) the Prophet went to his people and said:

a. *hāḏihi Makkatu qad alqat ilaykum aflāḏa kabidihā*
So Mecca has thrown to you the innermost pieces of its liver (i.e. its very best men)".[31] Nöldeke *ZGr.* 49.–17[32]

b. *yā bunayya hāḏā ššitāʾu qad hajama ʿalayka waʾanta taḥtāju fīhi ilā maʿūnatin*
"My son, look, winter has taken you by surprise and you will need some (financial) aid during this period". *Riwāyāt al-Aġānī* 2.–4

The words of (9)a are spoken by the Prophet prior to the scene of (8)b, i.e. while he and the Muslims are still awaiting the encounter with the enemy, who at this time had not yet come out from his assembling place behind the ʿAqanqal. At this stage the Prophet is trying to assess the strength of the enemy on the basis of intelligence brought to him. He has just learned that the enemy force includes a large number of the most prominent among the Qurayš. His words are spoken in direct reaction to this last piece of information: He realizes how seriously the

29 For the full context see *Aġānī* (first, 1868 ed.) VIII 81.13–14.
30 With the "resultative" perfect in (8)b and c, see note 26 above.
31 For the use of *aflāḏu kabidi Makkata* in this meaning see Lane s.r. *flḏ*.
32 For the whole story see Ibn Hišām I/1 436.1–436.–3 = Ṭab. I/3 1303.8–1305.2.

Meccans have taken the impending battle against the Muslims. Against this background one will understand the demonstrative presentative in (9)a as signalling this realization or conclusion, a meaning I attempted to reproduce above as "So Mecca has ..." (or alternatively, "Oh I see, Mecca has ...", or in Germ. "Da hat also Mekka ..."). In this interpretation, then, the structure of this sentence is proclitic[33] and the meaning inferential, to which compare the *types* of meaning (causal, explanatory, etc.) of the presentative sentences discussed in W. Fischer *Dem.* 159.–6ff. Given this context, an interpretation of (9)a on the model of the amplified structure, i.e. deictically "There is Mecca, having thrown to you ...", is far less probable. Thus, while the similarity of this sentence and (8)b might at first suggest the same analysis, a comparison of their contexts serves to highlight the difference. In (9)b a father wishes to convince his son to accept a sum of money as a gift from him (the sentence is followed by an explanatory parenthetical remark *wa'iḏā mālun ʿaẓīmun bayna yadayhi* "and there was a lot of money in front of him"). The meaning appears to be argumentative, perhaps more pertinently paraphrased by an informal English "Now look, my boy, winter has ...". For another proclitic sentence with an argumentative meaning cf. (4)b and § 3.3. An interpretation according to the amplified structure is here certainly not called for.[34]

4.5 The second, far rarer type of presentative sentence that exhibits no structure-determining criteria and therefore allows both interpretations (§ 4.1) is: demonstrative presentative + substantive + prepositional phrase. Nöldeke *ZGr.* 49.9–12, views the prepositional phrase as circumstantial ("Zustandsausdruck"), classifying the exx. exhibiting this sequence together with those with a *Ḥāl*- acc., i.e. (3). But I suggest that, here too, we recognize instances whose semantics point rather in the direction of the proclitic structure (i.e. the prepositional phrase being the predicate):

(10) "He approached (him) and said to him secretly:
a. *hāḏā l-Zubayru fī Wādī l-Sibāʿ*
Look, Al-Zubayr is in Wādī Al-Sibāʿ". IbnSaʿd III/1 78.23

33 Guillaume translates (9)a in Ibn Hišām as "This Mecca has thrown to you ...". Although this reading must be rejected for the reason mentioned above note 18 and more specifically Fleischer 749.–12, it does support our own interpretation indirectly insofar as it recognizes the verb in this sentence as the predicate, rather than a *Ḥāl*.

34 To be sure, in this particular ex. an attributive reading cannot be entirely ruled out ("this winter has ...") since the substantive has the definite article, unlike exx. (4)b, (9)a, see note 18.

"So I said (to them):

b. *tilkum*[35] *ṣāḥibatukum fī Banī Jumaḥa*
Look, your woman relative is with the Banū Jumaḥ". Nöldeke *ZGr.* 49.10

It is clear from the context of Ibn Saʿd that Al-Zubayr is not at the scene where (10)a is spoken but in Wādī Al-Sibāʿ, to which fact the speaker wishes to alert the addressee (as in other instances where a proclitic presentative is used with the alerting function, one may alternatively paraphrase with "Listen, Al-Zubayr is in ...", or [colloquially] "Hey, Al-Zubayr is ...", etc.). A deictic-concrete reading with *Ḥāl* syntax and semantics would be out of place, *"There is Al-Zubayr, (being) in ...". For much the same reason the proclitic interpretation of (10)b is more plausible than the *Ḥāl*-analysis proposed by Nöldeke, which would yield a meaning *"There is your woman relative, with the ...".[36]

4.6 Presentatives can be used to draw attention to the fact that a given period of time has elapsed. Viewed superficially, this is nothing but a special case of the alerting function. However, since this particular usage has special semantic properties (see below), there is some justification in regarding it as a type in its own right. The following exx. are from classical (a), modern colloquial (b), modern literary Arabic (c), Old Aramaic (d) and Bibl. Hebrew (e):

(11) "You told me that Taymāʾ is Laylā's abode as long as the summer lasts,

a. *fahāḏī*[37] *šuhūru ṣṣayfi ʿannī qadi nqaḍat*
but see, the summer months have passed me by". Reck. *AS* 288 n. 1[38]

b. *hayy ilarbʿīn yōm fātu wʾana ma muttʾš*
"Look, the forty days have passed and I have not died".
(Pal.) W. Fischer *Dem.* 177.–1

c. *hā qad marra sabʿatu ālāfi sanatin ʿalā wilādatī lʾūlā*
"Look, seven thousand years have passed since my first birth". Cant. II31

d. *hʾ ʿśr šnyn šlmʾ mn ywm dy npqth mn ḥrn*
"Look, ten years have elapsed from the time you departed from Haran". Fitzmyer 74.27

35 For *-kum*, the *Ḥarf al-Ḫiṭāb*, see Reck. *AS* 289 and n. 1.

36 With this contrast the deictic-concrete meaning of the (nuclear) sentence *ḏākum ṣāḥibukum fa-dḫulū ʿalayhi* "There is your man, come in to him", Nöldeke, ibid. For the context of this and (10)b see Ibn Hišām I/2 715.1, 878.–7.

37 *hāḏī*, for the more common *hāḏihi*, see W. Fischer *Gramm.* § 274 n.1.

38 For the full context see *Aġānī* (second, 1905 ed.) VII 89.26.

e. *kī hinnē hassətāw ʿāḇār*
"For lo, the winter is past". Ct 2:11

4.6.1 By simply describing this as a special case of the alerting function, one would not fully come to grips with the semantics of this sentence type. We are dealing once again with an extension (in the sense of § 3.5) of the rudimentary-concrete sense of the presentative, i.e. (put in a simplified way) from a use as in "Look, three men have come to you", where the speaker alerts to a concrete and visible event, to a use as in "Look, a month has passed". One will understand that in this latter type of use, here exemplified by sentences (11), the presentative is especially prone to acquire any of the abstract meanings (e.g. argumentative, explanatory, inferential) mentioned earlier.

4.6.2 There is another aspect of this sentence-type that can be seen in terms of a semantic extension, namely to a secondary *temporal* sense of the presentative. This is occasionally reflected in translations, e.g. Reckendorf's of ex. (11)a "jetzt sind mir die Sommermonate vergangen", or for that matter the alternative rendition of the Biblical ex. (11)e "... now the winter is past".[39] Notice also that the same semantic extension can be observed in the way (colloquial) American English uses its presentative "here", and renditions such as "here the summer is already gone" or "here the forty days are over" quite adequately reproduce this presentative-with-temporal sense that characterizes (11). Needless to say, the semantics of this sentence-type allow only an interpretation according to the proclitic structure, precluding amplified (*Ḥāl*) readings such as *"Here are the summer months ..." (in ex. c, moreover, the proclitic understanding is corroborated by the surface-structure criterion of § 2.8).

4.7 Occasionally a proclitic demonstrative presentative can be associated with no other function than that of resuming a narration, as in:

(12) "Then he went on to say:
hāḏā ʿAliyyunᵘ l-Uswāriyyu akala maʿa ʿĪsā bni Sulaymāna
ʿAli al-Uswārī ate together with ʿĪsā ..." Blau "Jāḥ." 286.6[40]

This use exhibits a demonstrative presentative that, depleted of its alerting function, has been reduced to a mere introductory signal. As is obvious, such a semantic depletion could have occurred only in the proclitic structure (and sentence (12) cannot be read other than according to this structure). A similar usage is found in some modern Bedouin dialects, where such an introductory demon-

39 As in the new translation of the *Jewish Publication Society of America* (differing from the wording of the *New Oxford Bible*, quoted above, (11)e.

40 For the context see Jāḥiẓ, *K. al-Buḫalā'* (ed. Van Vloten), 73.4.

strative presentative characteristically occurs at the beginning of a story, i.e. type:

hāḏa wāḥidin yesennid ʿala
"Someone addressed a poem to ..."[41]

4.8 Finally, a proclitic presentative may confirm a statement, emphasize its validity. This will be discussed in detail in connection with the semantic development of *inna*, see chapter V, §§ 1.1–2 and 2.5.2–3, but we may mention here that there is some (albeit limited) evidence also of the development of the demonstrative presentative in this direction, as in the following modern literary example. A contemporary scholar points out that the modern literary Arabic of Egypt is

luġa mustaqilla ʿanⁱ lluġa llatī ṭaraqat
bihā Miṣr abwāba lʿaṣri lḥadīṯ

(13) *fahāḏā Faraḥ Anṭūn yulaqqibuhā bi- "lluġa l-jadīda"*
"a language that is independent of the language
with which Egypt entered the modern era.
And in fact Faraḥ Anṭūn terms it 'the New Language'"
(or "and Faraḥ Anṭūn indeed, actually, etc. terms it ...").[42]

4.9 I hope to have shown in the preceding paragraphs that the determination of the underlying structure of a presentative sentence requires the consideration of formal as well as semantic criteria. In fact, the latter are ultimately more decisive, since formal criteria are often altogether missing, as we have seen. The essential contrast between the amplified (*Ḥāl*) and the proclitic structure is in the range and type of meanings involved: The amplified structure with its homogeneous (and relatively easily definable) semantic value, as against a heterogeneity of meanings of the proclitic structure.

5. *From Amplified to Proclitic Structure by Syntactic Reanalysis*

5.1 There are strong indications to suggest that the proclitic structure is historically secondary, resulting from a syntactic reanalysis (or shift) of the components of the amplified structure. Such a change could be conceived as a process by which the second component in the amplified structure (the "head" of the

41 For more on this type see § 5.1., below.
42 Al-Saʿīd Muḥammad Badawī, *Mustawayāt al-ʿArabiyya al-Muʿāṣira fī Miṣr* (Cairo 1973) 81.7.

nucleus) enters into a direct predicational link with the third component. The result is, on the one hand, formation of a new sentential unit whose predicate is the former circumstantial amplification; and on the other, reduction of the presentative to the status of a proclitic. The process may have started with cases where the morphology precludes an overt marking of the status of the circumstantial amplification, e.g. when it is a verb in the imperfect:

hāḏā Zaydun yanṭaliqu → *hāḏā Zaydun yanṭaliqu*

This state of affairs may have facilitated the reanalysis, since imperfects in Arabic can be *Ḥāl*s as well as predicates.

The notion of syntactic reanalysis occurs sporadically in the Arabistic literature, witness terms such as "Verschiebung der syntaktischen Gliederung", "Umdeutung der syntaktischen Beziehung" used e.g. Reck. *AS* 230.–10, W. Fischer *Dem.* 49.4 (though for developments other than the one under discussion). For a development which, despite differences in detail, bears much resemblance to the one proposed here see Blau *Emergence* 192 n. 1, where the Bedouin construction of the type *hāḏa wāḥidin yesennid ʿala* ... "There was someone who addressed a poem to ..." > "(Behold,) someone addressed a poem to ..." is discussed.

5.2 Let us examine critically the proposed syntactic shift. That the proclitic structure derives historically from the amplified one, rather than the other way around, is supported by a number of considerations:

5.2.1 There are examples of the proclitic structure in which the demonstrative presentative is inflected, e.g. (9)a, (10)b, (11)a (and possibly also (7)b, c – if they were formed as proclitic sentences, not amplified ones). Such inflection can hardly be understood other than as a diachronic "left-over" feature from the source structure, where this inflection is motivated by the sentential link with the second component, i.e. the head of the nucleus.

5.2.2 Inflected forms that become syntactically dislodged from a sentential link due to a shift of the kind described above occasionally tend to lose their inflection, the language developing an uninflected variant form in the third masc. sing. (i.e. the least marked member of the set). This is the case in Christian Middle Arabic, where the proclitic structure exhibits both inflected and uninflected demonstrative presentatives:

(14) a. *hāḏihi anbiyākum qad ayyasatkum*
"Behold, your prophets have driven you to despair".

b. *wahāḏihi asmāhum ʿindī maḥfūẓa*
"And behold, their names are preserved with me".

(15) *wahāḏā Āsiya wakull addunyā tasjud lahā*
"And behold, Asia and all the world worship her".[43]

Blau *Chr. Ar.* 463.–1, 464.1–3, 464.15

While the inflection of the proclitic demonstrative presentative in (14)a–b has the same (namely historical) explanation as proposed in § 5.2.1, the uninflected form in (15) is an innovation: It ought to be seen as an adjustment to the *synchronic* stage in which the inflection has lost its raison d'être due to the dissolution of the sentential link (see also § 5.3 below). One may surmise that, once so formed in a construction of type (15), this uninflected variant became productively used in the formation of new types of proclitic structure, such as (6)a–d.[44]

A word concerning the distribution of the uninflected proclitic demonstrative presentative. While it is well attested in (Christian) Middle Arabic, I know of only a single attestation in the classical language, *hāḏā ʿajiltum* ... (6)a.[45] However, since the form *is* thus attested, uninflectedness cannot be entirely ruled out also in classical examples such as (4)a–b, (10)a (or, say, (7)a in the proclitic reading) where a third person masc. sing. demonstrative presentative is followed by a masc. sing. subject. Of course, in order to *prove* uninflectedness in this type of proclitic structure one would have to have exx. such as (15), i.e. with subjects that are not masc. sing., and such exx. are absent in the classical material at my disposal. In view of its unequal distribution between classical and Middle Arabic (and excluding inconclusive examples from consideration), it is conce vable that the uninflected proclitic demonstrative presentative originated in an early Middle Arabic source whence it occasionally infiltrated classical texts.

43 Here too, a reading of these sentences according to the amplified structure would falsify their meaning. For a similar coexistence of an uninflected and an inflected proclitic demonstrative presentative in a modern dialect see Blau *BZ* § 18.

44 In Christian Middle Arabic the uninflected form also penetrates the nuclear structure, see *hāḏā nnār walḥaṭab* "Here is the fire and the wood" (var. *hāḏihi*, in agreement with *nār*), Blau *Chr. Ar.* 464.12 (on the other hand, this may be an inflected demonstrative, since *nār* also occurs as masc., see ibid. 136 n. 16). On the nuclear status of this sentence see note 67.

45 For the attestation of another uninflected proclitic presentative in a classical source (viz. *hā huwa ḏā*) see ex. (21)e.

5.2.3 The transition of the demonstrative presentative from nuclear to proclitic status is associated, in terms of diachrony, with various features of loss, i.e. the tendency to lose its inflection (as we have just seen) and, semantically, the tendency to lose its deictic-concrete meaning. For while it is unmistakably deictic in nuclear position and, as a proclitic, may still be associated with deixis when used in a purely alerting sense, there is certainly nothing of its deictic force left when it occurs with one of the extended meanings (argumentativity, inferentiality, etc.).

5.2.4 Finally, the direction of the development from a circumstantial amplification to a predicate (or, put differently, from a subordinated to a nonsubordinated predicate) has a parallel in the history of the *ḫabar kāna*, whose acc. case can best be explained as reflecting an original *Ḥāl*, as has long been recognized.[46]

5.2.5 To sum up: (1) The "left-over" character of the inflection of the proclitic demonstrative presentative; (2) its tendency to lose this inflection; (3) the large extent of loss of the original deictic-concrete meaning in proclitic position; (4) the typological support for the assumption of a transition from circumstantial amplification to predicate – all these features taken together point in the direction of a development from amplified to proclitic structure. These features would be hard to account for if one were to assume a development in the opposite direction.

5.3 Excursus: Syntactic Change and Loss of Inflection.

The loss of pronominal inflection discussed in § 5.2.2 may simply be seen as a manifestation of the well-known general phenomenon of language, i.e. the "drift" towards elimination of inflectional categories. However, since the inflectional loss in question occurs under a very specific condition of syntactic change, namely the *lowering of the syntactic status*, I prefer to view the loss of

46 So e.g. Fleischer 576–7, Nöldeke *ZGr.* 37, Brock. 107.–14 (where the development is in fact described in terms of a shift: "... gewinnt das Prädikativ den Rang eines Prädikats"), and Brock. 357. The theory advanced in Bravmann *Studies* § 56 can hardly replace the original explanation. But while the *Ḥāl*-origin of the *ḫabar kāna* is now widely acknowledged, the description of the feature occasionally suffers from a confusion of synchrony and diachrony, as when the acc. in question is said to be "in fact a circumstantial accusative", Cant. II 199.2, or a "Zustands-Akk." in W. Fischer *Gramm.* § 382a. Along the same lines, the Germ. term "Prädikativ(um)" is sometimes used indiscriminately for both the *Ḥāl* and the *ḫabar kāna*, e.g. Reck. *AS* 97.5 vs. 101.6, W. Fischer *Gramm.* § 380 vs. § 382a. There can be little doubt that in the grammatical system of Arabic the term in the acc. is a predicate, not a *Ḥāl* (as the very name *ḫabar kāna* indicates), and a synchronically and descriptively adequate nomenclature should reflect this fact, rather than the original state of affairs.

the inflection as a concomitant factor of this lowering[47] (to which compare e.g. the development of the invariable *hā huwa ḏā*, 6.3.1.) But comparable phenomena have been also observed in other languages. Consider e.g. the following feature of Hebrew syntax, described in Rubinstein *Ha-Ivrit Šelanu* 83–84. Hebrew has a pronominal copula that agrees with the subject (like Arabic), i.e. type

hadam hu hanefeš
"The blood is the life (lit. the soul)".
⟨the-blood (masc.) it (masc.) the-soul (fem.)⟩

This agreement is a diachronic left-over feature (Rubinstein calls it an "anachronism"), reflecting an early stage in which the pronoun in question was not a copula but a subject in a dislocation structure of the type S, S′ – P (where S′ is the subject pronoun in agreement with S). Now, modern spoken Hebrew developed a new copula in the uninflected third masc. sing., as in

Bolonya ze lo ir
"Bologna is not a city".
⟨Bologna (fem.) it (masc.)[48] not a-city (fem.),⟩

a development which Rubinstein sees as an adjustment to the synchronic state of affairs, the older inflectional type having lost its justification once the structure was no longer dislocational but copular.

5.4 We have seen earlier that there is a basic contrast, namely between semantically homogeneous nuclear and amplified structures on the one hand and semantically heterogeneous proclitic ones on the other. I believe this difference can be explained in the light of the syntactic reanalysis (shift) discussed in the preceding paragraph. As long as a presentative is an integral component of a nucleus, its meaning remains constant, namely deictic-concrete. But once dislodged from the nucleus due to the reanalysis, the presentative becomes exposed, as it were, to contextual influences and thus capable of acquiring new meanings – including meanings which quite substantially depart from presentativity in the strict sense, see esp. the semantics of sentences such as (13), and

47 For precisely this reason I believe that the feature under discussion ought to be separated from the occasional absence of masc./fem. gender distinction in demonstrative pronouns in Middle Arabic and modern colloquials, see Blau, *Jud. Ar.* 61, *Chr. Ar.* 135 and n. 12, 285, *Emergence* 112, W. Fischer *Dem.* 57.

48 It is immaterial to the point here under discussion that this new copula is formed from the demonstrative pronoun (masc. *ze*., fem. *zot*, *zo*, etc., contrasting with the older copula which is based on the personal pronoun).

below (18)d, (27)e–f. While this certainly does not explain how each type of meaning of the proclitic structures came into being, it does at least provide a basic frame for the understanding of the dualism (semantic homogeneity/heterogeneity) that is a central characteristic of presentative syntax.

5.5 At this point a methodological remark is in order. The proposed historical development ought not to be understood as resulting in the elimination of the old structure, but rather as an *addition* of a new (namely proclitic) one to the repertoire of the language: Not a stage of "only A" followed by a stage "only B", but rather a stage "only A" followed by one of "A and B". One could view this as a process of "loosening": An utterance, say, with an imperfect (see § 5.1), which prior to the syntactic shift could be generated only in one way, viz. as an amplified structure, could be generated after the shift *also* as a proclitic structure. It is of course possible that the synchronic coexistence of any such two diachronically related structures is only an intermediate station between an "only A" and an "only B" stage. But whether or not this is the ultimate direction of the development, it is precisely such a stage of "A *and* B" that classical Arabic presents to the observer in the case under discussion.

There is another consideration that could explain the coexistence of the source structure and the resultant structure. Even if one were to assume that the reanalysis altogether eliminates the amplified structure from the language (contrary to our above assumption), this structure could still be recreated *ab ovo* on the foundation of the (unamplified) nuclear structure, since the latter remains of course unaffected by the reanalysis.

6. *The Special History of Pronominal Nuclear Structures*

6.1 The nuclear pattern *hā huwa ḏā* and its development

6.1.1 When the head of a nuclear presentative sentence is a personal pronoun, Arabic uses a special pattern consisting of three components: *Hā* + personal pronoun + *ḏā/ḏī/ulāʾi* (the third component in agreement with the pronoun):

(16) *faqultu mā lḫabaru*
qāla qataltu ʿaduwwa llāhi (I)bna Ḫāzimin
a. *wahā huwa ḏā*
"So I said: What's the news?
He said: I killed Ibn Ḫāzim, the enemy of God,
and here he is". Ṭab. II/2 833.2

inna lfatā man yaqūlu
b. *hā anā ḏā*
laysa lfatā man yaqūlu
kāna abī
"The true man is the one who says:
Here I am,
not the one who says:
My father was ..." Fleischer 440.8

ilā an taqūlu l-Muġār
c. *hā anā ḏih*
"Until Al-Muġār says:
Here I am". Ṭab. *Gl.* 536.–7[49]

d. *hā naḥnu ulā'i*
ṯṯalāṯatu
"Here we are, the three of us". Cant. II 36

wa'ayna ḏālika lkitābu
qāla
e. *hā huwa ḏā*
yā sayyidī
"And where is that letter?
He said:
Here it is, Sir". Cant. II 36

The third component may be missing, as in:

faqāla ayna ssā'ilu ... qāla
f. *hā anā*
yā rasūla llāhi
"So he (the Prophet) said:
Where is the one who is asking? He answered:
Here I am, Messenger of God". Reck. *SV* 409.1[50]

and so may the first one:

waqāla afī nnāsi ʿAbdu l-Raḥmāni Bnu ʿAwfin
qālū naʿam yā amīra lmu'minīna
g. *huwa ḏā*
"And he (ʿUmar) said:
Is ʿAbd al-Raḥmān b. ʿAwf among the people (here)?
They said: Yes, Commander of the Faithful,
here he is". Ṭab. I/5 2723.–6

49 = M. J. De Goeje (*Annales ... At-Tabari ...*) *Glossarium*, Leiden 1901. *Ḏih* for *ḏī* is pausal, see W. Fischer *Dem.* 59.–8.

50 For the full quotation see Buḫ. (ed. Krehl) I 24.10.

There is no functional difference between the full, tripartite pattern and these shorter forms. This applies not only to the nuclear structure (16) but to all structures involving the pattern to be discussed in the following. The shorter forms will therefore be viewed as variants of the full pattern and not be treated separately.[51] Our analysis is based on data from classical, middle and modern literary Arabic.

6.1.2 It is our purpose to show, here again, that the nuclear structure is the base from which new structures developed. Like its counterpart with a substantival head, the nuclear presentative sentence with pronominal head can occur with a circumstantial (*Ḥāl*) amplification:

(17) a. *hā huwa ḏā marbūṭan*
"There he is, bound (tied)". — Reck. *SV* 410.6

b. *unẓur, hā hiya ḏī tanẓuru ilayka*
"Look, there she is, looking at you".[52] — Cant. II 36

6.1.3 And, here too, we encounter a type whose syntax and semantics are not circumstantial. The contrast, in purely structural-syntactic terms, is that in the amplified structure (17) the personal pronoun is an integral part of the nucleus (namely its head), whereas in (18) it is the subject of the sentence, the other term – verb, substantive, adjective, etc. – being the predicate.

(18) "Do you threaten every disobedient tyrant? (so says the infidel caliph Al-Walīd to God, in reference to Q 14:15, ... *waḫāba kullu jabbārin ʿanīdin*, all the while hitting a Qurʾānic *muṣḥaf* with arrows),

a. *fahā anā ḏāka*[53] *jabbārun ʿanīdu*
So look here, I am (such a) disobedient tyrant!" — A. Fischer "Schwur" 54.–4ff.

"Whenever I see wine, I feel that I must prostrate myself before it;

b. *fahā anā iḏā mā faqadtuhā faqīdu*
for look, if I am deprived of it, I have no existence". — A. Fischer "Schwur" 55

"They stopped in front of me and asked who I was, so I said:

c. *hā anā ḏā Ḫālidun*
Look, I am Ḫālid". — Reck. *SV* 410.5

51 On the question of the origin of the pattern see note 105.

52 Here and in (18) I am including the examples with finite verbs, i.e. whose morphology precludes case-marking, together with the marked examples.

53 For this *-ka*, the *Ḥarf al-Ḫiṭāb*, see Reck. *AS* 289 and n.1.

Speaker, having just related a series of successive and commonly known events, concludes his account by turning to his audience:

d. *wahā antum taʿlamūna mā ḥadaṯa*
"and you know, of course, what happened (in this particular instance)";
or "you know, don't you ...?", Germ. ihr wißt ja, ihr wißt doch ... Reck. *SV* 409.3

"Ibn Ṭūlūn said:
And as for the facility for the ritual bath,
I found in it uncleanness ...

e. *wahā anā abnīhā ḫalfahu*
wa'amara bibinā'ihā
and look, I am going to build it behind it (i.e. behind the mosque)",
and he ordered it built. A. Fischer "Schwur" 55.6

f. *wahā anā qādimun ilayka baʿda qalīlin*
"And look, I shall be coming to you shortly". Cant. II 36

"If we know our bounds ... we refuse to overstep them,

g. *wahā anta ḏā qad rafaḍta an tataʿaddā ḥudūdaka*
and here you have just refused to overstep your bounds". Bloch *Chr.* 74.5

h. *wahā hum ulā'i qad intaqalū*
fahal taṭma'innu qulūbuhum ḥaqqan
"And here they have just moved (viz. to a new neighborhood), but will they really find peace of mind?!"
Maḥfūẓ *Ḫān* 33.–11[54]

As this sample shows, structure (18) has a variety of meanings. Presentativity is perhaps most sharply profiled in (18)a: It is as if the caliph were saying, "Look at what I am doing here to your Holy Book!", using the presentative frame to point, as it were, to his very action. In (18)b we witness an extension (in the sense of § 3.5) from the purely alerting to a causal-explanatory meaning.[55] The same is true of (18)c, but the understanding of this sentence requires some background information. The speaker is convinced that those addressing him were sent by the caliph to bestow great honors on him, hence his astonishment that they don't know who he is. The special nuance could be reproduced in

54 For the full quotation of (18)c see Masʿūdī 115.2; for that of (18)d see Mubarrad, *Kāmil*, ed. Wright, Leipzig 1864, 576.12.

55 Notice that this is the same causal-explanatory sense that is often expressed by *fa'inna*, e.g. *daʿnī fa'innī maqtūlun* "Leave me, for I am dying", Reck. *SV* 466.1 ff. Since *inna* was originally a presentative (see ch. V), the prefixation of *fa-* to a presentative sentence as in (18)b may be seen as typologically akin to the prefixation of *fa-* to an *inna*-sentence.

English by some paraphrase such as "I am Ḫālid – don't you know that?!" Ex. (18)d shows especially well how far the meaning of this structure may deviate from presentativity in the narrow sense. Insofar as the speaker expresses his certainty that his audience knows what happened, the meaning here comes close to that of a "mood" category, which is relevant to the history of *inna*, see chapter V, note 8, § 2.5.2ff. In (18)e–f the speaker draws attention to an action he intends to undertake presently, in (18)g–h to one having occurred "just now" or very recently – two uses demonstrating an affinity between presentativity and actions in close proximity to the "speaker's present" (i.e. the moment of utterance).

6.1.3.1 This wide range and diversity of meanings put (18) in the same class as the proclitic structures (on which point see more below, § 6.1.4.2). Yet it must be emphasized that we are by no means dealing with a random diversity but with a semantic range that is typical also of presentative sentences elsewhere. Modern Hebrew, for example, possesses a presentative *hare* that covers the same semantic ground as sentences (18)b–d.[56] Furthermore, its Aramaic counterpart *'ry* of the Genesis Apocryphon is causal-explanatory in all of the attested uses.[57] Presentative sentences with an explanatory-causal sense are likewise found in a number of modern Arabic colloquials.[58] For the use of a presentative sentence specifically in relation to the speaker's intended action, as in (18)e–f, see the Bibl. Hebrew phrases of the type *hinənī* + participle.[59] Finally, note that presentative sentences with "here" in (colloquial) American English are used in much the same sense as (18)g–h, see the above renditions of these two exx. (and cf. § 4.6.2). Thus, in speaking of the semantic diversity which characterizes (18) (and the proclitic structures), we must at the same time keep in mind that it is a diversity *within* the category "presentative sentence".

6.1.3.2 The difference between structure (18) and the corresponding amplified structure (17) becomes particularly evident if one tries to read the former in terms of the latter. Thus, a circumstantial interpretation of, say, (18)d and e (or c and f, with an acc. instead of the nom.) would falsify the meaning of these sentences. Yet we must emphasize, here again, that the contrast is not absolute, for there are contexts admitting of either interpretation, such as (18)h, which

56 Thus, this presentative would render quite accurately (18)b–d: ... *vahare ani* ...; *hare ani Ḫālid*; *vahare atem yod'im* ...

57 Fitzmyer 227.4. Notice that the sentence quoted there has causal *kī* in the Biblical "Vorlage", Gn 13:14–15, 17.

58 W. Fischer *Dem.* 159.–6ff.

59 E.g. Gn 6:17 and passim. For *hinənī ēleḵā* in this meaning see P. Humbert, *Zeitschrift für die alttestamentliche Wissenschaft* 51 (1933), 101–8.

could also have been intended as a *Ḥāl* construction, "Here they are, having just moved ...", and cf. the discussion of (7)a–c in § 4.2.[60] It is precisely this occasional bivalence of a presentative sentence (or, put differently, the partial overlap between the two structures) that makes possible a syntactic change of the kind suggested § 5.1, by which an unmarked circumstantial amplification in a construction of type (17) is reanalyzed as a predicate, thus producing a new structure, (18).

6.1.4 The following synoptic juxtaposition (which disregards the shorter variants of the tripartite pattern) demonstrates, horizontally, the parallelism between the substantival and pronominal structures and, vertically, the similarity of their syntactic development:

substantival structure	its pronominal counterpart
hāḏā Zaydun (2)	*hā huwa ḏā* (16)
hāḏā Zaydun munṭaliqan (3)	*hā huwa ḏā munṭaliqan* (17)
hāḏā Zaydun munṭaliqun (4)	*hā huwa ḏā munṭaliqun* (18)

One structure which does not partake in this substantival-pronominal dichotomy must be added to this synopsis:

hāḏā (i)nṭalaqtum (6)

6.1.4.1 There are, then, on the one hand the nuclear and amplified structures, (2), (16) and (3), (17), in which the presentative forms a sentential unit (nucleus) with a substantive or pronoun, and whose meaning is *homogeneous*, being determined by the essentially deictic-concrete nature of the presentative in their nuclei; and on the other hand, the structures whose presentative does not form such a sentential unit and which are characterized by a *variety* of meanings, namely the proclitic structures (4), (6), as well as structure (18). It will be remembered that this semantic characterization includes also the morphologically unmarked manifestations of these structures.

6.1.4.2 A special explanation is here called for concerning the position of structure (18) within this system. This structure shares an essential *syntactic* property with the proclitic structures, namely the non-nuclear status of the two components, *hā* and *ḏā*, which constitute the presentative element (and which, in (16) and (17), are a part of the nucleus). Structure (18) also shares a *semantic*

60 It is the existence of such "neutral" contexts that can explain the occasional occurrence of a presentative sentence with the acc. in one text tradition, the nom. in another, as in Nöldeke *ZGr.* 49.–8 till –5, and cf. above note 17. We shall not deal with the acc. ~ nom. in Qur'ānic verses such as mentioned Nöldeke ibid. –4 till–1. This subject deserves a special study.

feature with the proclitic structures, viz. the diversity of its meanings. For these reasons, it is advisable to consider (18) as belonging typologically to the same class as the proclitic structures – even though its basic surface manifestation, *hā huwa ḏā munṭaliqun*, with its "discontinuous" presentative component flanking the personal pronoun, cannot be properly termed proclitic, in contrast to this structure's substantival counterpart, *hāḏā Zaydun munṭaliqun*. In counting (18) among the proclitic structures, we thus take its syntax and semantics as our criterion, disregarding its surface-structure peculiarity.

6.2 The pattern in the Qur'ān

6.2.1 It is a measure of the analytical intricacy of the constructions with the tripartite pattern (and its bipartite variants) that scholars have arrived at entirely different interpretations. To A. Fischer, for example, the pattern simply serves the "Emphatisierung der Peronalpronomina" – a semantic value which he represents by graphic prominence of the pronouns in question in his German translation of the examples.[61] But the semantic analysis of the data does not support this understanding. The device by which Arabic "emphasizes" personal pronouns is, above all, reduplication (see § 2. of ch. I) and to a more limited extent word-order reversal (see (5) of ch. V), whereas the constructions involving the pattern in question have the meanings and syntactic properties of presentative sentences, as we have seen in types (16)–(18) above. The same is true of the Qur'ānic usage (19) to be discussed presently.[62]

6.2.2 Nöldeke, on the other hand, adopts an analysis proposed in the indigenous Qur'ān exegesis to sentences of type (19), according to which *(hā)ulā'i* is a predicate and the finite verb a second predicate. This analysis, which amounts to suggesting two separate sentential units in asyndetic juxtaposition, yields very unlikely readings, e.g. (19)a, "Da seid ihr, liebt sie" ("There you are, love them")[63], or Arberry's "Ha, there you are; you love them", etc.

61 A. Fischer "Schwur" 53.–2 till 55. (The verse referred to ibid. 54 n. 3 is in Ṭab. I 1254, not 1245.)

62 Fischer (preceding note) deals only with exx. of type (18) and the Qur'ānic usage, not with types (16) and (17). But the latter two types would have lent themselves even less to his interpretation (not *"I killed Ibn Ḫāzim, the enemy of God, and *he*", etc.). The problem with Fischer's approach is that he puts on a par constructions with the pattern under discussion and certain externally similar oath formulas (type *hā la'amru llāhi ḏā qasaman*, etc.), completely disregarding the semantic gulf that separates these "Schwur- und Beschwörungsformeln" and our pattern. This is not to deny that there may have been *originally* some connection between these utterances, but if so, this connection has long ceased to be transparent and is therefore of no use to the understanding of the semantics of the pattern in question.

63 Nöldeke *ZGr.* 50.7–13. Nöldeke's alternative, likewise traditional interpretation also sees in

6.2.3 In my opinion these sentences are far more plausibly viewed as manifestations of structure (18), i.e. the personal pronoun being the subject and the finite verb the predicate:

(19) "O believers, take not for your intimates those that are outside of your community; such men spare nothing to ruin you; they yearn for you to suffer ...

a. *hā antum ulā'i tuḥibbūnahum walā yuḥibbūnakum*
Look, you love them, but they love you not". Q 3:119

b. *hā antum hā'ulā'i ḥājajtum fīmā lakum bihi ʿilmun falima tuḥājjūna fīmā laysa lakum bihi ʿilmun*
"Look, you have disputed on something about which you possess knowledge, so why then do you dispute on a matter of which you know not anything?" Q 3:66

c. *hā antum hā'ulā'i jādaltum ʿanhum fī lḥayāti ddunyā faman yujādilu llāha ʿanhum yawma lqiyāmati ...*
"Look, you have disputed on their behalf in the present life, but who will dispute with God on their behalf on the Day of Resurrection?" Q 4:109

To be sure, since the finite verb in question could in principle be as much a *Ḥāl* as a predicate, we might rather be dealing here with manifestations of the amplified structure, (17). But this interpretation is far less likely, for these three passages clearly do not possess the descriptive-situational semantics (the "scene" effect) typical of the amplified structure.[64] Moreover, notice that each passage involves two coordinated sentences with identical verbs, i.e. *aḥabba* X 2, *ḥājja* X 2, *jādala* X 2, and this distinctly parallelistic construction suggests similarity of the syntactic status of the verbs, i.e. predicate-predicate (as reflected in the above translations), rather than *Ḥāl*-predicate. As for the meaning: The "tone" in all three instances is that of a debate in which the speaker urgently reasons with the listeners and aims to

(hā)ulā'i the predicate, but views the finite verb as a *Ḥāl* (in this last respect thus corresponding to our amplified structure), "ihr seid da, indem ihr sie liebt". On this alternative interpretation see § 6.2.3.

64 As e.g. in (3), (17)a, and in unmarked exx. such as (8)a–c, (17)b. Nöldeke, who in another instance explicitly draws attention to the characteristic semantics of the amplified structure (*ZGr.* 49.–1 till 50.5), fails to apply this criterion to the Qur'ānic usage of (19)a–c, accepting instead the two traditional interpretations of these verses (cf. above and note 63) as equally plausible alternatives. In my view only one Qur'ānic occurrence of the pattern lends itself to an interpretation according to the amplified structure, Q 47:38: *hā antum hā'ulā'i tudʿawna litunfiqū fī sabīli llāhi* "Here you are, being called upon ...", although here too the reading according to structure (18) is equally possible.

convince them, which points in the direction of the *argumentative* use of presentative sentences, cf. § 3.3.

6.3 The invariable pattern

6.3.1 Apart from the inflected pattern – *hā anā ḏā, hā anta ḏā, hā huwa ḏā*, etc. – there also exists an invariable form of that pattern in the third masc. sing., *(hā) huwa ḏā*.[65] It is marginally attested already in the classical language (see ex. (21)e), but occurs more commonly in middle[66] and modern literary Arabic:

(20) a. *huwa ḏā mra'atuka*
"Here is your wife
(take her and be gone)". Gen 12:19 (*Al-Kitāb Al-Muqaddas*)

b. *huwa ḏā asrābu lḥamāmi waššaḥārīri*
"Here are the swarms of doves and blackbirds". Cant. II 32

c. *huwaḏāka* — *huwaḏāhu*
"Here you are". — "Here he is".
Blau *Chr. Ar.* 466.–3,–1[67]

(21) a. *huwa ḏā l'aḏrā'u taḥbalu*
"Behold, the virgin will be with child". Mt 1:23 (*Al-Kitāb Al-Muqaddas*)[68]

b. *walākin huwa ḏā nafsī tahmisu l'āna* ...
"But behold, my soul is now whispering..." Cant. II 32

c. *hā huwa ḏā anā ajlis*
"Behold, I shall sit" Blau *Chr. Ar.* 465.13

d. *hā huwa ḏā ulqī yadī 'alayhim*
"Behold, I shall shake my hand over them". Blau *Chr. Ar.* 465.11

e. *hā huwa ḏā qad qa'attumū lyawma minnī maq'adan*
"So you have made an attack against me today". Reck. *SV* 410.7[69]

While the inflected pattern is capable of functioning as a self-contained sentential whole, i.e. as in (16)–(17), the invarable *(hā) huwa ḏā* is syntactically

65 For the phonetics of the form in the light of its various spellings see Blau *Chr. Ar.* 465 n. 13, 466 n. 15.

66 In addition to the exx. from Christian sources in (20)–(21), see also Blau *Jud. Ar.* 174.

67 Blau renders "Behold, you" and "Behold, he", i.e. as a proclitic presentative followed by a one-term exclamation. I have no access to the source, but I have a hunch that this could also be understood as a nuclear presentative sentence and I am interpreting accordingly. I take the liberty to do so, because Blau consistently translates nuclear presentative sentences in this way, see e.g. Gen 22:7 in *Chr. Ar.* 464.13.

68 Also quoted Blau *Chr. Ar.* 467.–12.

69 Also quoted W. Fischer *Dem.* 161.–2.

a (presentative) *particle*, and therefore capable of occurring only in positions that are lower than the sentential level, namely in the two uses attested in the above examples: As the constituent of a nucleus, combining with a substantival or pronominal head (20), and as a proclitic (21). A similar link between uninflectedness (or, diachronically speaking, loss of inflection) and a reduced syntactic status was discussed in § 5.2.2 and § 5.3.[70]

6.3.2 With this in mind, let us examine the Middle Arabic forms in (20)c in the light of typologically similar forms of the modern colloquials. In various modern colloquials pronominal heads are suffixed to an invariable base, and these forms constitute an entire paradigmatic set. The historical analysis of some of these sets can explain the origin of our Middle Arabic forms. Pal., for example, exhibits the following two (functionally identical) sets:

1. *hay* + suffix, i.e. *hayni*, *hayyak*, *hayyo*, *hayha*, etc.
2. *hayyū* + suffix, i.e. *hayyūni*, *hayyūk*, *hayyūh*, *hayyūha*, etc.
   "Here I am", "Here you are", "Here he is" (etc. with all pronouns).

W. Fischer *Dem.* 179 has suggested that the second set is historically younger, being based on an older invariable ("frozen") form in the third masc. sing. of the first set to which in turn pronominal suffixes were attached.[71] This analysis allows us to point to a striking similarity between the second Pal. set and the Middle Arabic forms in (20)c: In both instances, a form in the third masc. sing., originally functioning as a member in a fully inflected set, serves as the base for the formation of a new nuclear sentence-type. And, of special significance to the feature of reduction: In both cases this invariable form comes to assume the status of a *constituent* of a nucleus (in (20)c and the second Pal. set), i.e. a position that is syntactically one step lower than the sentential level, a level where there is full inflection ((16)–(17) and the first Pal. set). A slightly different yet essentially compatible phenomenon is found in Eg., where the sentential level exhibits the inflected set *ahó*, *ahé*, *ahúm*, see below (22)a–c, but an invariable *ahó* occurs in a syntactically reduced status in forms such as *ahó-na*, *ahó-ntu*, Mitchell 56.

70 But while, then, syntactic reduction is conducive to loss of inflection, it by no means *necessarily* leads to such loss, witness the ("left-over") inflection of the proclitic demonstrative presentative, § 5.2.1 and cf. below § 6.6.4, steps 2 and 3.

71 Fischer reconstructs this older frozen form as *hayyū*, but the first set does not provide such a form with a long final vowel. Rather, I propose that *hayyo* of the first set had a variant form ending with *u* (this *u* still occasionally occurs in the first set, see ex. (27)d below) and that this *hayyu* → *hayyū* before suffixes, exhibiting the obligatory lengthening of a presuffixal vowel.

6.4 Incorporation of the post-nuclear substantival appositive

6.4.1 While in the classical and modern literary language nuclear presentative sentences with pronominal heads are typically formed by means of the tripartite pattern and its bipartite variants (§ 6.1.1), the modern colloquials construct these sentences in a variety of ways, some of which are presented here:

(22) a. *ilkitāb fēn* — *ahó*[72]
"Where is the book?" — "Here it is".

b. *ilʿilba fēn* — *ahé*[72]
"Where is the box?" — "Here it is".

c. *ilkutub fēn* — *ahúm*
"Where are the books?" — "Here they are".
a–c: Eg., Mitchell 55

d. *hayyūh*[73] *hayyūh warāh*
"Here he is, here he is, (run) after him!"
Pal. (Bīr Zēt), W. Fischer *Dem.* 179.–11

e. *tarāu*
"Here it is". — Bornu (Shuwa), W. Fischer *Dem.* 196.7

f. *šaḥḥon*[74]
"Here they are". — Syr., Cowell 565.–1

And a literary example (repeating (16)e above) for comparison:

g. *hā huwa ḏā*
yā sayyidī
"Here it is, Sir". — Cant. II 36

6.4.2 Consider now the following nuclear presentative sentences which are intimately related to those of type (22), as will be argued below:

(23) a. *aho-rrasmi ya bē(h)*
"Here is the plan, Bey". — Eg., W. Fischer *Dem.* 159.1

b. *ahe-lwara'a*
"Here is the sheet of paper". — Eg., Mitchell 55

c. *ahum ilkutub*
"Here are the books". — Eg., Mitchell 55

72 Mitchell lists these forms as *ahóh*, *ahéh* with pausal *-h*. For this and other phonetic vacillations (of stress, vowel length, etc.) in these forms see W. Fischer *Dem.* 170.

73 = Second Pal. set, § 6.3.2.

74 *šaḥḥon* for *šaʿhon*, see Cowell 565.–3.

d. *tarāha ṭṭarabeza*
"Here is the table". Sud. (Omdurman), W. Fischer *Dem.* 196.5

e. *šaʿon*[75] *maṣārīk*
"Here is your money". Syr., Cowell 564.–13

f. *hāu kursīk uhāu tāžek*
"Here is your throne and here is your crown".
Tun., W. Fischer *Dem.* 158.–4

And a corresponding ex. from the modern literary language:

g. *hā huwa ḏā lfirdaws*
"Here is 'The Paradise'". Bloch *Chr.* 78.–3

From a purely descriptive-synchronic point of view, it would be sufficient to state that (23) are nuclear presentative sentences with definite substantival heads, just as (22) are such sentences with pronominal heads. But such a description would be ultimately unsatisfactory, because it fails to take into consideration the relationship between these two sentence-types. There can be little doubt about the *existence* of such a relation, since the presentative constituent in sentences of type (23) is itself composed of ingredients that make up independent nuclear presentative sentences with pronominal heads, as in (22). How is one to explain this relationship?

6.4.3 A plausible answer lies in a diachronic analysis of sentences of type (23). I suggest that the presentative constituent in this sentence-type is the historical reflex of a nuclear presentative sentence with pronominal head, and that the definite substantive was originally an explanatory, or "epexegetical" appositive of the pronoun. Although this appositional structure is here postulated as a historical reconstruction, one occasionally encounters contexts that still allow such an interpretation (see below § 6.5.4). Normally, however, sentences of type (23) represent a unified whole in the synchronic system, the substantive no longer permitting an appositival "reading". I propose that the change be seen in terms of a syntactic shift by which the appositive is reanalyzed as the head of a new nuclear structure, i.e. schematically:

ahum ilkutub ⟶ *ahum ilkutub*
"Here they are, (i.e.) the books" "Here are the books"

resulting in the elimination of the syntactic boundary, real or ideal, separating the appositive from the nucleus in the source structure.

75 *šaʿon* for *šaʿhon*, see Cowell 541.1.

Insofar as sentences of type (23) result from the incorporation of a (originally appositival) substantive, we shall refer to them as "incorporating" nuclear sentences, thereby distinguishing them from nuclear sentences with substantival heads that have not emerged by this process, such as (coll.) *ha* + substantive[76], or the types (1)a–c, e, etc.

6.4.4 We have seen earlier that nuclear presentative sentences with pronominal heads (16) – just as their counterparts with substantival heads – constitute the starting point for the development of new structures, i.e. (17) and (18). Here then is yet another instance of a nuclear sentence with pronominal head, (22), forming the base for the formation of a new structure, (23). This development, however, differs from those described so far in this chapter in that its starting point is an *appositional* relationship.

6.5 The affective base

6.5.1 The preceding analysis needs some elaboration. Various constructions in Arabic and other Semitic languages have been explained as involving an "epexegetical" appositive of a pronoun[77], and related phenomena have been dealt with outside of the Semitistic literature under terms such as the already mentioned "epexegesis", as well as "right dislocation", "antitopic", "afterthought", etc.[78] I do not presume to deal here with the many aspects of this syntax[79], but merely would like to call attention to one particular domain of human language where this syntax seems to me especially common, namely exclamatory or otherwise emotive-affective sentences. I must emphasize right at the outset in order to avoid a misunderstanding that I do not claim that all manifestations of this syntax are affective in origin, only that affect is *one* of its sources. It is therefore no coincidence that one encounters this syntax especially in such typical forms of emotive language as curses, blessings, strong rebukes, exclamations, expres-

76 W. Fischer *Dem.* 163.2–5.

77 So above all the "analytical" constructions of types *hū gaḇrā, qaṭleh l-gaḇrā, bayteh d-gaḇrā* of Syriac, for which see esp. Polotsky's review of R. Schneider, *L'expression des compléments de verbe et de nom ... en Guèze*, *JSS* 6 (1961), 251–6, and the terms used e.g. by Blanc *CD* 131.–19 and Grotzfeld 72.16 for Arabic dialect correspondences of the last two types, and see Remark below.

78 For a critical appraisal of some of these terms (esp. the often used misnomer "afterthought" for these constructions) see Lambrecht 75ff.

79 Nor with the problem of the appropriate description: Is the substantive an appositive of the pronoun (the term "epexegesis" is commensurate with this view), or does the pronoun rather "anticipate" the substantive? The question, implied e.g. in Blanc *CD* 131.–19, is far from being just a terminological quibble, but concerns the very nature of these constructions. Descriptions such as Cant. II 430.9 are unfortunate amalgams of these two types of analysis.

sions of admiration, sorrow, bitter irony, etc. The following are examples from colloquial and modern literary Arabic:

(24) a. *šeft efʿālu hal-maġḍūb*
"I have seen the actions of this wretched person".
⟨I-saw the-actions-of-him this-wretched-one⟩

b. *yeʿmar dīn dīnu bayyek*
approx. "Three cheers for your father".
⟨long-live the-faith of-the-faith-of-him the-father-of-you⟩

c. *yeḥreq bay bayyu l-mannʿek*
"Cursed be the one who suckled you".
⟨may-burn the-father of-the-father-of-him the-one-who-suckled-you⟩

d. *sallem dayyāta l-ḥemltek*
"May (God) protect the hands of the one who bore you (in her womb)".
⟨may-he-protect the-hands-of-her the-one-who-bore-you⟩

e. *qallu ʿaqlātu haṣ-ṣabi*
"This boy doesn't have much brain".
⟨few-are the-brains-of-him this-boy⟩

f. *ʿemri ma šeft metlu ḫayyek*
"I have never in my life seen anyone like your brother".
⟨... the-like-of-him the-brother-of-you⟩

g. *ayš beddu yeṭlaʿ mennu ebn el-ʿawra*
"What can one expect of this son of the one-eyed woman?"
⟨what can come from-him the-son ...⟩

h. *mawš raḥ ensāha haš-šaġle*
"I shall never forget that thing".
⟨not (ever) will I-forget-it this-thing⟩
a–h: Leb., Feghali 210.–13ff., 297.–9, 298.12, 15.

i. *ma aḥlāni əʿəzmo hal-kalb*
"Wouldn't that be something, for me to invite that dog (fig.)".
⟨how nice-of-me to-invite-him that-dog⟩ Syr., Cowell 545 (16)

j. *wilič ẓālma, lēš tḥallīnhā ʿamya halḥdēṯa lḥilwa bintič*
"O you wrongdoer! Why do you keep her blind,
this lovely young daughter of yours?" Ir., Bloch *Chr.* 112.4

k. *mā llaḏī yanquṣuhā, hāḏihi lḥdēṯa lḥilwa*
"What's wrong with her, this lovely young girl?"
⟨what (is) that-which missing-her this...⟩ Ir., Bloch *Chr.* 114.7[80]

80 Mixed literary-colloquial style.

l. *ḫallenšūfhum lejjamāʿa*
"Let's see them, those boys!"
⟨let-us-see-them *L*-the-gang⟩ Ir., Blanc *CD* 129.5

m. *danšūfa bennādi l-Gaylān Rāmez*
"We see him at the club, that Gaylān Rāmez".
⟨we-see-him . . . *L*-Gaylān Rāmez⟩ Ir., Blanc *CD* 129.6

n. *w-ya zēno Abu Šādūf lamma . . .*
"And how fine (or elegant) he is, Abu Šādūf, when . . ."
⟨and-O the-beauty-of-him Abu Šādūf when⟩
Eg., 17th Cent., Davies 385.–8[81]

"I am not going to tell you how Jaffa fell,
o. *wakayfa nsaḥabū, ulāʾika lladīna jāʾū liyanjudūnā*
and how they withdrew, those who came to aid us".
Mod. Lit., Kanafānī 391.8

p. *hāʾulāʾi lfatayāt! law yaʿlamna kam hiya fāriġatun ruʾūsuhunna*
"Those girls, if they only knew how empty their heads are".
⟨. . . how they (are) empty the-heads-of-them⟩ Mod. Lit., Ḥaqqī 8.–2

q. *ma aḥlāhā ʿīšata lfallāḥ!*
"How sweet the fellah's life is".
⟨how sweet-it-is the-life of-the-fellah⟩ Mod. Lit., Maḥfūẓ *Ḫān* 282.–6[82]

Remark

The Lebanese, Syrian and Iraqi examples in this sample, (24)a–m, must be singled out for special comment. It will be noticed that the last two sentences in this group exhibit the "analytical" *L*- (i.e. the morpheme whose syntactic environments roughly correspond to those of Syriac *l*- and *d*-, see note 77), while it is absent from (24)a–k.[83] This may not be particularly noteworthy, since in these three dialects also the *regular*, i.e. nonaffective constructions of this type exhibit vacillation in the use of this *L*-.[84] On the other hand, the manifest preponderance

81 H. Davies, "Seventeenth Century Egyptian Arabic: A Profile of the Colloquial Material in . . . al-Širbīnī's Hazz al-Quḥūf", Diss. University of California, Berkeley, 1981.

82 The affective nature of most of these sentences can be mirrored quite adequately by appositional syntax in English, but I have chosen to demonstrate this in only a few of my translations. The punctuation marks in the Arabic of k, o–q, and in the Engl. of l–m are in the original text. Notice that *insaḥabū* (pl.) in ex. o marks the structure as appositional, for which criterion see also Reck. *AS* 25 n. 7 (as does of course the comma).

83 The *l*- in (24)c–d is a shortened form of the relative pronoun, see Feghali 310, not to be confused with the morpheme under discussion.

84 See Feghali 211.1, 298.17; Cowell 434 vs. 435; Blanc *CD* 128.–12. The question of the syntactic

of examples without *L-* among (24)a–m may not be entirely accidental. Insofar as this morpheme can be seen as a formal exponent of a comprehensive "nonagentive" case (marking the substantive in question for such relational roles as patient, possessor, etc.)[85], its scarcity in this group of examples may indicate a tendency of affective constructions of this type towards a "loose" apposition[86], i.e. one in which the substantive is unmarked for case.[87]

6.5.2 The following small sample will suffice to show that the proclivity of the language of affect for this (henceforth simply "appositive") syntax is not restricted to Arabic:

(25) Junger Mann: Ich liebe so sehr das Grün, das Licht und die ganze Welt da oben.

a. Asket: Tränen und Sünde ist sie nur, die Welt da oben.

b. Er soll krepieren, der kranke Hund.

(The little prince is sobbing. The speaker/author tries in vain to comfort him. He then goes on:) Je ne savais pas trop quoi dire ... Je ne savais comment l'atteindre, où le rejoindre ...

c. C'est tellement mystérieux, le pays des larmes!

d. It was a turkey! He never could have stood on his legs, that bird.

status of the substantive in the regular, nonaffective constructions of this type is largely unsolved. Cowell ibid. and Grotzfeld 72 describe this substantive in terms commensurate with an appositive or antitopic, but I suggest that in its most common uses the construction has become grammaticalized, so that the substantive can no longer be considered a separate component, but is an integral part of the syntagma (one may describe this in terms of an incorporation of the type § 6.4.3), in marked contrast to the substantive in affective sentences such as (24)a–m.

85 For the use of "case" in an abstract sense to denote semantic roles, see § 2.3.2 of ch. V.

86 In the sense of Havers 21, "eine lockere 'Anreihegruppe', die keine Kasuskongruenz zu haben braucht, was übrigens auch für den sogenannten Nominativ in der Apposition zu beachten ist".

87 This may be true also for such affective constructions elsewhere, as in this modern Hebrew sentence (from M. Talmi, *Habonbonim Haḫi Yafim* [Massada Ramat-Gan 1978] 61.–4):
ḫaserim lo kama ḫelke ḫiluf hamisken
"The poor fellow is missing a few spare parts". (humorous)
< missing to-him few parts of-replacement the-poor-fellow >, whereas a case-marked apposition would have:
lamisken
<to-the-poor-fellow>
(*la-* being the marker of a definite recipient/dative in Hebrew). This is of some general importance: While it is certainly true that antitopics are normally case-marked (see e.g. Lambrecht's explanation of this fact in Nonstandard French, 78–79), the evidence from modern Hebrew and Arabic adduced here suggests that this is not an *absolute* rule.

It is a cause of satisfaction and some wonder that
there is room for a new translation of Rilke's poems.

e. And a handsome one it is, this new version
by Stephen Mitchell.

f. I'll kill him for this, the ravishing thief.[88]

6.5.3 In view of the affinity of affective language for appositive syntax, it comes as no surprise that one also encounters this syntax in *presentative* sentences, especially since these sentences are often affective-exclamatory in character, on which point see W. Fischer *Dem.* 159.13ff. and cf. ibid. 161.9ff., 170.–16ff. Here are a few random examples of this syntax in presentative sentences outside of Arabic:

(26) a. But there she is, Patty Hearst, "back" – the euphemism
in the family for the phenomenon of being released on bail.

b. Here they are, the purple men.
(Announcing the coming of the "purple men")

And from modern Hebrew:

(A man is desperately looking for his lost horses.
When he hears a noise which seems to indicate their
presence, he exclaims:)

c. *hine hinam habriyot hayafot šeli*
"There they are, my beautiful creatures".

(A traveller, upon experiencing the views of the
Tyrol for the first time:)
"The country of fairy tales ... yodelling, lederhosen
and hats with a feather. Great God!

88 (25) a. N. Kazantzakis, *Komödie* (Propyläa Sonderheft), (Zürich 1969) 18.
b. F. Kafka, *Briefe an den Vater*, bilingual edition (New York: Schocken Books 1976), 54.15.
c. A. De Saint-Exupéry, *Le Petit Prince*, 28.
d. Ch. Dickens, *A Christmas Carol* (Mahwah, N.J.: Watermill Press 1980), 119.10.
e. *The New York Times Book Review*, January 30, 1983, p. 9 left col.
f. H. Ibsen, *Peer Gynt*, ed. J. W. McFarlane (Oxford 1970), 28.–2, paperback. This play is especially rich in the affective use of this syntax, see also ibid. 102.11, 113.1, 129.–5, 136.–6, 140.–15, 141.–9. Occasionally, appositive syntax occurs in combination with another affect-based feature, viz. fronting of the predicate (see a and e), but this feature is of no concern in the present context.

d. *hine hem kan, bemamaš – hayšišim hanṭuʿim befitḥe biqtotehem ...*
Here they are, in the flesh – the old men planted in front of their huts".[89]

6.5.4 The Arabic usage adduced in (24) and the broader aspect of the phenomenon documented in (25)–(26) suggest that the appositive syntax diachronically underlying the nuclear structure of the type *aho-rrasm* (23) is of an exclamatory-affective origin. The fact that the very category "presentative sentence" has a noticeable exclamatory component strongly supports this hypothesis. Here too, however, the original state of affairs must be separated from the synchronic usage: As is so often true, especially of constructions with a high degree of expressivity, the structure largely lost its original forcefulness, thus becoming free also for common, nonaffective use. This process of standardization or grammaticalization means, on the syntactic level, that the substantive loses its separate status as an appositive and becomes incorporated (reanalyzed) as the head of the new structure, see § 6.4.3. However, in this case too, diachrony may still coexist with synchrony (cf. § 5.5), because certain contexts permit a reading according to the *original* syntax and semantics postulated here, e.g. the context of (23)g:

> "I was constantly repeating to myself like a madman, without knowing what I was doing: The Paradise, The Paradise! So a passer-by pushed me into this place, saying:
> *hā huwa ḏā lfirdaws*
> Here it is, 'The Paradise'!"

alongside the reading according to the incorporating structure, "Here is 'The Paradise'".

6.6 The development of the incorporating substantival nuclear structure

6.6.1 Like other nuclear structures, the incorporating substantival structure, i.e. type *aho-rrasm* "Here is the plan" (23), can be viewed as the starting point for the formation of new presentative structures (see § 6.6.2). Consider the following colloquial exx.:

89 (26) a. *New York Times Magazine*, April 3, 1977, sec. 6, p. 20, col. 4.
b. TV program.
c. Mendele, *Sefer Haqabṣanim*, 6th ed. (Tel Aviv 1962), 71.–8.
d. Ḥ. Barṭov, *Piṣʿe Bagrut* (Tel Aviv 1965), 196.–7.

(27) "That's a plane that has come from America.

a. *šaʿhon ərrəkkāb nāzlīn mənha*
Amplified: Here are the passengers, descending from it",
or
Proclitic: "Look, the passengers are ..." Syr., Cowell 565.1

b. *šaʿha Ḥalab bānet*
"Look here, Aleppo has come into view". Syr., Cowell 545.–3

c. *ahe-ṣṣuffāra ḍarabit, yalla bīna*
"There! the whistle has just sounded, let's hurry!"
Eg., Mitchel 56, A 6

iʿfu ʿanni arbʿīn yōm tajīb ...

d. *uhayu liḫtyār illi ʿinde ḫrūjitna yičfalni*
"Grant me a respite of forty days so I can bring ...
and look, the old man who has our saddlebags will
be liable for me". Pal., Blau *Orbis* 206.–4

"Our neighbor killed a couple of pigeons
for him (viz. the sultan),

e. *hayyūh issulṭān aġnāh*
and behold, the sultan made him rich".
(Germ. "siehe da hat ihn der Sultan ...") Pal., Blau *BZ* 13.–2[90]

"If you don't listen to my words,

f. *aho abūki yigtilik*
your father will beat you". Eg., W. Fischer *Dem.* 160.–2

Since sentences of type (27) exhibit no structure-determining criteria, the assessment of their underlying structure depends entirely on considerations of meaning-in-context such as applied in §§ 3 and 4. Sentence (27)a allows an interpretation according to the amplified or the proclitic structure, i.e. the participle in this particular context may be a *Ḥāl* as well as a predicate, just as this is true of the participle in similar contexts, such as:

"And when the cock crowed,
iḏāhu Tiyādrus Al-Qiddīs rākib ʿala farasih(i)[91]
Amplified: there was St. Theodore, riding on his horse",
or
Proclitic: "behold, St. Theodore was riding ..."[92]
Blau *Chr. Ar.* 462.–5

90 For the full quotation of (27)d and e see Schmidt-Kahle II 74.–9, 152.–13.

91 It is immaterial that this particular ex. involves a different presentative form, viz. *iḏāhu* (< *iḏā* + *hu*), since it is only the phenomenon of structural bivalence that is under consideration.

92 Cf. the acc. ~ nom. in notes 17 and 60. Participles are prime candidates for this kind of contextual bivalence: Because of their inherent capability to describe situations ("scenes") and

In contrast, the remaining exx. in (27) are all unambiguously proclitic. Even this very small sample shows again the semantic heterogeneity that is a hallmark of proclitic structures, as we have seen. Alongside the plainly alerting function, as in (27)a in the second reading and (27)b, one also finds the proclitic structure in various specialized uses, as when it alerts to an event that has occurred shortly before the moment of utterance, i.e. in (27)c, to which cf. (18)g–h. In (27)d the proclitic structure[93] is used in an argumentative sense and in a context similar to that of (4)b, see the discussion in § 3.3. Quite a different function is exemplified in (27)e–f, where this structure marks the result or consequence of an action or event.[94] The latter use shows once again how the proclitic structures are capable of developing functions that are rather removed from presentativity in the strict sense.

6.6.2 From a purely syntactic point of view (leaving semantics aside), one may thus recognize these interrelated structures:

The incorporating substantival structure, (23);
this very structure with a circumstantial amplification,
as in (27)a in the first reading;
a proclitic structure, as in the remaining readings of (27).

Here too, the proclitic structure may be viewed as a product of a syntactic reanalysis of the unmarked amplified structure, see § 5.1, the coexistence of these two structures in the same stage of the language being explicable according to § 5.5.

6.6.3 The literary-language correspondences of (27) are sentences (28). This correspondence extends also to the genesis of type (28), if one considers the incorporating substantival structure of the literary language as the starting point of the development, i.e. type *hā huwa ḏā lfirdaws* "Here is 'The Paradise'", see ex. (23)g.

Just as (27), sentences of type (28) are in principle bivalent, but the exx. at my disposal favor a proclitic interpretation:

(28) a. *āh, hā hiya ssitāratu ssawdā'u tataḥarrak*
"Oh God, the black curtain is moving". Bloch *Chr.* 101.–5

processes, they are ideal vehicles for the *Ḥāl*, yet on the other hand they can equally well serve as predicates.

93 W. Fischer *Dem.* 179.12 and Schmidt-Kahle understand this as a nuclear sentence ("hier ist der Alte"), but see Blau *Orbis*, 206.–4 for the correct interpretation based on the context.

94 For further exx. demonstrating this particular function see W. Fischer *Dem.* 160.–13.

"Aḥmad wondered at the bad luck which has constantly befallen his family, for it had already lost one boy,

b. *wahā huwa Rušdī yuṣābu biddā'i lḫaṭīr*
and now Rušdī is afflicted with the serious disease". Maḥfūẓ *Ḫān* 234.6

"During the month of Ramaḍān he fell in love for the first time ... and now Ramaḍān has come again

c. *wahā huwa ḏā qalbuhu yanfuḍu ʿan ṣafḥatihi ḍḍabāba lbārida lqātima*
and behold, his heart shakes off from its caul (lit. covering, surface) the cold, dark mist". Maḥfūẓ *Ḫān* 95.3–7[95]

Far more rarely does one find this type in a *colloquial*, as in ex. d whose presentative element contains three components typologically corresponding to those of the literary language (presentative + personal pronoun + demonstrative, as in c), thus differing from the more common colloquial type with a bi-componential presentative element, (27):

d. *enhū ḏē*[96] *būkom ḏbaḥ ṭayretkom*
"Look, your father has slaughtered your bird".
Ḍofār, W. Fischer *Dem.* 184.–1

6.6.4 Viewing the material in a different way, one may speak of a step-wise process of *syntactic reduction* affecting pronominal nuclear structures. For the sake of clarity, let each step in this process be represented by an Egyptian and a modern literary example:

From step 1:	independent sentential status,	
as in	*ahó* "Here it is".	(22)a
	hā huwa ḏā "Here it is".	(22)g
to step 2:	constituent of a nucleus (through incorporation),	
as in	*aho-rrasm* "Here is the plan".	(23)a
	hā huwa ḏā lfirdaws "Here is 'The Paradise'".	(23)g
to step 3:	proclitic,	
as in	"(If you don't listen ...,) *aho abūki yigtilik* your father will beat you".	(27)f
	"(... Ramaḍān has come again) *wahā huwa ḏā qalbuhu yanfuḍu* and behold, his heart shakes off ..."	(28)c

Notice that this is a more extreme reduction than the one entailed by the shift of § 5.1, which involves only a transition from constituent of a nucleus (2) to

95 See also Maḥfūẓ, *Ḫān* 156.–8; Kanafānī (*Riǧāl Fī š-Šams*) 58.9.

96 For *en* as a colloquial presentative see below § 2.7.2–3 of ch. V.

proclitic (3). Notice also that here the inflection is retained in steps (2) and (3) – witness exx. such as *ahe-lwara'a* (23)b, *ahe-ṣṣuffāra ḍarabit* (27)c, *hā hiya ssitāratu … tataḥarrak* (28)a – which development differs from that observed (predominantly) in Middle Arabic, where steps (2) and (3) exhibit an uninflected form in the third masc. sing., see exx. (20) and (21). Here again, we view the inflection in steps (2) and (3) as a "left-over" feature from step (1).

6.7 Incorporation of the post-nuclear locative appositive

6.7.1 It was argued above that the presentative constituent in (23) – i.e. (representatively) the portion *aho* in *aho-rrasm* – is the historical reflex of a nuclear presentative sentence with pronominal head, and that the definite substantive was originally an appositive of the pronoun. An appositional relation of a different kind is involved in the following colloquial exx., where the nuclear sentence is followed by a locative expression (prepositional phrase or adverbial):

(29) *la tqūlūš il'arīs māt*
a. *šaḥḥu*[97] *bəl'alliyyi*
"Don't say that the bridegroom is dead,
there he is, in the upper room". — Leb., W. Fischer *Dem.* 200.7

qāl wēn binti? qāl
b. *heyha filqaṣir*
"He said: Where is my daughter? He answered:
There she is, in the castle". — Pal. (Bīr Zēt), Schmidt-Kahle I 210.–3

c. *hayyo hunāk*
"There it is, over there". — Pal., quoted Cowell 564.–9

And a corresponding ex. from the classical language:

"So Abu Bakr said: You are lying about him
(i.e. the Apostle). So they said: Not al all,
d. *hā huwa ḏāka*[98] *fī lmasjidi yuḥaddiṯu binnāsi*
there he is, in the mosque,
speaking to the people". — Reck. *SV* 414.–5[99]

This construction may have the referent of the pronoun preposed as the topic:

ṣṣābūn wəllīfe
e. *ša'hon bələḫzāne*
"The soap and the sponge,
there they are, in the cabinet". — Syr., Cowell 565 (3), and cf. (4)

97 For *ša'hu*, see Cowell 565.–3.
98 For the *-ka* see note 53 above.
99 For the full context see Ibn Hišām I/1 265.1.

maktab ilbusta
f. *aho ʿala y(i)mīnak*
"The post office,
there it is, to your right". Eg., W. Fischer *Dem.* 158.–14

In order to understand this appositional relation, let us remember above all the deictic nature of nuclear presentatives, § 3.2. Now, there are situations in which the nuclear sentence alone suffices to communicate to the addressee the location of the person or object to which the speaker is pointing, as is the case in (22)a–d, where the entity in question is in the visual field of both the speaker and the addressee. On the other hand, if the speaker wishes to identify this location with greater precision, he may do so as in (29), i.e. by adding a locative expression which, as it were, supplements the deictic gesture. The explanatory aspect of the construction becomes especially evident when there is more than one locative expression, as in

hā hōwa, qrīb, fdik llūṭa, ṛāha!
"There he is, nearby, in this plain,
over there (lit. there it is)!" Mor. (Ouargha), W. Fischer *Dem.* 189 n. 1

6.7.2 There is a similarity between this and the appositional phenomenon discussed earlier, insofar as in both cases the speaker moves toward a further specification, a "narrowing down" of a referent, i.e. schematically

There he is, (i.e.) Johnny
There he is, (i.e.) in the tree

the referent being a person in the first instance, a location (possibly marked by a deictic gesture) in the second. But despite this similarity, the two phenomena seem to have different roots. For whereas appositive-of-pronoun syntax has an affective base, as argued, constructions with locative appositives such as exemplified in (29) have a very specific *communicative* purpose, i.e. to further clarify a location. Manifestations of what may be called summarily "locative epexegesis" are found in many languages.[100]

6.7.3 But exx. of type (29) may also reflect another structure, namely one in which the locative expression is the *predicate* of the sentence. The relation between these two structures can be conceived in terms of a reanalysis

100 See Havers 49, 175. Also cf. Knobloch 153.–1, where Germ. *dort unten, in der Mühle* is adduced as a paradigmatic example of this type of epexegesis. This is not to deny, of course, that also such locative-epexegetical constructions may occasionally be exclamatory, as in the ex. § 6.7.1 end.

by which the personal pronoun changes its syntactic affiliation from head of the nucleus to subject of the sentential unity whose predicate is the locative expression:

šaḥḥu bəlʿalliyyi ——————→ *šaḥḥu bəlʿalliyyi*
"There he is, (i.e.) in the upper room" "Look, he is in the upper room"
(or, "Here he is in the ..."),

resulting in the elimination of the syntactic boundary (real or ideal) separating the locative expression from the nucleus in the source structure. Insofar as the presentative component in the resultant structure is no longer a constituent of the nucleus, we may speak of the resultant structure as "proclitic".

Here, again, it is the resultant structure that develops specialized nuances, witness e.g. the *temporal* meaning of:

(30) *elli ḏalmūk*
a. *hāhum taḥt īdek*
"Those that wronged you,
here (or now) they are in your hand".[101] Tun., W. Fischer *Dem.* 161.6

and from modern literary Arabic:

"The Suez Canal has long been
the object of our hopes,
b. *wahā hiya ḏī fī yadinā*
and here (now) it is in our hand". T. Al-Ḥakīm 54.8[102]

The temporal meaning puts (30)a–b in the neighborhood of (18)g–h, (27)c, (28)b, and see the general discussion in §§ 3.3, 4.6.2. It will be noticed that the prepositional phrase in (30) is not used in a concrete sense, but with its expanded, metaphorical-abstract meaning. This fact precludes an interpretation as in (29) and "forces" a reading according to the resultant structure, thus making sentences of type (30) symptomatic of the reanalysis. For a similar argument cf. §§ 1.4, 2.3, 3.3 of chapter III.

6.8 The special position of pronominal nuclear structures

6.8.1 In a number of ways nuclear pronominal structures hold a position of primacy over nuclear substantival ones. This manifests itself above all in a marked difference in the *generability* of these two types of nuclear structure. Thus one often finds that the formation of the substantival type is in one way or

101 Topicalized, like (29)e–f.
102 T. Al-Ḥakīm, *ʿAwdat al-Waʿy*, Beirut 1974.

another "blocked" as compared with the formation of the pronominal type. E.g., in the dialects of the Ḥōrān a presentative *hāḏā* (or its shortened variant *hāḏ*, both invariable) combines with pronouns to form nuclear sentences, i.e. *hāḏ(ā) hu*, *hāḏ(ā) hi*, etc., but not with substantives.[103] A similar preference can be observed in the Eastern *šaʿ* and the North African *ra* and *ha* – three presentatives which combine freely with pronouns, but far less commonly with substantives.[104] The *diachronic* expression of this primacy is the remarkable phenomenon discussed earlier: We have seen that various modern dialects developed a nuclear structure with substantival head by exactly the same procedure, namely by "grafting" a substantive onto a preexisting nuclear pronominal structure (see § 6.4.3), thus yielding type (23). The importance of the phenomenon is highlighted by the fact that this development occurred independently in each dialect group, as emerges clearly from the componential diversity of the various versions of (23).

6.8.2 Among the nuclear pronominal structures discussed, *hā huwa ḏā* (16) deserves special attention. Its unique feature is that the pronominal head is interposed between the components *hā* and *ḏā*, markedly contrasting with the position of the head in the corresponding substantival structure *hāḏā Zaydun* (2).[105] To be sure, it is a well-known fact, notably in the Romance languages, that personal pronouns under specific conditions do not appear in the same position as the corresponding substantives.[106] But no special conditions could be

103 W. Fischer *Dem.* 186.11 ff.

104 In Syria *šaʿ* combines exclusively with pronouns (suffixes), see Cowell 564.–13, while in Daṯīna it is also capable of combining with substantives, W. Fischer *Dem.* 199.–13. For *ra* and *ha* see ibid. 189.1–3, 189.–7, 163.7, 164.5–8.

105 A point of clarification: Only in a purely descriptive-synchronic sense may one speak of the pronoun in (16) as "interposed" (or, alternatively, of a "discontinuous" presentative component flanking the pronoun), because the diachrony of (16) presents a different picture. It appears that *hā* got only secondarily prefixed to historically older bipartite nuclei, namely a pronominal *huwa ḏā* (an echo of which may have been preserved in *hum ulāʾi* of Q 20:84) and a substantival *ḏā Zaydun*, for whose early attestation see Reck. *SV* 409.6–7. But this is irrelevant to the essence of the present discussion, because these bipartite nuclei likewise exhibit the positional contrast between pronoun and substantive.
It is of interest to the typology of presentative sentences that Biblical Hebrew has a nuclear construction that corresponds componentially to the Arabic one with substantival head, i.e. presentative + demonstrative + substantive, as in *halō ze Dāwīḏ* ... *halō ze haddāḇār ašer dibbarnū* ..., see I Sam 29:3, Ex 14:12, and also Gn 44:5, Jud 9:38, I Sam 21:12, 29:5, Jes 58:6 (for a most perceptive account of the function of this *halō* see R. Steiner in *Afroasiatic Linguistics* 6/4 (1979) 149).

106 I have in mind formal conditions, such as shortness and absence of stress leading to fronting and cliticization, as e.g. in French. For this phenomenon in general see Hetzron "Clitic Pronouns" 189 n. 1 (where last word in line 3 should read "verbs").

named to explain the position of the head in (16), for in nominal sentences (I am choosing these as the class most closely akin to nuclear presentative sentences) personal pronouns consistently hold the same position as the corresponding substantives, i.e. (with Cl. Arabic as the representative model) *Zaydun ḥasanun/ aḫī/fī lbayti* = *huwa ḥasanun/aḫī/fī lbayti*, etc. Notice that positional identity of substantive and corresponding pronoun holds true also in inversion, as in *a-qā'imun Zaydun?* = *a-qā'imun huwa?*, etc.[107] I have no explanation for this phenomenon, but the following considerations may be relevant. We have seen that *hāḏā Zaydun* is semantically bivalent, i.e. may have a presentative as well as identifying meaning (§ 2.5). Now, it is significant to the problem at hand that *hāḏā Zaydun* "pronominalizes" to yield *hā huwa ḏā* only when the meaning is presentative, not when it is identifying ("This is Zayd"): In the latter case there is, again, no positional difference between substantive and pronoun, i.e. *hāḏā Zaydun* = *hāḏā huwa*. This suggests that the positional peculiarity of the pronominal head in *hā huwa ḏā* is a peculiarity characteristic of *presentative* syntax. Here again, we are dealing with a more general phenomenon that manifests itself not only in Arabic: Notice that in English, too, nuclear presentative sentences show pronouns holding a different position than substantives – *Here is Johnny*, but *Here he is* – in contrast to other sentence-types where they occupy the same position.[108] In this sense, then, the position of the pronominal head of these nuclear presentative structures may be said to be "systemically unique" in both Arabic and English.

7. *Conclusion*

The aim of this chapter was to describe some of the major types of Arabic presentative sentences and discuss their syntactic and semantic development. The following dichotomy was found to be fundamental to Arabic presentative syntax: On the one hand, structures – here termed "nuclear" and "amplified" – in which the presentative forms a sentential unit (nucleus) with a substantive or pronoun and, on the other, "proclitic" structures in which the presentative does not form such a sentential unit. This syntactic dichotomy has a semantic correlate, insofar as the meaning of the nuclear and amplified structures is

107 For exx. with inversion see Reck. *AS* 8.–4, Wright II 257B, Cant. I 30.

108 I.e., *This is Johnny* = *This is he*; *Where is Johnny?* = *Where is he?*; *(I told you) where Johnny is* = *(I told you) where he is*; *It is Johnny (who did it)* = *It is he (who did it)*, etc. The positional peculiarity of the pronoun in *Here he is* may be the same as found in exclamatory-affective sentences such as *(Into the car and) away we go*, or *Up she rises*, which would once again point to the connection between presentativity and affective language, see § 6.5.3.

homogeneous, being determined by the deictic-concrete nature of the presentatives in their nuclei, while the proclitic structures are characterized by a diversity of meanings.[109]

It will be understood from the approach underlying this chapter that the assessment of whether a given presentative sentence is amplified or proclitic depends upon criteria of form (surface structure) as well as meaning. The latter criteria, in fact, are the ultimately decisive ones when a sentence exhibits no structure-determining markers, in which case only its semantic analysis in context (as demonstrated § 4) may suggest a "reading" of its underlying syntactic structure. To be sure, there are contexts where both interpretations are equally possible. But this does not refute our contention of the amplified/proclitic contrast: Rather, it is precisely the hesitation, on the part of the observer of such a sentence, as to which of these two interpretations is the one intended that serves to highlight this dichotomy.

Evidence was adduced to suggest that the proclitic structures are historically secondary, deriving from the amplified ones by a process of syntactic reanalysis described § 5. The contrast between semantically homogeneous nuclear and amplified structures on the one hand, and semantically heterogeneous proclitic ones on the other, can be understood in terms of the change brought about by the reanalysis: As long as the presentative is an integral component of the nucleus, its meaning remains constant; but once released from its nuclear position into the status of a proclitic, the presentative becomes exposed, as it were, to contextual influences and may acquire new meanings – including meanings which depart quite substantially from presentativity in the strict sense, see e.g. the account of the semantics of sentences (13), (18)d, (27)e–f. Thus, the semantic heterogeneity of the proclitic structures is seen here as a historically secondary phenomenon, developing as a consequence of the syntactic reanalysis.

Two further types of syntactic reanalysis were discussed, both resulting in the incorporation of appositional-epexegetical components that follow a nuclear presentative structure. In one development, a substantival appositive of the pronominal head becomes itself the head of a new nuclear structure, see § 6.4.3, and in the other an epexegetical locative expression becomes the predicate of a new proclitic structure, see § 6.7.3.

In our understanding, then, nuclear structures are the very building stones of Arabic presentative syntax. While the first part of this chapter traced the way

109 It will be remembered that on account of its syntax and semantics, the structure *hā huwa ḏā munṭaliqun* (18) is counted here among the proclitic structures, i.e. irrespective of its "recalcitrant" surface manifestation, see § 6.1.4.2.

that leads from nuclear over amplified to (by reanalysis) proclitic structures, the second part concentrated on a specific category of nuclear structures, namely those with pronominal heads. It was shown that this category is particularly productive in the creation of new presentative structures, see especially the historical analysis of (18), (20)–(21), (23), (27)–(30).

Chapter V

The Historical Syntax and Semantics of inna

1. The Function of inna

1.1 Description

1.1.1 Classical Arabic *inna* emphasizes the speaker's certainty (in questions, his doubt) that what is said in a sentence is a fact, is true, will indeed take place, etc. – a function quite adequately rendered with *indeed*, *certainly*, *surely* and the like.[1] Despite a large degree of conventionalization of its use, the particle's full force is sufficiently recognizable in familiar exx. from the cl. language[2] such as (1):

(1) a. *inna llāha ʿalā kulli šay'in qadīrun; inna llāha ʿazīzun ḥakīmun*, etc.
"God is indeed powerful over everything"; "Surely God is All-mighty, All-wise". Q 2:20, 8:10 and passim

b. *našhadu innaka larasūlu llāhi*
"We bear witness that thou art indeed the Messenger of God". Q 63:1

c. *a'inna lanā la'ajran; a'innā lamabʿūṯūna*
"Will we really be rewarded?"; "Will we indeed be resurrected?"
Q 26:41, 23:82 (and cf. Q 6:19, 13:5)

1 I shall not deal with the functionally identical "lighter" particle, the so-called *In al-Muḫaffafa*, Wright I 283 B; W. Fischer *Gramm.* § 339 n. 2; and esp. Nebes, "*'In Al-Muḫaffafa* und *Al-Lām Al-Fāriqa*, I" *ZAL* 7 (1982), 7–22. This particle differs from *inna* in several respects, above all in that it allows a verb-initial word order and leaves the subject in the nom. case – facts which strongly suggest that its historical syntax differs from that of *inna*.

2 On the other hand, it is rather doubtful whether *inna* still fulfills any emphasizing function in the modern literary language, as is claimed in Cant. II 232–3. Rather, its use is more likely governed by such factors as the specific genre of the text; the idiosyncrasies of particular writers; the particle's manifestly "classicizing" flavor. On the connection between the frequency of its occurrence and the SVO word order on the one hand, and certain literary genres on the other, see Parkinson, "VSO to SVO in Modern Standard Arabic: A Study in Diglossia Syntax", *Arabiyya* 14/1–2 (1981), esp. 34.

d. *innaka latajidu ʿUmara bna l-Ḫaṭṭābi fī l-Tawrāti*
"Do you indeed find ʿUmar b. Al-Ḫaṭṭāb mentioned in the Torah?!"
Spoken by ʿUmar to Kaʿb b. Al-Aḥbār, after the latter told him that he had found in the Pentateuch knowledge about ʿUmar's impending death. Ṭab. I/5 2722.–2ff.

e. *ṣadaqā wallāhi innahumā li-Qurayšin*
"These two have spoken the truth. They do belong to the Qurayš".
Said by the Prophet to his men who had captured and interrogated two Qurayši watermen. The latter had identified themselves as Qurayšis, but the Prophet's men refused at first to believe them. Ibn Hišām I/1 436.1–9

On the (optional) use of *la-* in the *inna*-sentence, see § 1.2.2.

1.1.2 *Inna* most typically occurs with affirmations, but may also be used with questions, as in (1)c–d, and negations. In these three basic uses, its function may be rendered in informal glosses such as:

X is certainly ...
Is X really ...?
X is certainly not ...

1.1.3 The medieval Arab grammarians that I consulted describe *inna*'s function in terms of *Ta'kīd* (*Tawkīd*) "emphasis". Although their formulations vary, they are all united in the correct recognition that this function pertains to the sentence *as a whole*, on which point see § 1.3 below. Thus, in the words of Sībawayhi II 338.19: *Inna tawkīdun liqawlihi Zaydun munṭaliqun* "*Inna* emphasizes a sentence (such as:) *Zaydun munṭaliqun*, Zayd is departing" (in other words, *inna Zaydan munṭaliqun* means "Zayd is surely departing"). To this compare the similar definition of Ibn Yaʿīš, 125.3–4: *Inna lita'kīdi ljumlati* "*Inna* serves to emphasize the sentence".[3] On another occassion Ibn Yaʿīš explains this function by saying that it is "as if one repeated the sentence" (*ka'annahu fī ḥukmi lmukarrari naḥwa Zaydun qā'imun Zaydun qā'imun*), 1120.22–23.

1.2 The larger picture: Devices functionally corresponding to *inna*

1.2.1 I suggest that, for functional reasons (see more § 1.3), *inna* must be classified together with devices such as:

- *Qad* with the perfect in the function of *taḥqīq* "to indicate absolute certainty", Wright II 4B;

3 It is immaterial to the point under discussion whether Ibn Yaʿīš means *jumla* in the sense of "statement" or "sentence".

- the energetic, and *lan* (with its subjunctive), in the meaning of "certainly will/will not", respectively;
- strongly asserting oath-words such as *wallāhi, laʿamrī*, when preceding a statement;
- *la-* in its various uses (see § 1.2.2);
- the perfect of *kāna* in the Qur'ānic formula of the type *wakāna llāhu ʿalīman raḥīman*;[4]
- nominalizing structures of the type *alwāqiʿu anna* "it's a fact that ...";

or, in Biblical Hebrew,

- the cognate absolute infinitive preceding the finite verb;[5]
- the particle *āḵēn*, preceding a statement,[6]

etc.

1.2.2 Of the devices named in § 1.2.1, *la-* deserves a few words since this particle exhibits an especially wide variety of uses. These can be classified under two headings:

1. *La-* as a certainty-emphasizing device in its own right, as in *lalmawtu ḫayrun min ḥayatin ʿalā ġamḍin* "Surely death is preferable to a life in obscurity" W. Fischer *Gramm.* 334, and for further exx. see *WKAS* II 1.7–14 left; Q 2:221, 12:8, 109, 16:30, 93:4–5.

2. In combination with another such device, most typically one of those mentioned above: the pre-perfect *qad* (i.e. *laqad faʿaltu*); the energetic (*la'afʿalanna*); the oath-words (*wallāhi* + *la-* ...). Here belongs also the use of *la-* in combination with *inna*, see some of the exx. under (1) above, and Reck.*AS* § 65.3. The point of this exposé is this: The more *la-* has become a conventionalized, automatic concomitant (one may call it a "satellite") of the other device, the more its own force tends to diminish, to the point that it may be altogether annulled. This is most conspicuous in the energetic, whose *la-* has all but become an integral part of the verbal form, see Reck. *AS* § 11. The same applies to *la-* in sentences with *In Al-Muḫaffafa* (see above note 1) which, devoid of all emphasizing force, is conceived as a mere disambiguating device in the indigenous grammatical tradition, hence its name *Al-Lām Al-Fāriqa (Al-Fāsila)*, see discussion in Fleischer 423.–11 ff. There are other aspects of the use

4 "God is indeed, is truly ..." On this function of the formula see W. Reuschel, in *Studia Orientalia in Memoriam Caroli Brockelmann* (Halle [Saale] 1968), passim, esp. 152 last paragraph ("ist in der Tat/tatsächlich/wirklich, ganz bestimmt"). Because it has an unmistakable *ta'kīd* function in the Qur'ānic formula, this *kāna* does more than "mark a fact", so W. Fischer *Gramm.* § 181 n. 2, or "denote the present", as in Blau, "Jāḥ." 279.–4.

5 See Muraoka 65, Goldenberg 69–70.

6 See Muraoka 101.

of *la*- that cannot be discussed here[7], but our main purpose was to highlight this one point: Only in type 1. does *la*- appear as a fully functioning device in its own right (not a "satellite"), here exhibiting its undiminished force.

1.3 Difference from other "emphasizing" devices, notably those for focusing and topicalization

Obviously, the devices listed § 1.2.1 are radically heterogeneous, structurally and syntactically. Yet they deserve to be classified together with *inna* for the one important *functional* aspect which they share with it, namely that they, like *inna*, pertain to the factual status of what is said in the sentence[8], and for this reason must be sharply distinguished from devices such as those for focusing or topicalization, which pertain to a specific component of a sentence, i.e. the subject, object, etc.[9] I am stressing this difference because *inna* has been recently described by W. Fischer as a particle that "emphasizes the subsequent substantive or pronoun as the topic".[10] A look at sentences such as (1) clearly does not support this interpretation of their meaning.[11] If a *component* of a sentence is to be put into relief – be it in terms of topicalization or focusing – this is not done by means of *inna* but by other devices. Thus, for topicalization Arabic typically uses

(2) dislocation, as in:

a. ... *wallaḏīna yamkurūna ssayyi'āti lahum ʿaḏābun šadīdun*
"and (as for) those who devise evil deeds – theirs will be a terrible chastisement". Q 35:10

7 Such as the component to which it typically attaches in the *Inna*-sentence and the *In (Al-Muḫaffafa)*-sentence.

8 With this in mind, their function(s) – as well as *inna*'s – may be classified under a broadly defined category of *mood*, in the sense of Lyons *Introduction* 307.

9 For essentially the same distinction, albeit formulated differently, see Goldenberg 70.–2ff.

10 "Die Partikel ... weist ... auf das folgende Substantiv oder Pronomen hin und hebt es als Thema (topic) hervor, über das eine Aussage (comment) gemacht wird", W. Fischer, "Daß-Sätze" 28. The words in parentheses are in the original.

11 It is unfortunate that Fischer here in effect resurrects a misconceived notion of *inna*'s function which ought to have been laid to rest through Fleischer's masterfully lucid statement (correcting De Sacy): "... indem diese Partikel (viz. *inna*) keineswegs zur Hervorhebung des von ihr unmittelbar angezogenen logischen Subjectes – sei dieses Nomen oder Pronomen – sondern zur Verstärkung der durch den Satz ausgedrückten Bejahung oder Verneinung dient", Fleischer 744.–1ff. Cf. Carter's correction of a similar misconception of Schub in *ZAL* 7 (1982), 79.16. See also J. Huehnergard in *JAOS* 103/3 (1983) 569 n. 1.

b. ... *wazzāniyatu lā yankiḥuhā illā zānin*
"and the fornicatress – none shall marry her but a fornicator". Q 24:3

(3) or dislocation reinforced by *ammā – fa-*:
ammā qatlan falastu qātilan
"As for killing, I am not going to do it". Reck. *AS* 371.7

while focusing is commonly expressed by

(4) pronoun reduplication, see § 2 of chapter I

(5) word-order reversal, as in
(*wamā tawfīqī illā billāhi*)
a. *ʿalayhi tawakkaltu wa'ilayhi unību*
"*In Him* I trust and *to Him* I turn in penitention". Q 11:88

b. *iyyaka naʿbudu*
"*Thee only* we serve". Q 1:5

c. *Tamīmiyyun anā*
"*I* am a Tamimite". Fleischer 747.7[12]

(6) various clefting constructions involving clause nominalizations by means of a relative pronoun or *mā*[13], as in

a. *ahāḏā šiʿruka llaḏī anšadtahu*
"Is this *your* poem that you recited?" Blau "Obs." 174.–17

b. *kānat ummī hiya llatī aḫbaratnī*
"*My mother* was the one who informed me". Reck. *AS* 283.1

c. *liljaddi mā ḫuliqa l'insānu*
"It is *for luck* that man has been created". Nöldeke *ZGr.* 62.2

1.4 Use of *inna* as an independent morpheme

1.4.1 Nowhere is the strength of *inna*'s function more clearly observable than when the particle is used in isolation, in the meaning of "yes indeed!":

12 Similarly, the regular VS order may be reversed for contrastive comparison of two coordinated subjects, Reck. *AS* 10.8. In a sentence such as *inna lʿāqila yattaʿiẓu bil'adabi walbahā'imu lā tattaʿiẓu illā bilʿaṣā* "A reasonable man learns through education, cattle learn only by beating" the contrastiveness is of course expressed by the reversal, not by *inna*, as correctly in W. Fischer (ed.) *Grundr.* I 75.–6.

13 For a discussion of cleft sentences with *mā* and *innamā* see Goldenberg 78; Polotsky *Études* 65–67. I am using "clefting" in a broad sense: The common element that is shared by the three types represented in (6) a–c is that the portion containing the given, or known information is a nominalized clause (the "glose").

(7) a. *yaqulna šaybun qad ʿalāka waqad kabirta faqultu inna(h)*
"... While saying (fem. pl.): Grey hair covers you, and you have become old. So I said: Yes indeed!" Reck. *AS* 127

b. *qāla (I)bnu Faḍālata laʿana llāhu nāqatan ḥamalatnī ilayka qāla (I)bnu z-Zubayri inna warākibahā*
"Ibn Faḍāla said: God curse the (lit. a) she-camel that carried me to you! So Ibn Zubayr said: Yes, and its rider too!" Reck. *AS* 127

c. *qālū ġadarta faqultu inna warubbamā nāla lʿulā wašafā lġalīla lġādiru*
"They said: You have acted treacherously. So I said: True, but a treacherous man often achieves an exalted rank and gratifies his desire". Reck. *AS* 127

d. *qālū aḫifta faqultu inna waḫīfatī mā in tazālu manūṭatan birajāʾī*
"They said: Were you afraid? So I said: Yes, but my fear is all the while attached to my hope". Howell I p. XXI

e. *waqāʾilatin asīta faqultu jayrin asiyyun innanī min ḏāka inna(h)*
"And there was many a woman saying: You have become mournful. So I said: Yes, (I am) mournful, I am truly thus (lit. of that), indeed". Howell III 560

f. *inna salīṭan fī lḫasāri inna(h) awlādu qawmin ḫuliqū aqinna(h)*
"The Salīṭ are truly losers, indeed! Descendants of people who were born as slaves". Jarīr, *Naqāʾiḍ* (ed. Bevan) I 4

g. *lā uqīmu bidāri ḏḏulli inna walā ātī ilā lġadri ...*
"I shall not dwell in the abode of disgrace, indeed (not), nor shall I commit an act of treachery". *Ḫiz*. IV, 486[14]

1.4.2 While there is no doubt about the meaning of this *inna*, it is far less certain how to explain its use as an independent morpheme.

The occurrence of a particle without the remainder of the utterance has parallels elsewhere in the classical language. Consider the following:

14 A few details about these exx.: (7) a, Qays b. al-Ruqayyāt, born 620 CE; b, Ḥadīṯ ʿAbdallah b. al-Zubayr, died 692 CE; for a var. see *Lisān* s.r. *ʾnn*; c, Masʿūd b. ʿAbdalla al-Asadī, no year; see *Ḥam*. Buḥturī (ed. Cheikho) 12.7; for alternative reading *wašifā lġalīli* see Ibn Yaʿīš 448.3; d, Anon.; e, Al-Muṯaqqib Al-ʿAbdī, died 587 CE; f, Jarīr, died 728–9 CE; var: *abnāʾu qawmin* in *Lisān* s.r. *qnn*; g, Sāʿida b. Juʾayya of Huḏayl; his Rāwī, Abū Ḏuʾayb, died 649 CE; for var. see *Lisān* s.r. *ḫmj*. The (*h*) in a, e and f is pausal; so already Sībawayhi II 303.–3 (in ch. on *waqf*), Ibn Yaʿīš 1133.–3ff., and cf. Brock. 18.2ff. for discussion.

(8) a. *afida ttaraḥḥulu ġayra anna rikābanā lammā tazul biriḥālinā waka'an qad(ī)*
"The time of departure arrived, except that our camels had not yet moved off with our gear. But it was as if they had already done so". Lane s.v. *qad*

b. *qālat banātu lʿammi yā Salmā wa'in kāna faqīran muʿdiman qālat wa'in*
"The uncle's daughters said: O Salmā, and if he turns out to be a destitue pauper?! She said: Even if! (i.e., so be it)". Howell I p. XXII

Here the contexts unquestionably suggest implicit portions such as *zālat bihā* after *qad* in a and *kāna faqīran muʿdiman* after *wa'in* in b – portions which, for descriptive convenience, may be said to be "deleted" from the surface structure. The same applies to utterances ending in *walam*, *iḏā lam*, *wa'in lam*, or in *walammā*, see Ibn Yaʿīš's model sentence:

c. *yurīdu Zaydun an yaḫruja walammā*
"Zayd wants to go out, but he hasn't yet",

to which Ibn Y. adds the comment *ay walammā yaḫruj*.

Ibn Yaʿīš 1165.9–10

While exx. (8)a and b are verse, c suggests – and the following d strongly supports – that usage of this kind was not restricted to poetry:

d. *qāla nnāsu yā amīra lmu'minīna amāta Abū ʿUbaydata qāla lā waka'an qad*
"The people said: O Commander of the Faithful, has Abu ʿUbayda died? He said: No, but it is as if he had already". Ṭab. I/5 2518.6[15]

Here, again, the immediately preceding context, i.e. the question: *amāta A. ʿU.*?, leaves little doubt that the reply contains an implicit *māta* following *qad*.

1.4.3 It is on the basis of examples such as (8)a–d that Zamaḫšarī, Ibn Yaʿīš and Fleischer explain the use of *inna* here exemplified in (7) as likewise involving deletion.[16] I believe that this is a *possible* explanation, although the very com-

15 (8)a, Al-Nābiġa, born 525–50 CE; b, Ru'ba, born approx. 699 CE; c, for *walam, iḏā lam, wa'in lam* in this use see Ibn Yaʿīš 1165.16–17, and Fischer-Bräunlich 221–2. I owe knowledge of many of these rhyme-end occurrences of particles to Michael Zwettler. For *ka'an qad*, as in a and d, see *WKAS* I 4.3ff. left, where further exx.

16 Zamaḫšarī 131.2 (= Ibn Yaʿīš 1070.9), where the words *waka'an qad(ī)* – alluding to the verse

parison between types (7) and (8) runs into some serious methodological difficulties:

1.4.3.1 Utterances of type (8) are recognizably truncated, requiring a portion to be mentally supplied by the hearer/reader in order to be understood. There can be little doubt as to what these portions are, since they are easily "retrievable" from the immediately preceding contexts, as we have seen. In contrast, *inna* in (7) is a semantically self-contained unity, an independent "sentence-word" with an affirmative meaning – just as are words like *naʿam*, *ajal*, *balā*. The assumption of a deleted portion is here as superfluous as it would be in the case of any independent affirmative, and the variety of suggestions as to the exact nature of the deleted portion in fact points to the arbitrariness of the procedure. Thus, among the paraphrases for (7)a, we find *inna ššayba qad ʿalānī*, *innahu qad kāna kamā yaqulna*, etc., see *Ḫiz.* IV, 486.6, 10–11. What, along these lines, would be the deleted portion in a sentence such as (7)b?!

1.4.3.2 Examples (8) represent a special *type* of deletion, namely one involving segments consisting of, or beginning with, a finite verb. The particles involved – *qad*, *lam*, (the conditional) *in*, etc. – normally impose a verb-initial configuration (one may exclude clearly exceptional cases where this principle is violated, as in Reck. *AS* 46 n. 2, § 156.3). Put differently, the use of these particles elicits an "expectation of a finite verb" (*tawaqquʿ fiʿl*) on the part of the hearer, to borrow Ibn Yaʿīš's expression, 1165.12. Yet this very fact disqualifies the type of deletion of (8) as a model for explaining (7), because *inna* disallows any verb-initial word order.[17]

1.4.3.3 A feature related to verb-deletion is verb-replacement, i.e. the use of *faʿala* as a "pro-verb", as in *qultu lahu an yadḫula walākinnahu lam yafʿal*. The fact that Arabic possesses this device, but has no corresponding device for, say, the replacement of a sequence SV, strengthens my belief that exx. (8) constitute a very special phenomenon within Arabic syntax, viz. one pertaining specifically to finite verbs.[18]

(8)a – are mentioned in connection with the *ḥaḏf*-interpretation for *inna*. See also Fleischer 425.–1.

17 It is only by replacing *inna* with *naʿam* in his paraphrase that Ibn Yaʿīš manages to claim a *fiʿl maḥḏūf* in (7), see note 20.

18 Although at first glance reminiscent of Engl. usage as in "I asked him to come in but he didn't", it is quite certain that Arabic verb deletion as in (8) or the use of the pro-verb *faʿala* never acquired the same established status as in Engl. It is possible that usage of type (8) betrays the influence of spoken language. For this aspect of deletion (in general) see Blau *Jud. Ar.* 266 and n. 1; Blau *BZ* 268. It would be of some general linguistic interest to know the constraints on the use of *faʿala* (only "action" verbs?!, etc.), in the sense of Lyons *Introduction* 325.18, 340.–6.

1.4.4 One will have to understand this explanation of (7) in the light of what by the time of Zamaḫšarī and Ibn Yaʿīš had become the standard method of grammatical analysis. It was not possible, with the now strictly defined terminology, to acknowledge an *inna* with an independent status, because *inna* was classified among the *ḥurūf*, and a *ḥarf* was *by definition* barred from occurring unaccompanied. But if there could be no such thing as an independent *ḥarf*, then an *inna* in isolation presented an obvious dilemma. The postulate of a deleted portion in (7) was therefore necessary in order to bring this particular use of *inna* in line with the definition of *ḥarf*.[19] Since *naʿam*, *balā*, etc., are likewise *ḥurūf*, the two mentioned grammarians apply the same explanation when these words occur in isolation.[20] This contrasts with the strictly descriptive-functional (and methodologically unbiased) presentations of Sībawayhi and Aḫfaš who, recognizing in this *inna* the independent affirmative which it is, simply paraphrase it with *ajal* or *naʿam* and let the matter stand at that.[21]

1.4.5 To summarize: There *are* genuine phenomena of deletion in Arabic, and the usage exemplified in (8) is a case in point. On the other hand, not every use of a particle without the remainder of the utterance necessarily involves deletion, and it behooves us to examine critically each instance in which this explanatory principle has been applied in the indigenous grammatical tradition. Specifically, in view of the objections raised in § 1.4.3.1–3 it seems rather doubtful that type (8) can serve as an explanatory model for the use of *inna* as an independent morpheme (7).

1.4.6 I would like to propose an alternative explanation for the emergence of the use of *inna* as an independent morpheme, one that is not based on the assumption of a deleted portion. A close look at the exx. in (7) reveals that the independent *inna* is used in two distinct functions:

1. As an affirmative by which a participant in a dialogue voices agreement with his interlocutor's statement, see (7) a–d. In this case the particle functions

19 See the wording Zamaḫšarī 130.–1 – 131.2.

20 Thus, Ibn Yaʿīš 1070.16–17 says that *inna(h)* in (7) a implies: *naʿam qad ʿalānī ššaybu*, just as a *naʿam* that occurs in answer to a question *aqāma Zaydun*? is stated by him to imply *naʿam qad qāma*, the portion *qad* + verb being considered as deleted in both cases. These very paraphrases, of course, highlight the fact that *inna(h)* possesses here the same independent ("sentence-word") status as *naʿam*.

21 Sībawayhi I 424.1, II 303.–3. For Aḫfaš see the quotation *Ḫiz.* IV 486.3. The difference between their and Ibn Yaʿīš's approach is not just a matter of nuance: The latter expressly insists that the *inna* in isolation does not express its meaning *by itself*, but only by means of the deleted portion (*bitaqdīri lmaḥḏūf*), see Ibn Yaʿīš 1070.11–12. To be sure, all these affirmatives (including *inna*) are *ḥurūf* also to Sībawayhi, but for him the term *ḥarf* does not yet have the strict definition given to it by the later grammarians, see Mosel 215–20.

as a reply word, and it is this particular function that the grammarians have in mind when they speak of *inna*'s occurrence *fī ljawāb*, Sībawayhi I 424.1, and cf. Ibn Yaʿīš 1070.16.

2. To reconfirm emphatically the validity of the speaker's *own*, immediately preceding statement. This function is exemplified in the following excerpts from (7)e–g (repeated here as (9)a–c):

(9) a. *innanī min ḏāka inna(h)*
"I am truly thus, indeed!"

b. *inna salīṭan fī lḫasāri inna(h)*
"The Salīt are truly losers, indeed!"

c. *lā uqīmu bidāri ḏḏulli inna*
"I shall not dwell in the abode of disgrace, indeed (not)!"

In (9)a–b (ex. c will be discussed separately below) the emphatic reconfirmation of the statement is expressed through the repetition of *inna* after the sentence-break. Now, it is significant that Arabic possesses a similar pattern of emphatic reconfirmation involving *negations*:

(10) a. *šarafan mā nālahū ʿArabiyyun lā*
"An exalted rank that no (other) Arab ever attained, no!" Reck. *AS* 335.–7

b. *lam tubqi baʿlan lā*
"They left no husband alive, no!" *WKAS* II 19.21 right

c. *laysa hāḏā mustaqīman lā*
"This is not right, no!" *WKAS* II 19.22 right

d. *ayyāma lā Kisrā yunāwiʾu maʿšarī lā*
"In the days when Kisrā would not defy my people, no!"
WKAS II 19.10 right

Exx. (10)a–d bring to the fore an essential point, namely that this pattern of emphatic reconfirmation involves a "switch" from any one of the dependent negations to the independent negation *lā* (corresponding to a switch in English from *not* to *no*), i.e. schematically:

mā/lam/laysa/lā (etc.) . . ., *lā*[22]
(the comma marking the sentence-break)

22 That (10) does indeed involve the device of repetition can be seen from the fact that the negation can be repeated more than once, see exx. in *WKAS* II 19 right, passim. Another instance where repetition for "emphasis" involves a switch from a bound to a free form is pronoun reduplication for focusing, see § 2 of ch. I.

The obvious similarity between the affirmative pattern of emphatic reconfirmation in (9)a–b and the negative one in (10)a–d points to a plausible "locus" for the emergence of the use of *inna* as an independent morpheme: If this morphologically bound particle was to be repeated (for emphasis) following the sentence-break, this *necessarily* involved creation of a new use for it, namely as a free form. My hypothesis is based on the assumption of a close association between the affirmative and negative patterns of emphatic reconfirmation – an assumption supported by the existence of an ex. such as (9)c, which is an amalgamation of these two patterns. I propose that once thus established as an independent form due to its use in the repetitional frame, *inna* could be used also outside this frame, i.e. to confirm another person's statement, as in (7)a–d.

1.4.7 The exx. with the independent *inna* place this usage in the preclassical and classical periods, see references in note 14. Although attested mostly in verse, the independent *inna* was apparently not confined to poetry, witness the prose dialogue in (7)b, and consider also Sībawayhi's *inna yā fatā* "indeed, young man" (I 424.1), which sounds much like prose conversation. However, to my knowledge this feature completely disappears in the later periods of the literary language, where *inna* is used only as a dependent (sentence-proclitic) form.

1.5 The bi-directionality of *inna*

Let us sum up this first section of the present chapter: Two manifestations of *inna* were discussed, i.e. its regular use as a dependent, sentence-proclitic form, (1), and its use as an independent affirmative, (7). In both of these uses we are dealing with essentially the same function, namely confirmation of what is said in a sentence. The difference between these two uses may be formulated in terms of different directions in which *inna* operates, viz. progressively to confirm the immediately following sentence (1), or regressively when it confirms the preceding one – be it another person's, (7)a–d, or that of the same speaker, (7)e–g. In both of these uses the particle reveals its central characteristic, i.e. its pertinence to the facticity (validity, certainty, etc.) of what is said in a sentence. It was argued that because of this characteristic, *inna* must be sharply distinguished from devices such as those for focusing or topicalization, which pertain to a component of a sentence.

2. *Inna Zaydan: Vestiges of a Historically Primary Nuclear Structure*

2.1 The evidence

2.1.1 There is yet another view of *inna*'s function that ought to be examined critically. One occasionally finds the particle described in terms of a presentative or, alternatively, paraphrased by words such as *look*, *behold*, *siehe*, *ecce*, which suggest a presentative function.[23] This understanding does not seem to be based on observation of actual use of the particle in this sense, but on theoretical considerations – above all, its identification with etymological cognates such as the Biblical Hebrew presentative *hinnē*[24] – since there is to my knowledge no textual attestation of *inna* with a presentative meaning. This is also supported, indirectly, by the Arab grammarians who, while recognizing presentatives elsewhere (e.g. § 2.4 of ch. IV), describe *inna* only in terms of sentence confirmation, see § 1.1.3, not as a presentative.

2.1.2 There is, however, good evidence to support the notion of an *originally* presentative *inna*. I am basing my argument on a vestigial use of the particle which was observed by the medieval grammarians but was paid little attention in our Western grammatical works. For the following usage see Sībawayhi I 244.14–21; Zamaḫšarī 15.8–12 (Ibn Yaʿīš 127.4–7, 22–23). We are told that one says:

(11) a. *inna mālan wa'inna waladan wa'inna ʿadadan*
"There is money", and "there is a boy", and "there is a quantity (or a crowd, multitude)".[25]

Then an actual situation is described in which this use of *inna* may occur. A man who is being asked by another:

hal lakum aḥadun? Inna nnāsa albun ʿalaykum
"Do you (pl.) have anyone to stand by you? The people have really ganged up against you",

may reply:

23 E.g. W. Fischer *Gramm.* § 339: "*Inna* 'siehe' lenkt die Aufmerksamkeit auf die folgende Aussage" (which differs from Fischer's later view, see above note 10); Blau *Emergence* 85, *Chr. Ar.* 511, *An Adv.* 4 n. 5.

24 E.g. Barth *Pron.* 99, where Nöldeke is quoted. Cf. also the rare old Arabic demonstratives *hinnā*, *hannā*, *hunnā* Reck. *SV* 420 n. 1, Wright I 288 A. In general see Cohen s.v. *'/HNN*.

25 It is immaterial whether (11) a is analyzed as reflected in the above translation or rather as representing a single speech act, i.e. "there is money and there is ..." In the latter interpretation, one may prefer to read *wuld* (pl., kindly suggested by R. Talmon), or *walad* (collective, cf. Q 71:21, so A. Ambros), which alternatives would fit well with the other two substantives – both mass-words.

b. *inna Zaydan wa'inna ʿAmran*
"There is Zayd and there is ʿAmr".

One also says:

c. *inna ġayrahā ibilan wašā'an*
"There are camels and sheep other than these",
lit. "there are other than these, camels and sheep",
with *ibil* and *šā'* in the *Tamyīz* acc., as confirmed by
Sībawayhi's analysis.[26]

The following attests this usage in poetry:

d. *inna maḥallan wa'inna murtaḥalan*
wa'inna lissafri iḏ maḍaw mahala(n)
"There is a time (or place) of staying and there is
a time (or place) of departing; and indeed the travellers,
once departed, have (but) a respite".[27]

Finally, a report by Al-Farrā', quoted Sībawayhi (Būlāq ed.) I 284 right margin (and cf. Ibn Yaʿīš 127.22–23), suggests that this use of *inna* was also known among Bedouins. Someone said to a Bedouin:

azzabābatu lfa'ratu
"A *zabāba* is the same as a *fa'ra*"[28],

whereupon the Bedouin replied:

e. *inna zzabābata wa'inna lfa'rata*
"There is a *zabāba* and there is a *fa'ra*",

to which Al-Farrā' adds the comment:

ay inna hāḏihi muḫālifatun lihāḏihi
"This means, the one is not the same as the other".

(*Zabāba* "large, red-haired rat that is deaf" see *Lisān* s.v.; *fa'ra* "mouse".)

26 I 241.20: *wa ntaṣaba l'ibilu waššā'u ka ntiṣābi fārisin iḏā qulta mā fī nnāsi miṯluhu fārisan.*

27 Verse generally attributed to Aʿšā l-Kabīr, born before 570 CE. For the version quoted here see Ibn Yaʿīš 127.16. For the various variants, all pertaining to the second hemistich, see *Dīwān al-Aʿšā* ... Muḥ. Ḥusayn, ed. (Cairo 1950), no. 35, p. 233, where also the question of Aʿšā's authorship of this verse is discussed; *The Diwan of Al-Aʿšā*, R. Geyer, ed., Gibb Memorial New Series 6 (1928), no. 35, p. 155; *Ḫiz*. IV, 381 ff.; Šantamarī, in Sībawayhi (Būlāq ed.) I 284.–10. *Safr* "travellers" can also be meant in the sense of "those who die", see e.g. Lane. For *maḥall* and *murtaḥal* as referring here to time or place see *Ḫiz*. IV 383.4–5.

28 On this type of identifying predication see e.g. Reck. *AS* 5.–6 ff. The def. article in both words is generic (*Lām al-Jins*). On the use of the singular of animates as generics see Reck. *AS* 182.1 ff.

2.1.3 Since use of the type *inna Zaydan* completely disappears from the later stages of the literary ʿArabiyya, the question arises as to the historical setting of exx. (11)a–e. The very scanty background information on these sentences, however, allows no more than the suggestion that the type was used in an early period – notice that *inna maḥallan* ... (11)d is from a Qaṣīda generally attributed to Al-Aʿšā, see note 27 – and that it was not confined to verse, witness the unmistakable prose-conversational character of some of these exx., above all *inna zzabābata* ... (11)e (the latter example, moreover, may reflect Bedouin usage, which is of some interest in view of the modern evidence, see § 2.7). But the circumstantial details concerning the "when", "where", "by whom", etc. of this type's use are ultimately less relevant than the plain fact that it *is* attested in Arabic. In the remainder of this chapter we shall try to see how this type can shed light on the historical syntax of *inna.*

2.2 The semantic range in a general linguistic perspective

2.2.1 The meanings of (11)a–e range from deictic-presentative to purely existential. Although absence of sufficient contextual background makes it difficult to determine with certainty which of these two meanings applies in each case, it seems that ex. (11)b favors a presentative interpretation, especially if we are dealing with a concrete situation in which Zayd and ʿAmr are actually on the scene (one could imagine the speaker pointing to them: *Voilà Zayd et voilà ʿAmr*[29], to which compare the coordinated nuclear presentative sentences of ex. (2)d in chapter IV!), while exx. (11)d and e are unmistakably existential.[30] In (11)c a presentative-deictic reading cannot be entirely ruled out, but an existential understanding is more likely (for a similar use of a *ġayr-* phrase as the head of an existential sentence see *hal ġayru hāḏā* "Is there anything other than this?", Reck. *AS* 356.–3).

2.2.2 This particular range of meanings suggests a distinct direction of semantic development. As is well known, expressions of existence in many languages derive historically from expressions of concrete deixis, consider e.g. *there* in Engl. existential *there is/are*; Fr. *y* in *il y a*; Ital. *ci* in *ci sono*; and cf. Germ. *da* in

29 In this specific use, then, *inna* is not only the etymological but also the functional cognate of Bibl. Hebrew *hinnē* in cases such as Gn 12:19, 22:7, 30:3, see § 2.6.1 below.

30 Existential sentences characteristically exhibit indefinite heads, see e.g. Lyons *Introduction* 390 (and this feature is in fact considered criterial for this category of sentences by Clark 6.–12), but since the heads of presentative sentences may be definite ("there is Johnny") as well as indefinite ("watch out, there is a snake!"), definiteness/indefiniteness in itself is not a sufficient criterion for the distinction between these two categories of sentences.

das Dasein "existence", lit. "the being there";[31] and the same is true also of various Arabic existentials, see § 2.2.3. In the light of this general phenomenon, I suggest that (11)a–e are surviving vestiges of a historically primary, nonderived sentence-type composed of *inna* and a term in the acc. case; that the historically primary meaning of this sentence-type was deictic-presentative (i.e. that it was originally a "nuclear presentative sentence", to use my own term)[32], but that it had largely lost this meaning and become predominantly existential by the time these vestiges emerge before our eyes in the recorded ʿArabiyya.

2.2.3 Within the realm of Arabic, the most familiar instances attesting a transition from an originally deictic to an existential meaning are the particles *ṯammata, hāhunā, hunāka, hunālika.* Another example is provided by the demonstrative presentatives. In the classical language they retain their deictic meaning in nuclear status, see exx. (2)–(3) of chapter IV, but exhibit the change to an existential meaning in the nucleus of the Bedouin construction of the type *hāḏa wāḥidin yesennid ʿala* "there is/was someone who addressed a poem to ..." (since the construction with the *existential* meaning does not undergo the shift described end of § 5.1, of ch. IV; cf. end of § 2.5.3 below). Consider also the colloquial Iraqi existential *aku*, which Diem reconstructs as consisting of a deictic particle **ak* and a third masc. sing. pron. **hu*[33], and his explanation of existence-negating *ma-allōš, ma-hallūš* of Yemen as likewise originally containing a deictic particle.[34]

2.2.4 But while the connection between expressions of deixis and existence is fairly evident (even on formal-etymological grounds alone) and is rarely disputed, it is far less clear how one is to conceive the transition from the concrete notion of deixis to the abstract notion of existence.[35] I shall not attempt to solve this problem, but merely try to show on the basis of an example how a

31 See e.g. Lyons "Possessive, Existential ..." 390, and Lyons *Introduction* 390; Bravmann *Studies* 140.–5 – 141.11. This is not to say that there is a total consensus on this question. For different conclusions see Breivik "On the Interpretation of Existential *there*", *Language* 57/1 (1981), 1–25.

32 All nuclear presentative structures are, at least in their origin, deictic in nature, see §§ 2.1 and 3.2 of ch. IV.

33 W. Diem, "A Historical Interpretation of Iraqi Arabic *ʾaku* 'There is'", *Orbis* 23/2 (1974), 448–53.

34 W. Diem, "Studien zur Frage des Substrats im Arabischen", *Der Islam* 56/1 (1979), 30.–2ff.

35 Bravmann *Studies* 139–50 must be credited for having clearly recognized and formulated the problem, even though his explanation is not fully convincing.

presentative particle may acquire a secondary existential meaning in a specific context.

From the Biblical language modern Hebrew inherited the presentative *hinnē* (now *hine*). While in the common usage its meanings clearly fall within the semantic scope that one would expect of a presentative particle, its meaning in an instance such as the following is worthy of notice. A contemporary scholar speaks of the wealth of synonyms that have come into modern Hebrew by virtue of the fact that it inherited words from the Biblical as well as the Mishnaic tradition, and how the language tends to make use of this wealth by secondarily differentiating between such words. In his own formulation:

> Since we inherited word pairs, it is but natural that we would want to make distinctions between them. (E.g.,)
>
> *hine "doreš" vehine "tovea"*
> Here is *doreš* and here is *tovea*,
>
> (two words) between which there is no difference at all, the Bible using *doreš* and the Mishna *tovea* (both meaning "to demand"). But one now (i.e. in modern Hebrew) makes a distinction, in that *doreš* is used in the plain sense of "to demand", while *tovea* is used specifically in connection with monetary and legal matters.[36]

I have rendered *hine* as a presentative, but it is not difficult to see that in a context such as this the particle is used in a different way than usual. *Hine* does not point here to a concrete entity – as it would, say, in *hine David* "Here is David" – but refers to the existence of an abstract concept, "here is a word *doreš* and a word *tovea*". I am by no means claiming that *hine* has become an existential particle in modern Hebrew, which it definitely has not.[37] Rather, it is an ad hoc use in an extended (one might say "symbolic") sense of a particle which otherwise is strictly presentative. But precisely the fact that such ad hoc usage is possible suggests that there are contextual *loci* that make possible the transition from the concrete notion of deixis (which underlies any nuclear presentative sentence) to the abstract notion of existence.[38]

36 Abba Bendavid, *Lešon Mikra u-Lešon Ḥaḇamim* (Vol. I, Tel Aviv 1967), 7.12–15. The portions in parentheses are my explanatory additions.

37 For the expression of existence Hebrew uses *yeš*, see Rubinstein *Ha-Mišpaṭ Ha-Šemani* 199.

38 When a presentative is used to refer to a *word*, as in the Hebrew example just quoted, the meaning is necessarily existential.

2.3 The acc. of the head and other expressions of case notions

2.3.1 In the following we shall attempt to show that the acc. of the sentence-type *inna Zaydan* (11) can be explained within a larger frame of Arabic syntax and that, more importantly, it expresses a specific (functionally defined) case notion that is characteristic of nuclear presentative structures not only in Arabic.

2.3.2 In order to understand the meaning of the acc. case in sentence-type *inna Zaydan*, it will be useful to compare it with the acc. in other verbless utterances such as:

(12) a. *alhilāla wallāhi*
"The new moon, by God!" (exclamation upon seeing the new moon)

b. *ḥadīṯaka*
"Your story!" (i.e. "tell your story!")

c. *alkilāba ʿalā lbaqari*
"The dogs onto the antelopes!" (command to hunters to let loose the dogs)

d. *al'asada*
"The lion!" (warning upon seeing a lion)

e. *ruwayda Zaydan*
"Treat Zayd gently!"

f. *ḥayyahala ṯṯarīda*
"Come quickly to the stew!"

g. *halumma šuhadā'akum*
"Bring here your witnesses!" a–g, Wright I 294.–2, II 75–78

Although the acc. in (12)a–g stands for a variety of meanings, these can all be subsumed under a single, broadly conceived notion of *object*, if this term is understood to encompass relations such as: thing/person[39] perceived (i.e. by the speaker, or which the addressee is called upon to perceive), as in a, d; thing/person handled, treated, acted upon, brought ("patient"), as in e, g; thing brought into existence, produced, as in b;[40] thing/person approached, come to, arrived at ("target"), as in f, etc.[41] Thus, I use *object* as a comprehensive case

39 Here and in the following, "thing/person" is a shorthand symbol for any entity term.

40 I.e. something that comes into being only as a result of the action itself, as in *sing a song*, *write a book*, *light a fire*, etc. See also Knobloch 71, under "Accusativus effectivus"; Lyons *Introduction* 439, under "object of result".

41 We are not concerned here with the question of a possibly interjectional origin of the *-a* in utterances of type (12), see Brock. 8, Reck. *AS* 108 (and cf. Nöldeke *ZGr.* 47.1 and n. 1). In the

category – "case" being understood in a semantic-functional sense, for which see e.g. Lyons *Introduction* 295. (Alternatively, one may speak of these relations in terms of "semantic roles" in the sense of Comrie 51–56.)

2.3.2.1 It could be argued that semantic relations of so great a diversity as those just mentioned ought not to be subsumed under a single umbrella-term such as "object". It is important to remember, however, that Arabic treats all of these relations as (direct) object relations, marked by the acc. case, also *outside* of utterances of type (12), i.e. in verbal sentences, and this fact justifies their subsumption under a single heading.

2.3.2.2 As is known, traditional grammar usually postulates an "implicit" verb in utterances of type (12). This approach can be accepted at best as a heuristic explanatory device, because any claim that a specific verbal form is underlying in a given case is necessarily arbitrary (as when (12)b is said to be underlyingly *hāti ḥadīṯaka* "Give your story!", or d *iḥḏari l'asada* "Beware of the lion!", see Wright l.c.). Moreover, these verb interpolations run the risk of violating the principle of meaning preservation, for which see below § 2.4.2 and note 61. In the grammatical system of the ʿArabiyya these are verbless utterances, and I propose that their acc. case be seen as autonomously expressing objecthood. The concept of "autonomous" objects – in the sense of object relations that do not require the presence of a verbal form – is useful in the description of the semantics of a fairly large number of verbless constructions of Arabic, see also chapter III.

2.3.3 My interpretation of *inna Zaydan* (11) as the reflex of an original nuclear presentative sentence-type and of its acc. case as the exponent of a notion of object (in the sense of the definition in § 2.3.2) gains support from a comparison with another type of nuclear presentative sentence whose head is likewise in the acc.:

(13) a. *hāka naẓman*
"Here is a poem for you". — Wright II 77.–1

b. *hāki ssayfa*
"Here's the sword for you (fem. sing.)". — Wright II 78.1

c. *hākumā maʿbada*[42] *ššamsi*
"Here, you two, is the temple of the sun". — Cant. II 31.–2

grammatical system of the ʿArabiyya these are unmistakably accusatives – or have been so reinterpreted, if their origin was interjectional, see Reck. *AS* 109.1 – and it is only the "case" values expressed by these accusatives (in the sense defined above) that are here under consideration.

42 So, not *mabʿad* as in Cant.

This type differs from (11) in that it involves an additional component, viz. an inflected second person pronoun suffixed to the presentative particle *hā*[43], representing the addressee(s).[44] But the really essential element in the comparison between *inna Zaydan* (11) and *hāka ssayfa* (13) is of course the feature that both sentence-types have in common, i.e. the acc. case of the head. In type (13) it marks the thing/person which the speaker presents (introduces, offers, hands, shows, points out, etc.) to the addressee, and one may surmise that at a time when (11) was still exclusively presentative in meaning its acc. stood for a similar range of object notions. The evidence of the Biblical Hebrew nuclear presentative sentence with *hinnē*, the etymological cognate of *inna*, points in the same direction, see (17) below, especially the meanings of exx. a–c. But apart from this comparative evidence, it is above all the existence of a presentative sentence-type such as (13) in the synchronic – i.e. nonreconstructed – system of Arabic that provides good typological support to the proposed historical analysis of (11), and particularly to the interpretation of the acc. of this type as an original exponent of objecthood.

2.3.4 But Arabic also possesses nuclear presentative sentences whose head is in the nom. case, e.g. type (14):

(14) a. *ṯumma sāra arbaʿa marāḥila waʾiḏā jubaylun*
"Then he travelled for four days, and there was suddenly a small mountain". Reck. *SV* 478.3

b. *aġarnā ʿalā ahli l-Muṣayyaḫi waʾiḏā rajulun yusammā* ...
"We raided the people of al-Muṣayyaḫ, and there was suddenly a man there named..." Reck. *AS* 357.–4

c. *iltafattu faʾiḏā nnabiyyu*
"I turned around and there suddenly was the Prophet".[45] Brock. 36.3

43 The presentative *hā*, termed in the indigenous tradition the *Ḥarf al-Tanbīh* "the particle that calls attention", Wright I 268 A, occurs also in environments other than (13). It has been mentioned passim in ch. IV.

44 Insofar as in (13) this suffix represents a special kind of addressee, namely one *to whom* something is given, offered, shown – i.e. (in semantic role terminology) a "recipient", "benefactive", etc., the designation "vokativisch", for which see Reck. *SV* 408 n. 2, is somewhat too narrow. The term "Directionssuffix" used by Fleischer 522.–11 comes closer to the point.

45 For other examples of type (14) see Reck. *SV* 312.2, 3; Bravmann "Linguistic Taboo" 479.5. It is essential to distinguish between these sentences and those of an identical surface structure, such as *takallamat faʾiḏā aʿrābiyyatun faṣīḥatun* "she spoke and behold, she was (i.e. turned out to be) an eloquent Bedouin woman", Reck. *AS* 358.3, where *iḏā* is not nuclear but proclitic with the subject pronoun deleted. The underlying structure of a sentence such as the one just quoted manifests itself in cases where that pronoun is explicit, e.g. *naẓartu ilā lmaqtūli faʾiḏā huwa l-Ḍaḥḥāk* "I looked at the killed man and behold, it was Al-Ḍaḥḥāk", Reck. *SV* 476.

The *iḏā* in this and the related types (see ch. III) is the *Iḏā l-Mufāja'ati* "the *Iḏā* of Suddenness".[46] Like many other presentative particles, it is of an originally deictic meaning.[47]

The existence of nuclear presentative sentences with the head in the nom. case alongside others whose head is in the acc. demands an explanation. I believe this dichotomy is rooted in the very nature of the category "nuclear presentative sentence" and is, therefore, of some general linguistic interest. Simply put, it is a reflection of two different ways in which language chooses, as it were, to "look" at the entity in question: as an object, in the sense of the term defined above; or as a thing/person that is *located* (sits, stands, etc.) in a given place. One may see this contrast in terms of a "dynamic" (or "directional", "target oriented") and a "static" view of that entity, respectively.[48] The linguistic representation appropriate to the second view is the nom. case – just as locative sentences of the type *jumla ẓarfiyya* take their "head" in the nom. (*ʿalā ljabali qaṣrun*), or – to choose a word category akin to *iḏā* – just as the originally deictic words of the set *ṯammata, hunāka*, etc. have the head in the nominative.[49] Thus, what at first glance may appear as an unmotivated case contrast can be explained as a manifestation of these alternative "views".

2.3.5 It was shown that one of the characteristics of the presentative type *hāḏā rrajulu* is nonoccurrence of the copula, § 2.5 of ch. IV. This is also shared by all types of *jumla ẓarfiyya*, as well as by type (14) (where any interposing pronoun is not a copula but a subject, see note 45). Typologically and functionally, therefore, the presentative type *hāḏā rrajulu* belongs together with type (14), and this applies also to the nom. case of its head which likewise reflects the "static" view of the entity in question.

2.3.6 Apart from the case marking of the head, this notional dichotomy is also reflected to some extent in the very expressions which languages in general tend to use as presentatives. Especially conspicuous are of course presentatives that derive historically from some form of the verb *to see* (often an imperative), thus reflecting the "object view" of the head, at least in their original meaning, e.g. Fr. *voici, voilà*. For coll. Arabic, consider Maġr. *ṛa*, Omdurman *tara*, Pal. *arīh* ("there he is"), and the various manifestations of *šaʿ* < **iqšaʿ* "see!" in a number of dialects.[50] Moreover, it is a measure of the strength of the object view that

46 For the alternation *wa'iḏā* ~ *fa'iḏā* in (14) see note 2 of ch. III.

47 On its deictic nature see Reck. *SV* 475.

48 On this dichotomy as a general phenomenon of language see Lyons *Introduction* 300.

49 In fact, some grammarians speak of *Iḏā l-Mufāja'ati* as a locative particle, see the terms *makāniyya, ẓarf makān*, Fleischer 113, 425.

50 W. Fischer *Dem.* 188.–4ff., 192.–15, 199.

even when the presentative is not derived from a verb *to see*, a head in the first person singular will still often exhibit the object form of the pronominal suffix, e.g. Pal. *hayni*, *hayyūni*, § 6.3.2 of chapter IV, or Bibl. Heb. *hinnenī* "Here I am." On the other hand, there are presentatives like Engl. *here*, *there*, whose very etymology suggests the locative view.

2.3.7 There are other areas of syntax where a nom./acc.-dichotomy reflects a notional contrast in the sense of the foregoing discussion. Ethiopic uses the preposition *ba-* to express possession, as in *bōtū welūd* "He has sons" ⟨with (*bei*, *chez*, etc.)-him sons⟩, where the term for the thing possessed is in the nom. case. However, this term may alternatively exhibit the acc., *bōtū welūda*.[51] Each of these representations has its own logic in terms of relational notions: The (historically older) construction with the nom. reflects the original "locative" syntax, in the sense of *bei ihm*, *chez lui*, while the acc. has been superimposed secondarily to represent a relational notion of object, as it were "He possesses sons".[52] It is immaterial that this dichotomy differs from the one observed in the presentative sentences, insofar as the Ethiopic feature involves an older and a younger (superimposed) representation.[53] What alone counts in the context of the present discussion is the general phenomenon: We see that language makes use of two different ways to treat the head of a nuclear presentative and a nuclear possessive sentence, namely as reflecting an entity located in a given place, or as an object. In this sense, then, these two nom./acc.-dichotomies are a similar phenomenon of language.

2.4 The medieval grammarians' deletion hypothesis and its modern counterpart

2.4.1 The interpretation proposed here for the sentences of the type *inna Zaydan* (11) differs sharply from the one given in the indigenous grammatical

51 Brock. 90. For *ba-* with still a purely locative sense in Eth. see e.g. *babēta abūya* "in my father's house", ibid. 363.13.

52 This is essentially the interpretation of Brockelmann, Dillmann and Prätorius, which Bravmann (*Studies* 146 n. 1) attempts to refute with the argument that "Ethiopic ... does not possess ... a verb which from the outset expresses the abstract notion of possession". This may well be true, but it is safe to assume at the same time that the inventory of Ethiopic has always contained at least a few basic verbs with sufficiently similar meanings – *hold*, *get*, etc. – to allow a transfer of their acc. to the construction with *ba-* under discussion.

53 In its superimposed nature, this acc. is similar to the one discussed in § 3.5 of ch. III. One may mention here also the standard (and historically older) prepositional construction denoting possession of Hebrew, type *yeš li ha-sefer* ⟨is to-me the-book⟩ "I have the book", and the younger substandard type *yeš li et ha-sefer*, with the obj. market *et* prefixed to the thing possessed.

tradition. The medieval grammarians I consulted did not accept these sentences as they are – and indeed could not have done so within their system of grammatical analysis. The reasons are essentially similar to those described above § 1.4.4, but the details vary. Seen in terms of this system of analysis, sentences of type (11) exhibit an *ism inna* (the term in the acc.)[54], but no *ḫabar* to go along with it, i.e. a single component where two are expected. The method of explanation adopted by most medieval grammarians since Sībawayhi demands that in cases like this the "harmony" be restored by the assumption that the other component occurs virtually (*taqdīran*) and is merely deleted (*maḥḏūf*) from the surface structure. The grammarians' approach to the type with *inna* under discussion must be understood in the light of this explanatory principle.[55] Their usual procedure with respect to this particular sentence-type is to postulate a prepositional phrase as the "missing" *ḫabar* (but see also Al-Farrā''s suggestion below). Thus, we are told that (11)a–b are underlyingly as on the right:

(11) a.	*inna mālan*	*inna lanā mālan*
b.	*inna Zaydan*	*inna lanā Zaydan*

with *lanā* being considered deleted in the surface structure, and the other exx. of type (11) are treated in the same vein.[56] It is worth mentioning for comparison that sentences with *Lā li-Nafyi l-Jins* ("*Lā* that negates the genus") receive the same analysis. Thus, it is claimed that e.g. (15)a–c are underlyingly as on the right:

(15) a.	*lā ḥawla walā quwwata*	*lā ḥawla walā quwwata lanā*
b.	*lā ilāha illā llāh*	*lā ilāha fī lwujūdi illā llāh*
	lā fatā illā ʿAliyy	*lā fatā fī lwujūdi illā ʿAliyy*
c.	*alā mā'a bāridan*	*alā mā'a lanā bāridan*

a–b: Ibn Yaʿīš 131.9–18
c: Sībawayhi I 245.1

with the missing *ḫabar* that "ought" to accompany the *ism* (in this case it is the *ism lā*) here again supplied by the grammarians, i.e. *lanā* in (15)a and c, *fī lwujūdi* in b. The similar way in which the grammarians treat these two sentence-types is of interest in view of their typological similarity: The mean-

54 So, rather than *ḫabar inna*, as erroneously in Cant. II 227.6.

55 On Sībawayhi's use of *Taqdīr* to demonstrate underlying "harmony" in other instances see Baalbaki, esp. 13 where the tenet of the mutual indispensability (*ʿadam istiġnā'*) of the two components of a nominal sentence is discussed. In another connection, the principle of mutual indispensability is mentioned specifically with respect to *inna* and its "sisters", Sībawayhi I 338.4.

56 Sībawayhi I 244.15–20; Zamaḫšarī 15.8–12; Ibn Yaʿīš 127.13, 15.

ing of type *inna Zaydan* (11) ranges from deictic-presentative to existential, as we have seen (§ 2.2.1), while type (15) is purely existential.[57]

By ascribing the mentioned underlying structures to these sentences, the grammarians in effect distort their real meanings. Thus, *inna maḥallan wa'inna murtaḥalan*, (11)d, simply says that there is a time (or place) of staying and a time or place of departing, not that "we have" (*lanā*) such a time or place, as the grammarians' interpretation would have it. The *fī lwujūdi* in (15)b shows especially well that these are scholastic interpolations, not integral components of the meanings (or, if you will, the underlying structures) of these sentences, as is implied in the *Taqdīr* approach.[58] Since the purpose is to restore the "harmony" it is immaterial what kind of *ḫabar* is postulated in a given instance: it can be a prepositional phrase, as we have seen; or a substantive, as is the case when Al-Farrā' maintains that

(11) e. *inna zzabābata wa'inna lfa'rata*

is underlyingly:

inna zzabābata zabābatun wa'inna lfa'rata fa'ratun
Sībawayhi (Būlāq ed.) I 284 right margin

or an adjective[59] – and it is not surprising that at times two different ways are proposed to "restore" the same sentence.[60] All of this points to the arbitrariness of the procedure, but also to the one true motivation behind it, viz. to force sentences (11) and (15) into the prescribed mold of *ism* and *ḫabar*.

2.4.2 Inasmuch as these interpolations in one way or another change the meaning, they in fact violate a regulatory principle which was specifically introduced by Arabic medieval grammatical scholarship for the purpose of preventing such misuse of *Taqdīr*, namely the principle that the resulting construction not deviate in meaning from the construction before the application of *Taqdīr*. In reality, of course, this principle was not infrequently broken[61] – and the treatment of the types with *inna* (11) and *lā* (15) is another case in point.

57 The *Lā li-Nafyi l-Jins* is put on a par with *inna* also from the viewpoint of its government, see Sībawayhi I 300.13.

58 It is hard to imagine anyone but a linguist to come up with such a postulate for the *Šahāda*!

59 Cf. *muṣaddaqun* in Zamaḫšarī 15.13–15 = Ibn Yaʿīš 127.7–9.

60 Thus, in dealing with the sentence *inna ḏāka* (in the passage referred to in the preceding note), Ibn Yaʿīš contemplates two different underlying representations, i.e. *inna ḏāka muṣaddaqun*, 128.11, and *inna laka ḏāka*, 128.13.

61 On this principle – and its violation – see Baalbaki 10, and esp. n. 24 (where the reference to Sībawayhi [Būlāq ed.] I 47 should read I 147). It is worth remembering that "meaning preservation" used to be debated among transformational linguists in recent years.

2.4.3 To be sure, even if our assessment is correct that the grammarians' interpretation of these two sentence-types is motivated by their "restorational" approach, this interpretation still merits an examination on its own grounds, all the more so since there are indeed genuine phenomena of deletion in classical Arabic, as we have seen. But it is precisely the comparison with these phenomena that helps to put into relief the decisive differences. Sentences such as (8) are unmistakably truncated, requiring a portion to be mentally supplied by the hearer/reader in order to be understood. Moreover, in (8) the portions in question are integral to the meaning of these sentences and are retrievable from the immediately preceding context. In contrast, sentences (11) and (15) are semantically self-contained. The only ex. that *might* differ in this regard is *inna Zaydan wa'inna ʿAmran* (11)b, where an implied/deleted *lanā* "we have" is at least conceivable, since this sentence is in answer to the question *hal lakum* ...? – although even here a reading without the assumption of a deleted component seems more natural. But certainly no such assumption is justified in any of the other exx. of these two sentence-types, where the supposedly deleted portions are neither integral to the meanings nor contextually retrievable.[62]

2.4.4 The Arab grammarians' analysis is of some interest to the history of linguistic methodology. There is a modern approach to existential sentences which, though based on a different premise, leads to a similar interpretation and must ultimately be rejected for much the same reason as the approach of the grammarians. Thus, John Lyons observes that existential sentences "do not normally occur without a locative or temporal complement", which is an unobjectionable statement as long as "normally" simply refers to a greater statistical frequency. But Lyons then goes a bit too far in suggesting that "it might appear reasonable to say that all existential sentences are at least implicitly locative (the term "locative" being taken to include both temporal and spatial reference)".[63] This is an example of how an empiricist-philosophical approach to language may lead to an artificial grammatical analysis. Lyons bases his suggestion on the axiom that if something exists, it must exist somewhere. But this by no means implies that locativity necessarily inheres in *statements* about existence. The contrivedness of this view becomes clear if one considers common existential sentences such as:

62 Ibn Yaʿīš 127.10–14, in an apparent attempt to justify his claim that it is the context (*qarā'in al-aḥwāl*) that makes possible the *ḫabar*-deletion in (11), says of the lead sentence *inna mālan* ...: *ka'anna ḏālika waqaʿa fī jawābi hal lahum mālun*. But his very formulation with *ka'anna* ("it is as if") in effect acknowledges that the question-answer frame, at least in this particular example, is no more than an explanatory ploy.

63 Lyons "Possessive, Existential" 390. For a similar position see now Beeston "Reflections on Verbs 'To Be'", *JSS* 29 (1984), 9–10.

There is a kind of banana that keeps fresh for months.
If there's love there's hope.
There is a time for playing and a time for studying.

or, for that matter –

There is a modern approach to existential sentences which ...

In statements of this kind one can legitimately recognize no more than the bare existential sentence-nucleus, "there is/are X".[64] The assumption of implicit locativity would be here as unjustified as is the postulate of a "missing" portion in the Arabic sentences of types (11) and (15)[65]

2.4.5 A word more on existential sentences in Arabic may be in order. It will have been understood from the method adopted throughout this work that "existential sentence" is taken here as a *functional-semantic* class that is confined to no single formal type (cf. § 1.2). Thus, to this class also belong types such as (sample representing various periods):

(16) a. *walaqad taraknāhā āyatan fahal min muddakir*
"And We left it for a sign. But is there any that will remember (or, will be warned)?"[66] Q 54:15 (also verses 17, 22, 32, 40)

b. *kāna tājirun (wākana lahu ...)*
"There was a merchant (and he had ...)" Wright II 99 D

c. *ahāhunā wāriṯun ġayrukum*
"Is there an inheritor other than you?" Reck. *SV* 421.6

d. *hāhunā nafarun min al-Yahūd*
"There are some Jews (whom ...)" Blau *Chr. Ar.* 255.–1

e. *hunāka ṭirāzun wāḥidun min arrijāli aḥtarimuhu*
"There is one kind of men that I respect". Bloch *Chr.* 148.9

f. *baynamā tūjadu šuʿūbun ġaniyyatun*
"While there are rich nations"
Kropfitsch (mod. lit.) 35.–3, and cf. 33.–3, 34.1

64 Lyons himself, apparently a bit uncomfortable with his suggestion in his (later) *Introduction*, adds a qualifying "whether or not this last point is accepted", 390 second par. For a criticism of Lyons see also G. Goldenberg, "On Syriac Sentence Structure", in *Arameans, Aramaic and the Aramaic Literary Tradition*, M. Sokoloff, ed. Bar-Ilan University, Ramat-Gan (1983), 130.

65 For a few more existence-negating sentences of type (15) without any amplifiction see e.g. Reck. *AS* 120.3,–1; 121.–2; 122.1. On the self-containedness of this type see also Blau "Remarks" 224. For a model treatment of existential sentences in a modern language see Rubinstein *Ha-Mišpaṭ Ha-Šemani* 199 ff.

66 And cf. the numerous exx. with *hal min*, *mā min* in Reck. *AS* 357.

g. *mā bə'tə'ed fī wa't ləlḥādse*
"I don't think there's time for talking". Cowell (Syr.) 415

Just as argued above for the types with *inna* (11) and *lā* (15), these sentences do not imply locativity, in the sense of Lyons; nor do they suggest a missing portion, in the sense of the Arab grammarians. Rather, when such portions do appear in the surface structure, the meaning is not existential but possessive or locative: E.g. contrast (16)a with sentences such as *hal lakum min abin* "Do you have a father?", *mā birrabʿi min aḥadin* "There is no one in the camping place".[67]

A rigorously semantic approach also requires preclusion of sentences that look like existentials but have a different meaning. Thus, alongside sentences that are genuinely existential, Cant. II 197–8 adduces those like:

ḥattā kāna l-Islāmu
"Until Islam appeared".
ḥattā kāna yawmun mina l'ayyāmi ḏāqa ṣṣabiyyu fīhi l'alama
"Until a day came when the boy felt the pain".
walākinna šay'an min ḏālika lam yakun
"But none of this happened".

which are better classified together with common verbal sentences marking the occurrence (or nonoccurrence) of an event, i.e. "X came/happened/occurred".

Along the same line, one must also set apart usage such as (Syr.):

kīf mərrūḥ ʿal-Aṣṣāʿ
fī l-bāṣ wət-tramwāy wət-taksi
"How shall we go to Qassa?"
"There's the bus, the streetcar, and taxis". Cowell 415

where the meaning is obviously not existential. This interesting usage, which characteristically occurs in *listings* (so also in spoken Am. Eng.), deserves a special, cross-language examination.

2.5 The syntactic and semantic development

2.5.1 Assuming that the type *inna Zaydan* indeed reflects an original nuclear presentative sentence as argued in § 2.2.1–2, one may expect to learn about the possible direction of its historical development by looking at the development of other presentative sentences. Ideally, a hypothesis on this matter ought to be based on knowledge of how presentative sentences tend to develop *in general*,

67 Exx. Reck. *AS* 267.

but in the absence of such cross-language information[68] a language-internal comparison is the next best approach.[69] A clear picture of the processes by which new presentative sentences have been formed from historically older ones in Arabic is provided by the presentative sentences with demonstrative pronouns discussed in the preceding chapter. We have seen that these exhibit three structures – nuclear, amplified and proclitic – and arguments were adduced to suggest that the proclitic structure is historically derived (secondary), resulting from a syntactic reanalysis of the components of the amplified structure, see § 5.1 and especially § 5.2 of chapter IV. This provides a typologically plausible model for a hypothesis on the history of the *inna*-structure under discussion. I propose that this structure was capable of occurring unamplified, i.e. as in (11)a–e, as well as with a circumstantial (*Ḥāl*) amplification, and that the amplified structure underwent a syntactic reanalysis such as was described for the demonstrative presentatives, thus producing the proclitic structure. Here too, the process may have started with morphologically unmarked *Ḥāls*, i.e. (schematically)

inna Zaydan yanṭaliqu → *inna Zaydan yanṭaliqu*

in other words, a shift by which the *Ḥāl* assumes the status of a predicate, cf. § 5.1 of chapter IV. This, then, is a synopsis showing the parallelism of the two developments, as proposed:

Nuclear	Amplified	Proclitic
hāḏā Zaydun	*hāḏā Zaydun munṭaliqan*	→ *hāḏā Zaydun munṭaliqun*
inna Zaydan	**inna Zaydan munṭaliqan*	→ *inna Zaydan munṭaliqun*[70]

Given this development, the acc. in the proclitic *inna*-structure is a "left-over" of the earlier stage in which it was motivated by its nuclear status, see § 2.3.2-3, just as this is true of the inflection of the proclitic *hāḏā*, see § 5.2.1 of ch. IV.

68 E. Clark's study is universal in outlook and contains much information that is, even if only indirectly, relevant to our subject, but its approach is purely synchronic and thus does not concern itself with the kind of questions here under discussion.

69 The great importance of language-internal evidence for historical reconstruction has been demonstrated by R. Steiner in a different matter, see *JAOS* 100/4 (1980), 513–18 (consider esp. his general remark on methodology, n. 16).

70 It will be remembered that this development must be understood as resulting in the creation of a new, *additional* (viz. proclitic) status for *inna*, not as eliminating the original nuclear one, cf. § 5.5 of ch. IV. This explains how the two manifestations could coexist in the same historical stage, as in exx. (11) b and d.

It will have been noticed that all these structures are actually attested[71], with the sole exception of the amplified *inna*-structure (*), which has not survived.[72]

2.5.2 And from the syntax to the semantics: How did an originally deictic (presentative) *inna* come to have the emphasizing meaning it possesses in classical Arabic? The most plausible solution is to assume a semantic change. This is what Fleischer seems to have in mind when he states that *inna* is "originally a deictic particle and later on a particle of confirmation" ("von Haus aus eine Hinweisungs- und weiter eine Bestätigungspartikel");[73] similarly Brokkelmann: *Inna Zaydan karīmun* "siehe (wahrlich) Zayd ist ...", where "siehe" represents the original function, "wahrlich" (in parenthesis) the secondary one;[74] and likewise Wright: *Inna* "certainly, surely, truly", literally "lo! see! en, ecce!", where the word "literally" is meant to indicate the particle's original meaning.[75]

All of these approaches have in common a rather easy attitude towards what, after all, are two distinct meanings. The common trait appears to be here the tacit assumption that these two meanings are sufficiently similar to allow a mere *assertion* that a change has taken place.

It may be noted in passing that in his treatment of *alā* and *amā*, Reckendorf displays a similar laxity towards precisely these two meanings when he states that these particles "serve to draw attention to what follows, to stress its factuality". But the first of these two clauses is a description of presentativity and the second of sentence-emphasis![76]

71 I shall not deal here with the so-called "sisters" of *inna*, a number of particles which behave structurally like *inna* itself. In view of their widely differing functions and syntactic origins, their uniform structural behavior is rather striking and suggests that strong processes of analogical levelling have been at work. For a few brief remarks on their history see Nöldeke *ZGr.* 40 n. 2; Fleischer 510.4, 561.1ff., 646.–12ff., but much is still unexplained.

72 A reflex of such an original amplified structure may have been preserved, however, in the noncanonic type *inna Zaydan munṭaliqan* – that is, if the second acc. reflects an original *Ḥāl*. But this type may have other interpretations, see Rabin 173, Fleischer 561.7.

73 Fleischer 421.–3.

74 Brockelmann *Arabische Grammatik*, 16th ed. (Leipzig 1958), 174.

75 Wright I 284.–2. Understandably, and in keeping with its predominantly diachronic character, Bergesträsser's *Einführung in die Semitischen Sprachen* (Darmstadt 1963) 142.–4 speaks of *inna* only in terms of its original function, "deiktisch".

76 "... haben die Wirkung, die Aufmerksamkeit auf das Folgende zu lenken, seine Tatsächlichkeit zu betonen", Reck. *SV* 79. The fact is, rather, that both *alā* and *amā* are presentatives, as also described by the grammarians (*tanbīh*, see Fleischer 458.–3), so that only the first of Reckendorf's clauses is justified. If the combinations *alā inna*, *amā inna* express both functions (which remains to be investigated; it is equally possible that one of the two functions is annulled), then it is precisely the combination with *inna* by which this is achieved.

2.5.3 It may not be possible to explain why a given semantic change takes place, but it is the researcher's task at least to look for conditions under which it might have occurred. Our study of the Arabic presentatives has shown – and the evidence of Biblical Hebrew *hinnē* (see § 2.6.1) provides strong outside confirmation – that there is a close relation between the type of structure and the range of meanings: Nuclear (and amplified) structures are semantically homogeneous, because their meaning is determined by the essentially deictic-concrete character of the presentative, whereas proclitic structures are capable of expressing a wide spectrum of meanings, including sentence-emphasis, see e.g. in chapter IV: §§ 2.1, 2.3, 2.6, 3.2–3, 4.8, 6.1.3, 6.6.1 and passim; in the present chapter: §§ 2.3.3–4, 2.6.1. This rather substantial difference in the semantic range was explained (on the model of the demonstrative presentatives) as a consequence of the syntactic shift: Embedded in the nucleus, the presentative retains its deictic meaning; but once dislodged from this position into the status of a proclitic, it becomes exposed to contextual influence and may acquire new meanings, depending on the context.[77] The fact that sentence-emphasis is one of the meanings of the proclitic demonstrative presentatives and proclitic *hinnē*[78] allows the conjecture that this may have been true at first also of the proclitic *inna*, but that in this case this meaning gained the upper hand so as to become predominant. While this of course remains a hypothesis, it is a hypothesis that is based on a comparison with the semantic range of other proclitic presentatives, which puts it typologically on a relatively sound foundation.

In nuclear position, on the other hand, *inna* over time lost its deictic meaning and became predominantly existential, as attested in the vestigial sentences (11). In this respect, then, *inna* went a step further in its development than the demonstrative presentatives and *hinnē*, which fully retain their deictic meaning in nuclear status, and more closely resembles the (likewise originally deictic) particles *ṯammata*, *hunāka*.[79]

Finally, it must be emphasized that the nuclear/proclitic-dualism is a prerogative of *presentative* particles, while existential ones are confined to the nuclear position (in support of this point, consider here again the existential particles *ṯammata*, etc., which are inherently nuclear and do not occur proclitically). For the history of *inna* as proposed here this implies that the syntactic shift occurred before the emergence of the particle's existential meaning.

77 Specifically, notice how the basic alerting meaning of a proclitic presentative may develop in different directions, see the discussion in § 3.3–5 of ch. IV.

78 It *may* also be one of the meanings of proclitic presentatives in some modern Arabic colloquials, see Landberg 496.4.

79 However, for an instance in which a demonstrative presentative becomes existential see § 2.2.3 above.

2.5.4 Of the Western grammarians, only Reckendorf, as far as I know, devoted a fully detailed discussion to the historical syntax of *inna*, Reck. *SV* 354 ff. Reckendorf acknowledges the examples of the type *inna Zaydan* (11), but accepts the grammarians' deletion hypothesis, thus failing to recognize this type's potential for the reconstruction of the original syntax, ibid. 357 n. 1. Moreover, unlike Fleischer et al., see § 2.5.2, Reckendorf does not believe that *inna* could have been originally deictic, because the "really" deictic particles *iḏ* and *iḏā* ("... welche wirklich deiktisch sind", ibid. 354 n. 2) never take the acc. case. This argument is fallacious for the following reasons: (1) The deictic (presentative) *hā* does take the acc., namely in the type *hāka ssayfa* (13), a type not considered by Reckendorf. (2) The originally deictic nature of *inna* is suggested by its etymological and functional cognates in other Semitic languages, notably Biblical Hebrew *hinnē* (and see note 24 above). (3) If a deictic particle behaves in one way, it by no means follows that another particle which behaves differently cannot therefore be deictic as well. We have argued that the contrast between the nom. of *iḏā* and the acc. of *inna* reflects a notional dichotomy which, in fact, lies in the very nature of presentative sentences, see § 2.3.4–6.[80]

2.6 The Biblical Hebrew evidence

2.6.1 Our argument concerning the relationship between the types of meaning of a presentative and its syntactic status receives support from the Biblical Hebrew presentative *hinnē*. This particle is consistently deictic-concrete in nuclear position:

(17) a. *wəʿattā hinnē ištəḵā qaḥ wālēḵ*
"Now then, here is your wife, take (her) and be gone". Gn 12:19

b. *hinnē hāʾēš wəhāʿēṣīm wəʾayyē hasse ləʿōlā*
"Here are the fire and the wood, but where is the lamb for a burnt offering?"[81] Gn 22:7

80 In one important aspect, however, our analysis resembles Reckendorf's, namely in the assumption of a syntactic shift (reanalysis), See ibid. 355, and cf. also Beeston 64.

81 For this reading of Gn 22:7 see e.g. Lambdin 170.10. The parallelistic construction of Isaac's words confirms *hinnē*'s nuclear status ("Here is X, where is Y?"), disqualifying renditions of the type "Behold, the fire and the wood; but where is ...", as e.g. in the *New Oxford Bible.* Similarly, contrast the appropriate rendition of the Aramaic parallel of Gn 12:19 in the Genesis Apocryphon, *hʾ ʾnttk* "Here is your wife", in Fitzmyer 65.–2, with the meaningless "Behold thy wife" of Avigad-Yadin, *A Genesis Apocryphon* ... Jerusalem (1956) 44.27.

c. *hinnē amāṯī Ḇilhā bō(') ēlēhā*
"Here is my maid Bilha; go to her". Gn 30:3

"While they were walking and talking,
d. *wəhinnē rekeḇ ēš wəsūsē ēš*
there came a chariot of fire and horses of fire". 2 Kings 2:11

In proclitic status, on the other hand, the particle is characterized by semantic diversity. We shall not describe here the many meanings of proclitic *hinnē*, but single out one that is less common. In the following verses the particle is used in an emphasizing sense:

(18) "He will not let your foot stumble; your guardian will not slumber.
a. *hinnē lō(') yānūm wəlō(') yīšān šōmēr Yiśrā'ēl*
Indeed, the guardian of Israel will neither slumber nor sleep". Ps 121:4

b. *hinnāḵ yāp̄ā raʿyāṯī*
"Indeed, you are beautiful my beloved (or, you are truly/certainly ...)". Ct 4:1, and similarly Ct 1:15, 16

Biblical *hinnē* is all too often treated as if it were invariably alerting. But the speaker in these particular verses does not alert – hence the inappropriateness of translations such as "See, the guardian of Israel ...", or "Behold, you are beautiful ..."[82] – but confirms these facts, emphasizes their truth and validity. This is recognized in Joüon's grammar, 502, where this meaning is quite fittingly reproduced by "certes, il ne dort pas" and (Ct 1:16) "oui, tu es beau". Moreover, witness that (18)a essentially repeats, and thus reinforces, the immediately preceding statement ("your guardian will not slumber") and that, similarly, *hinnāḵ yāp̄ā* occurs twice in the same sentence in both Ct 1: 15 and Ct 4:1 – details which strongly point in the direction of confirmation and emphasis rather than any other function.[83]

2.6.2 The relevance of this evidence to the history of *inna* lies not so much in the fact that the Hebrew particle happens to be *inna*'s etymological cognate, but in that it confirms a more general assumption we made with respect to *inna*, namely that a presentative particle can fulfill functions so *dissimilar* as concrete deixis, on the one hand, and sentence-emphasis on the other. We assume that

82 See the *New Oxford Bible*, the *Revised Standard Version* and the trans. of the *Jewish Publication Society of America* (the latter, however, departs from this pattern in the Ct verses, rendering "Ah, you are fair ...").

83 For another use of the device of repetition in this sense see § 1.4.6 above. Cf. also Ibn Yaʿīš's opinion, end of § 1.1.3 above.

such a substantial semantic contrast could develop only in what are two fundamentally discrete syntactic positions (nuclear/proclitic) held by each of these presentatives, in Arabic as well as Hebrew.[84]

To be sure, the similarity between the two particles does not go all the way. For whereas in Arabic *inna*'s emphasizing function carried the day, this function remained quite marginal with Biblical Hebrew *hinnē*, which is more commonly alerting, causal-argumentative, etc.

2.7 The modern colloquial evidence

2.7.2 A remarkable reflex of *inna* with an unmistakable *presentative* meaning has been preserved in a number of modern, mostly Bedouin dialects:

(19) a. *w'ana wəlbunayya ṣaʿadna ʿaljabal waṣalna larās marqab wənn nabʿ əlmā'*
"And I and the girl went up the mountain. We reached a high elevation and there was the source of water".
ʿAnaze (Syr. desert) Landberg 351.11

b. *ma šāf illa ḥormi bitféyyiqu fattaḥ ʿayūno*(!) *winnha mart ʿammu*
"A woman suddenly woke him up. He opened his eyes and behold, it was his uncle's wife". Ḥōrān area (Syr.) Landberg 351.–9

c. *ṭagg ʿala lbāb wənn ənnagrāt b-ə́ḏənha*
"He knocked at the door and behold, the knockings reached her ear". ʿAjārma (Jor.) Palva 86.1[85]

d. *ṭuḫḫuw álwalad hāḏ winnhum gāṭmīn rijlah*
"They shot at the boy and lo, they broke his leg".
Rašāyda (Judean desert) Rosenhouse-Katz 77.–4

e. *wiʿīt fallēl win jimālī(h) mahu fī mạḥṛakah*
"I woke up at night and behold, my camel was gone from his place". Ẓullām (Negev) Blanc "Negev" 145.13

f. *wraššit fauġoh ma' min waṣt gārūrah winn gaḏḏa' itnaʿfat wgām*

84 Bakr (I thank G. Goldenberg for this reference) correctly applies *hinnē*'s positional dualism to the syntactic analysis of *inna*, but his hypothesis of a deleted subject pronoun is unfounded in both cases, 48–50.

85 Palva's text is especially rich with presentative use of this particle, see also 58.4; 66.4; 68.12; 70.3, 12, 14, 15,–14; 80.–2, –14; 84.–7, –6; etc. The high frequency and formulaic nature of much of its use (typically in the frame *yōm … wənn …*), however, suggest that the particle is often defunctionalized.

"And she sprinkled water on him from a bottle,
so he suddenly jerked and stood up".

Yemen (Jewish) W. Fischer *Dem.* 184.–10, and cf.–8[86]

2.7.3 The following background information will explain the significance of this usage. While functional correspondences of classical *an/anna* are quite common in various modern dialects in the role of the regular subordinating (complemental) conjunction – manifesting themselves in forms such as *inn/ənn*, *in/ən*, or with suffixes *i/ənni*, *-ak*, *-o*, etc.[87] – it is much less usual to encounter genuine correspondences of classical *inna*. To be sure, certain constructions involving emphatic assertions preceded by oath-words have been interpreted at times as exhibiting reflexes of *inna*, e.g.

wiḥyāt laḥmit halʿīd ... in ma ʿalēč ḥaqq
"By the meat of this feast, you are not to blame".
walla innak zēn
"By God, you are a nice man".

i.e. with the clause viewed as nonsubordinated (an interpretation which puts these dialectal constructions syntactically on a par with classical ones such as *wallāhi inna Muḥammadan rasūluhu*, or *ḥalafa innahu kaḏā*).[88] But this interpretation is far from certain, because such dialectal constructions may equally be subordinating-conjunctional, i.e. "By the meat ... (underlyingly = I swear) that you are not to blame", "By God (underlyingly = I swear) that you are a nice man".[89] The essential point in the present context is, however, that even if these should turn out to be genuine reflexes of *inna*, they certainly do not reflect its *presentative*, but rather its emphasizing function[90], with semantic values (at least originally) such as "By the meat ..., you are certainly not ...", "By God, you are indeed ..."[91] It is against this background of an otherwise

86 With the exception of a, which is my phonetic approximation of Landberg's transcription in Arabic characters, all exx. in (19) follow as closely as possible the original transcription.

87 Due to a tendency of *a* to pass to *i*, the forms *an* and *anna* have largely blurred and become indistinguishable from *inna* already in Middle Arabic, see Blau *Emergence* 85 and n. 2, and Blau *Chr. Ar.* 510 and n. 2.

88 E.g. Wright II 175 D; Lane s.v. *ḥalafa*.

89 For these two interpretations and further exx. see Blau *BZ* § 141.

90 It is therefore somewhat misleading that § 141 of Blau *BZ* is contained in the chapter that deals with presentatives.

91 It is safe to assume, however, that such a use of nonsubordinating *inn* in a modern dialect would be largely restricted to formulaic expressions, rather than being fully productive (in contradistinction to the subordinating *inn*). Needless to say, when the particle occasionally appears in a dialect in its full disyllabic form it is a loan from the classical language, as in Marçais *Gl. Takr.* 155 s.v. *ʾenna*.

total or near-total absence of reflexes of *inna* in the modern dialects that the evidence of (19) is striking, all the more so since these reflexes have a presentative meaning.

The presentative clauses in (19) are non-initial, with a *w-* prefixed to the particle, yielding a form *win(n)/wən(n)*. The particle is also attested without *w-*, namely (as one would expect) in initial position[92], although this use is far less common.[93] In its function to call attention to a sudden or unexpected turn in a narration, and with this characteristic connective prefixed to the particle, (19) is the exact typological cognate of the noncolloquial presentative constructions with *fa'iḏā*, see (14) above and (1)–(2) of ch. III, or of the very common Biblical Hebrew ones with *wəhinnē*, e.g.,

wayyāḇē(') yāḏō bəḥēqō wayyōṣi'āh
wəhinnē yāḏō məṣōraʿaṯ kaššāleġ
"And he put his hand into his bosom, then took it out
and, behold, his hand was leprous (and white) as snow". Ex 4:6

2.7.4 The particle holds a proclitic status in all of (19), with the sole exception of a, where it is nuclear. This ex. is thus of a special significance, since it exhibits the same primary, bipartite sentence structure (type *inna Zaydan*) whose vestiges we encountered in the classical language in (11)a–e. The attestation of this very structure with a recognizable deictic-concrete meaning in a modern dialect lends substance to our reconstruction of these vestiges as reflecting an original nuclear (and thus deictic-concrete) presentative sentence-type.

2.7.5 At the same time the evidence highlights a more general point, namely that the modern dialects may preserve an ancient feature of the Semitic languages more faithfully than classical Arabic.[94] For while the particle's original presentativity is suggested on comparative-etymological grounds[95], and also can be quite plausibly reconstructed from its existential meaning on the basis of general linguistic (diachronic) considerations, as we have argued in § 2.2.1 ff. above, all this still remains only inferential – and thus indirect – proof: Within the domain of Arabic it is in the modern dialects alone that the particle's presentativity has actually been kept alive and thus can be directly *observed*. It is undoubtedly not

92 See the few exx. from Ḍofār and Aden in W. Fischer *Dem.* 184.–1 ff., exhibiting the particle with pronominal suffixes (*enhū*, *enhei*, etc.), as well as in combination with demonstrative forms, see ex. (28)d in ch. IV.

93 In fact, the particle is listed only with *w-* in Barthélemy, s.r. *'nn*, *wnn*.

94 On this subject in general see Blau *Jerusalem Studies in Arabic and Islam*, 3 (1981–82), 223–35.

95 I.e. by its cognates in the other Semitic languages such as Bibl. *hinnē*, and see note 24 above.

coincidental that the feature is mostly found in Bedouin dialects, which tend to be more conservative in general than the sedentary vernaculars.[96]

3. *Conclusion*

We argued that *inna* was originally a presentative in a primary, nuclear sentence-structure of the type *inna Zaydan*. There is evidence of a vestigial use of this structure in the early ʿArabiyya, albeit in a predominantly "reduced", i.e. existential meaning (11). The acc. case of the head of this structure was explained as the exponent of a broadly defined relational notion of "object", and this notion was shown to manifest itself in a variety of ways in nuclear presentative sentences in general.

It was suggested that by a process of syntactic reanalysis of an amplified structure the nuclear presentative came to assume the proclitic status it possesses in the classical language. The postulated steps – from nuclear to amplified to proclitic structure – are supported by evidence from the historical syntax of the demonstrative presentatives outlined in the preceding chapter. The semantic change involved, namely from presentativity to sentence-emphasis, was likewise documented by reference to parallel instances, notably in Biblical Hebrew. This change is seen as having occurred after the procliticization of *inna*, due to contextual influence.

It is highly significant to our interpretation of the vestigial type *inna Zaydan* that evidence of both the nuclear structure itself and of the particle's original presentative meaning has survived in some modern dialects.

96 To mention but one other aspect of this conservatism, witness the well-known phenomenon of vestigial *Tanwīn*, Blau *Emergence* 187ff., Blau *Tarbiz* 25/1 (1955), 27–35, esp. 32ff.

I. English Index

Abstract cases *See* Semantic roles
Acc. case
alternating with bi- 50
alternating with nom. case in Qur'ān 79
of the ḫabar kāna 72
alternating with the nom. in nuclear sentences 118–121, 122
in other verbless utterances 118
Affect XIX, 86–91, 96, 99
Amplified structure XVIII, 55–62, 63, 69–74, 76, 81, 99, 100, 128, 130, 136
Antitopic *See* Appositival syntax
Appositival syntax XIX, 84–91, 96
Arab grammarians XIV, XX, 4, 7, 30, 37–38, 56, 103, 108, 109, 110, 112, 113–114, 119, 122–126
Aramaic
Biblical Aramaic
pronoun reduplication (apposition) 5, 6, 12, 13
presentatives (h', 'ry) 67, 78
Syriac
utterance of address 39
Autonomous (verb-free) cases XVII, 53, 119

Bedouins, Bedouin dialects XX, 68–69, 70, 114, 116, 133–136

Category ("genus") XVI, 22–24, 25, 28, 34, 40
Change
syntactic, semantic change XIV, XVI, XVII, XX, 43, 48, 69–74, 85, 93, 94, 97, 127–131
Circumstantial amplification *See* Ḥāl
Clefting 2, 106
Colloquial Arabic, the colloquials XIV, 5, 30, 31–33, 67, 78, 83, 87–89, 92, 94, 95–96, 98, 127, 133–136
Comitativity, comitative XV, XVI–XVII, 12, 41, 43, 44, 47, 48, 50, 51, 53

Deletion *See* Ḫabar deletion, Verb deletion

Demonstrative pronouns as presentatives 56–74, 116, 121, 128, 130
Direction of diachronic development XX, 70–72
"Discontinuous" presentative component 80, 98
Dislocation, dislocation structure 73, 105, 106

Emotive, exclamatory syntax *See* Affect
"Emphatic" indirect relative clause XVI, 25–27, 40
"Envisaged scene" 44–47
Epexegetical syntax *See* Appositival syntax
Existential sentences, existential semantics XX, 115–117, 125, 126–127

Focus, focusing XV, XVI, XIX, 1, 2, 10, 11, 105, 106

Glose (in cleft sentences) 106

Hebrew
Biblical Hebrew
presentative (hinnē) XX, 55, 62, 68, 78, 98, 113, 117, 120, 122, 130, 131–133, 135, 136
pronoun reduplication 3, 6
sentence emphasis (āḵēn, cogn. absol. infinitive) 104
Mishnaic Hebrew 117
Modern Hebrew
appositival syntax 89–91
balancing 9
presentative (hare) 78, 117
pronominal copula (ze) 73

Imbalanced coordination 14

"Left-over" features XVIII, 70, 72, 73, 95, 128
Locative epexegesis 95–96
Loss of inflection 70–73

Meaning preservation 119, 124
Medieval grammarians *See* Arab grammarians
Metaphors (in relative clauses) 34–36
Middle Arabic XIV, 59–60, 70–71, 82–83
Mood (as relating to the semantics of inna) 78, 105
"Movement with" XVII, 47–51

Nuclear structure XVIII, XIX, XX, 55–62, 73, 74–99, 115, 118, 121, 128, 130, 136

Object, objecthood XVI, XVII, XX, 41, 43, 47, 48, 50, 53, 118, 119, 120, 136
"On/off the scene" XVI, 30–34, 40, 115

Parity
  syntactic parity 7–9, 11–13
Particles
  in rhyme-end position 107–111
Phoenician
  pronoun reduplication (apposition) 5
Presentative XVIII, XIX, XX, 54–101, 115, 117, 130, 135
  presentative semantics 55, 61–69, 77–79, 81–82, 90–91, 93, 113, 115, 129, 131–133
Proclitic structure XVIII, XX, 55–62, 63, 69–74, 78, 92, 93, 97, 99, 100, 128, 136
Pronouns
  pronominal copula 57, 73
  pronoun reduplication XV, XVI, 1, 2, 4, 5, 7, 8, 10–13, 80, 106
  resumptive pronoun XVI, 16

Proximity XVI, 41, 43, 44, 47, 48, 53

Qur'ān, Qur'ānic language 28, 79, 80–82

Reanalysis *See* Change
Repetition
  for emphatic confirmation/negation 111–112
Right dislocation *See* Appositival syntax

Self-contained (as opposed to classified, categorized) XVI, 24, 40,
Semantic (abstract case) roles XVII, 41, 53, 89, 118–119, 120, 136
Sentence emphasis XIX, XX, 102–105, 112, 129, 130, 132, 134
Specificity XVI, 18–22, 23, 25, 27, 29, 30, 32, 33, 40
Stress XV, XVI, 2, 9, 10
Superlative 23, 24

Topic, topicalization XIX, 105–106

Verb
  deletion (or "implied" verb) XVII, 42, 49, 108–110, 119
  replacement (faʿala as pro-verb) 109
Vocative, vocativic utterances 12, 13, 18, 27–34

Word-order reversal 80, 106

II. Arabic Index

Ahó, ahé (Eg.) 83, 84
ʿĀ'id 16, 19, 21, 37, 38
Ajal 109–110
Aku (Ir.) 116
Alā, amā 129
ʿAlā
of directionality ('towards') XVII, 48
Allaḏī
as pronominal head 15, 16, 21, 22
ʿAlayya bi-Zaydin 47–50, 53
Ammā – fa- 106
Anā laka bi-Zaydin XVII, 47, 48, 53
Arīh (Pal.) 121

Balā 109–110
Bi- *See* Comitativity, comitative

Ḍamīr al-Faṣl 57
Ḍamīr al-Ša'n 73
Ḍarūrat al-Šiʿr 4

Hāhunā (hunāka, hunālika) 116, 121, 130
Hā huwa ḏā
inflected 74–82, 85, 98–99
invariable 82–83
Ḫabar, ḫabar deletion 123, 124
Ḫabar kāna 72
Hāḏā *See* Demonstrative pronouns as presentatives
Ḥaḏf, ḥaḏf fiʿl *See* Ḫabar deletion, Verb deletion
Hāka ssayfa 119, 131
Ḥāl XVIII, 45, 58, 64–70, 72, 76, 79, 81, 92, 128, 129
Hal lī bi-Zaydin 48, 53
Ḥarf al-Ḫiṭāb 76, 95, 120
Ḥarf al-Tanbīh 120
Ḥarf, Ḥurūf 110
Ḥasan (gramm.) 4
Hayni, etc., hayyūni, etc. (coll. presentative) 83, 84, 122
Hayy (coll. demonstrative, presentative) 57

Iḏā, fa'iḏā
of suddenness (presentative) 44, 52, 121, 131, 135
Iḏā anā/huwa bi-Zaydin XVII, 41, 42, 52, 53
Iḏā bi-Zaydin 41, 42, 52, 53, 55
Iḏā Zaydun 55, 120
Ilṣāq 43
In (cond.) 109
In al-Muḫaffafa 102, 104, 105
Inna XIV, XVIII, XIX, XX, 69, 78, 102–136
as an independant morpheme 106, 112
used fī ljawāb 111
inna(h) 107, 111
inna Zaydan 113–136
and its "sisters" 123, 129
Innamā 106
Ism, Ism Inna 123, 124

Jā'a bi-Zaydin 47, 48, 50, 52, 53
Jumla Ẓarfiyya 121

-Ka *See* Ḥarf al-Ḫiṭāb
Ka'annī bi-Zaydin 44–46, 53
Kāna (for sentence emphasis) 104
Kayfa lī bi-Zaydin XVII, 47, 49, 53

La- 103–105
Lā 111
Lā li-Nafy al-Jins 123, 124
Laʿamrī 104
Lafẓ 38
Lam (neg.), also walam, iḏā lam, wa-in lam 108–109
Lām
Lām al-Jins 22, 24
Al-Lām al-Fāriqa 102, 104
Lammā (neg.) 108
Lan 104
Li-
of directionality ('towards') XVII, 48
with jussive 39

Mā (relative)
as pronominal head 15, 16
(conj.)
in a cleft sentence 106

Ma-allōš, ma-hallūš (Yem.) 116
Maḥḏūf *See* Ḫabar deletion, Verb deletion
Makāniyya, Ẓarf Makān 121
Man (relative)
as pronominal head 15, 16, 21, 22, 25, 27
"emphatic" use 26
in a vocative utterance 29
Man lī bi-Zaydin 48, 49, 52, 53
Maʿnā 38
Min
specifying min-phrase 21
Min ayna lī bi-Zaydin 48, 53
Mulābasa 43
Muṣāḥaba 43

Naʿam 109–110
Naʿt Sababi 15, 31

Qabīḥ (gramm.) 4, 37
Qad 103, 104, 109

Ṛa (Magr.) 121
Ruwaydaka bi-Zaydin 50

Šaʿ, Šaʿo, etc. (Syr.) 84–85, 121
Šāḏḏ 30

Taḥqīq 103
Taḫṣīṣ 19
Ta'kīd (Tawkīd) 103, 104
Ṯammata 116, 121, 130
Tanbīh 56, 129
Taqdīr 123, 124
Tarāu, tarāha, etc. (Sud.) 84–85, 121
Taʿrīf 19
Tawaqquʿ fiʿl 109

Wajh (gramm.) 37
Wallāhi 104
Wāw al-Ḥāl 45
Win(n)/wən(n) 135

Yā (coll. ya, yalli, ya mīn) 26, 28, 29, 30, 31, 32, 33

Ẓarfiyya 43